ROME
THE ENCHANTED CITY

The start of a carriage ride through Rome

ROME
THE ENCHANTED CITY

FRANK J. KORN

OUR SUNDAY VISITOR, INC.
NOLL PLAZA, HUNTINGTON, INDIANA 46750

ISBN: 0-87973-857-X
Library of Congress Catalog Card Number: 76-41315

Cover Design by Eric Nesheim
Cover Illustration by Clete Olinger

Published, printed and bound in the U.S.A. by
Our Sunday Visitor, Inc.
Noll Plaza
Huntington, Indiana 46750
857

Dedication

To My Beloved Wife
— *loyal companion of all my Roman adventures.*

To My Dad
— *lifelong benefactor and dearest friend.*

To My Angel Mother
— *boundless source of wisdom and counsel, Requiescat in Pace.*

F.J.K.

Contents

Preface

I try to think of some word to describe my reaction to this book. What comes is a word I do not use ordinarily. But there is only one word to describe it. Delightful.

I am no expert on guidebooks of any kind or guidebooks to Rome, although I have read a few. But this is not a guidebook, although it serves admirably as a guidebook. It is a memoir of a man's love affair with Rome.

What makes it a wonderful book is not just that the author has told us of the city but he has managed to blend in the history of the city. It is a complete history and yet so carefully blended with the narration that you are not aware of reading history. He doesn't say, "Now we will give you some history." He takes you somewhere and tells you in passing who has walked these stone streets before; who has stood at these columns in the Forum.

It is a personal story. He lets you know his wife, Camille, and his three sons. You come to know Mama Irma, his landlady, and you get to understand the people.

I think this is a great book. It is simply a lover's description of his beloved and he loves her so much he makes the reader love her, too.

He manages all the things tourists should know —

where they should shop, where they should eat, where they should look for antiques. He describes all the things that must be seen but never in a way that suggests this is a tourist's guide. You learn far more from it than any tour guide I've seen but you do not learn it in the lecture-presentation of a tour.

I am very strong in my praise for this book because it is beautifully written, because it moves, because it charms.

DALE FRANCIS

Introduction

In 1969 the United States State Department selected me as a Fulbright Scholar for a year's study of classical civilization in Rome. Whereupon I applied for and was granted sabbatical leave from my positions as a high school teacher of Latin and Italian and college professor of English rhetoric.

On the evening of June 24th of that year I departed from John F. Kennedy Airport in New York via a 747 jet for Leonardo Da Vinci Airport outside the Eternal City. The flight itself seemed eternal but, knowing that beyond this eternity the splendor of Rome awaited me, my spirits remained high.

And high over the Alps we were suddenly coasting, already in our descent, as some fellow Fulbrights and I tried to decide which of the passes that we could discern had been Hannibal's choice.

On the morning of the 25th I came, I saw, and I was instantly conquered by what I saw. But my first order of business was not a visit to the Colosseum nor to St. Peter's. Rather it was to find an apartment for my family who would be joining me in a few (lonely) weeks. After hunting for three days, I found a place I knew we would all love. The landlady (about whom I will have much to say later in this volume) and I entered into a lively negotiating session which resulted for me in a sizable discount on the rent. It seems she has always had a soft spot in her heart for members of the teaching community.

When at last the gang arrived we became a live version of the television program popular at that time: *To Rome With Love* — but with a few differences. In the show an American family of three daughters, a dog, and the widower (played by John Forsythe) move to Rome where he works as a teacher at the American Overseas School. While in our show there are three sons: Frank, then ten years old; Ronald, eight; and John, six; a dog Princess, then one; a pretty mother of Italian ancestry, Camille, whose age I've been forbidden to publish; and a father (played by me), a student at the American Academy.

Our acclimation to life in the honey-colored city was surprisingly rapid. We learned quickly to keep our eyes and ears and even our noses on constant twenty-four hour alert when we realized that Rome's delights to the senses are truly endless.

Still there was something special beyond these tangible delights, something almost spiritual that we could not see nor articulate, something that held us totally in thrall, something that was to make this the happiest experience of our lives. How often I would find myself reflecting on a line of poetry I had learned ages ago in high school:

"Our hearts were drunk with a beauty
That our eyes could never see."

Superfluous to say, the time passed all too quickly and the hour for singing *Arrivederci Roma* had arrived. Before our departure however I had managed to land summer jobs in Rome, as a writer for a small newspaper and as a guide for English and Italian speaking tourist groups. The news was hailed by my loved ones, for this of course ensured our return next year. We did go back the next summer and have done so every June since. My family and I have become part-time Romans, summer patricians you might say. For we have retained that same apartment we had in our Fulbright year, in a lovely quarter of the Eternal City, to which we hasten each year on the last day of the school term for a stay of almost three months.

It is only after we arrive here at our street, struggle with the luggage through our tiny courtyard, make the four story climb, are greeted by our "Roman Mamma," the extraordinary woman who owns the building, unlock the door, throw open the shutters, and step out on the balcony, that I get the feeling that at last I am back home where I belong.

Long ago, the philosopher Lucretius maintained: a) that man consists of atoms; b) that these atoms have always been, and always will be, part of the universe; c) that upon death a man's atoms disperse back into the universe, scatter in every direction, and eventually join with others coming from anywhere and everywhere to form another man. Accordingly, it is possible that atoms which have been floating around in Asia, Africa, on every continent, in countless countries, can assemble and constitute a new human being, say, in France.

For those of us who have ever experienced the phenomenon, *déjà vu,* perhaps Lucretius' theory explains it best. I have often wondered if a high percentage of my atoms have spent years, decades, or even centuries scurrying about in the atmosphere of the city of Rome, thus making my arrival here each year seem more like a homecoming than a peregrination.

Or might it be simply that I am desperately trying to disprove Thomas Wolfe's line: "You can't go home again," in which the playwright submits that a man, however much he may endeavor to, can never return to the world of his youth, for change is inexorable and that world exists no longer. For somehow I have discovered in Rome so many of the simple joys and human values and so much of the world I knew in boyhood, and I long to, "go home again."

Here the sound of church bells wakes me gently each morn, the *angelus* rings out joyously each noon and evening. Here it is still possible to hear a Latin Mass accompanied by Gregorian Chant. Here the priests still walk the streets in their cassocks and three-cornered *birettas* and the nuns still wear their habits long.

In Rome, Saturday evening is still the most convivial time of the week. We like to sit at our favorite sidewalk café in Piazza Santa Maria in Trastevere in those precious hours, and watch the magnificent human drama unfold in the huge square, a perfect stage.

Robust Roman matrons rumble by with their market bargains for tomorrow's weekly feast. The men of the community, having doffed their peasant work clothes and donned their best suits and spiffiest ties, are beginning to cluster. Their conversations grow more animated, and louder, as the evening progresses. A chubby Franciscan friar ambles along, oblivious to the tiny mutt stalking him. Two Carabinieris, smartly dressed in their summer whites, survey the scene. Soldiers on leave ogle everything feminine, while hippies in rough velvet clothes stake their claim to a corner of the piazza. Young lovers stroll dreamily by as the strains of *Anema E Cuore* or *Santa Lucia* waft from an apartment overhead out over the square. The singer, a Trastevere *mamma mia* at peace with the world, is soon joined in song by many others below. Kids begin to spill out of the sandstone buildings, fresh and vigorous from the traditional Saturday night bath, knowing enough to be seen but not heard.

And so it goes in every quarter of the ancient city. Streets, squares, cafés teem with people. Clamorous, spirited, contented, energetic people. A festive atmosphere pre-

vails into the wee hours as the *Frascati* flows. For indeed
tomorrow is Sunday, in Italy still genuinely the day of rest,
so live with gusto tonight.

I can recall a like spirit in our neighborhood in New
Jersey before television converted all families into "loners"
behind locked doors, hopeless addicts to the tube. Here
with but two channels offering but a few hours of pro-
gramming each day, the Italian still favors a good book,
good wine, good conversation for his leisure.

Sunday, as it was once in our neck of the woods, is
still, totally, family day in this city. The family, a close knit
unit often including a *nonna* and a *nonno*, sits down to a
midday feast of fresh meat, fresh vegetables, fresh fruit. TV
dinners, frozen pizza, canned vegetables, synthetic foods
are all anathema to the Roman. The session at the table
lasts literally for hours but no one cares about the clock.
The dialogue is lively, the laughter uninhibited, the vino
marvelous. There are no generation gaps. A Roman father
is completely at ease communicating with his father or his
son and feels no embarrassment whatever in kissing either,
regardless of his age. The art of discipline, without high
handedness, is still well practiced today throughout the
sun-drenched Italian peninsula, both in the home and in
the school. There remains a sincere respect for one's elders
and a high regard for their judgment.

Evening is on its way. What an ideal time for a family
ride or — what's better — a walk, through a medieval villa,
now a public park, or perhaps along the historic Tiber to a
small café for a strong espresso. From there it's on to a
gelateria like *Tre Scalini* in Piazza Navona.

The popular sport of walking in parks, down twisting
narrow side streets, or in dimly lit back alleys has not
become the perilous diversion we know it to be back in the
U.S.A.

Are you old enough to remember when a bus ride cost
less than a dime? I can travel to any point in my adopted

home town from any other point, or even make a complete circuit tour of it for 50 lire. (That's eight cents, my friend.)

Do you remember fondly, as I do, the men's clubs that abounded in the decades B.T. (Before Television)? I need only to walk to the corner each summer evening to watch a hot *bocce* match, or kibbitz at a spirited card game.

Do you go back to the days when it wasn't necessary to be friends, or even acquaintances, to exchange "good morning," to strike up conversations on trains, in restaurants, or even on the street? In Rome expect a *buon giorno* from anyone and be prepared to discuss, with vigor, the weather, the traffic, the cost of living with the person next to you, while waiting for a bus, standing in a line, sitting at a sidewalk table.

Have you forgotten how, whenever a member of the family was ill, the entire neighborhood was concerned and would be at your door with offers of assistance? How when your car was disabled the man downstairs insisted you use his; how a man's worth was measured not by his position, nor his income, nor the size of his home, but by the quality of his character?

These values (frivolous some might call them but dear to me and mine) and so many more like them are still a vital part of the fabric of life in Rome and throughout Italy. The Romans — I find them to be at least — are an unpretentious people, not yet afflicted by the "keeping up with the Joneses" syndrome. They are not petty but rather magnanimous as a race, simple in many respects yet profound in others, scatterbrained and intellectual one and the same. They can argue strenuously on politics, religion, morality, wines, women, and song — on anything under God's sun, without offending or taking offense.

I have witnessed more than once an accident where the two drivers accuse and denounce each other to the heavens, and after five or six hours of vigorous debate, before an ever mushrooming crowd and countless police, repair to the nearest bar, arm-in-arm — strangers no more but rather partners in a warm, new friendship.

But do I, on a mere academician's salary, retreat so frequently to this *City of the Caesars,* this *City of the Seven Hills,* this *City of the Popes,* to try to recapture my lost youth?

Indeed not. There is so much more that draws me irresistibly to Rome that one article, one book, many volumes would not be enough for me to convey it. I have drunk deeply of the same heady atmosphere that intoxicated the souls of Shelley, Keats, Goethe, et al.

I come to Rome because I admire the Romans' eye for beauty — natural, archaeological, architectural, spiritual, and to be sure, feminine beauty. Their respect, nay reverence, for the past moves me.

In Rome, I can stroll along and enjoy the plaintive cry of the ragman and the rhythmic clopping of his horse, the simple beauty of a rooftop garden and the awesome elegance of a Renaissance palazzo, the roaring waters of a baroque fountain and the soft fluttering of pigeons in a campanile.

The challenge of bargaining with a shopkeeper or street vendor never fails to delight me.

In Rome my wife and I can dine out inexpensively at some small, intimate trattoria and be favored by a violinist or two or occasionally a Neapolitan singer. And from there we can drop in on friends, be warmly welcomed, and upon taking our leave be thanked profusely for the visit. Making our way home on foot we may pass such enchanting places as the Bridge of the Angels, the Tomb of Hadrian, the walls of the Vatican, before we climb the winding road up the Janiculum Hill, where we reside.

On nights when the mood moves us, we take a cab for about a half-dollar to the Baths of Caracalla and take in the opera *Aida* or *Rigoletto* or some other Verdi hit, under the stars and umbrella pines, amidst the brooding ruins.

After the show, humming the arias along with everyone else as we leave the Baths, it's home again via a romantic horsedrawn carriage or a clangorous trolley car.

Rome's sultry summer days bother us not. For Mediterranean beaches await us merely 30 minutes away by Fiat. There are times when we choose to take an aged, wooden-seated train through the Roman Campagna to Ostia Lido where the waves are better. The sea is not the only way to beat the heat however. A picnic in the Castelli Romani, the Alban Hills south of Rome with their charming medieval hamlets, will serve the same purpose.

On a particularly ambitious day, a two-hour scenic ride down the autostrada brings us to the Bay of Naples, the cliffs of Sorrento, the Isle of Capri. There is no problem agreeing with the Neapolitan's description of his land as *"un pezzo di cielo caduto sulla terra"* (a piece of heaven having fallen on earth).

Four hours or so in the opposite direction such fairytale places as Florence and Siena beckon us.

And while we ordinarily make annual pilgrimages to all these points, I would ask for nothing more than to be free to roam the Eternal City, unlocking more and more of her endless and timeless secrets.

I come to Rome because I believe in the old Roman conviction that one is inadequately educated until he has traveled extensively in another country, been exposed to another culture, mastered another language. On that score I believe our three sons have a jump on their peers.

They have cultivated warm friendships with their summer pals, they speak Italian, they have seen personally and often the Holy Father. They have viewed great works of art, visited countless museums, enjoyed sipping wine and *cappuccino.* They are fast becoming thoroughly bi-cultural and bi-lingual.

I come to Rome, not only in summer but at other times during the year, because it is here that I indulge my insatiable interest in archaeology, the Papacy, the Renaissance, the Risorgimento, the Italian Language, in everything that is Roman.

Here I can each day stroll out on our balcony and watch the late afternoon sun transform Rome into a gloriously pink city. Here I can live the life of poetry and romance I thrive on, enveloped by the city's fabulous sights, sounds, and even smells.

Yet while Rome is a Garden of Eden for me, I can recommend it only for most, not for all. For I have seen some Americans driven out of their trees by the maddening idiosyncracies and eccentricities of the Roman life style.

However while I am here I heed closely the advice of St. Ambrose to St. Augustine *Quum Romae, Romano vivite more*. (When in Rome, live like the Romans) . . . and I get along just fine.

Even as I write this I paraphrase in my mind the words of Browning: "O to be in England now that Spring is there" to, "O to be in Rome now that summer's here." And then I count my blessings.

For we love Rome, her crumbling stones, her people, her spirit, and we will spend the rest of our lives urging others to come here, like a self-appointed Chamber of Commerce.

It is my hope to show you through the eyes of myself and my family, via the following essays, the almost endless charms of Rome that never fail to captivate the eyes, and ears, and heart of every beholder.

If this little volume enables the lucky reader who has been in Rome to reminisce a bit; the reader fortunate enough to be going to Rome to be a bit more prepared for his sojourn; and the reader who does all his traveling by pictures and books to envision a bit what Rome is truly like, the purpose of the author will have been accomplished.

Buon viaggio!

Author seated on an ancient tombstone near the historic Appian Way

I

The History of Rome

Rome, 1975

It is summer of this Holy Year and I sit here lunching ascetically (cheese, olives, bread, wine) with my wife on the breezy terrace of our apartment high upon the summit of the Janiculum Hill. The view is glorious — St. Peter's to one o'clock from my seat, Santa Maria Maggiore to three o'clock, the Colosseum at four-thirty, San Giovanni in Laterano at six, the Pyramid of Cestius and Porta San Paolo at quarter after seven, the Tiber just below us, the Castelli Romani in the distance. Songs of Giuseppe Di Stefano and Giuliano Virgili serenade us through the windows via a stack of their records on the stereo inside. Puffy white clouds float by in the heavenly blue Roman sky. There may be a more idyllic spot somewhere on the face of this earth but if so, I'm not aware of it, nor do I care to become so. For I have discovered my own private Utopia right here. Our sons Frank, Ronald and John burst upon this Eden, importuning Camille for food and drink, and me for some coins. They'll need the latter for admission to the swimming pool out in Mussolini's Forum where the 1960 Olympic games were held.

Soon calm is restored, for the dishes have been cleared

away, Camille is back at her book (Carlo Levi's *Christ Stopped At Eboli*), and the bambini with some Roman chums are on their way to their vicarious Olympiad. In the lazy air of late June I let my thoughts drift back across the sands of time in an effort to put together a résumé of the fascinating life story of Bella Roma. To appreciate further a visit to Rome, one ought to have some knowledge of what took place here before he arrived. Cicero warns that, "not to know the past is to remain forever a child."

On April twenty-first last, Rome observed her 2,728th birthday. In the spring of 753 B.C. Romulus, according to tradition, inaugurated the village on the Palatine Hill which was to evolve into the most enduring civilization the world would ever know and one which would leave an indelible influence on all succeeding ages. The village was given the name of *Rome* in honor of its founder and king.

Because of a severe woman shortage, Romulus soon sought a friendship with neighboring tribes, all of whom rejected his petition for intermarriage in order to propagate the Roman race. He then in desperation resorted to treachery. A tribe from the nearby hills, the Sabines, with a coincidental abundance of young maidens, was invited to the new city for a day of feasting and games. They came unarmed, suspecting nothing. Then when all were intent upon the banqueting and sports, Romulus had his troops seize all the unescorted women, an act immortalized in literature and art as "The Rape of the Sabine Women." The helpless Sabine men protested in vain and vowed to retaliate. Some days later they returned and a fierce battle was joined. Only the intervention of the maidens, who liked the treatment they were receiving at the hands of their captors, prevented wholesale bloodshed. An accord was reached which resulted in a coalition of the two tribes, so that Rome's population more than doubled overnight.

As the decades passed, Rome, through more such coalitions with other hill tribes expanded to encompass the seven gentle hills on the left bank of the Tiber. Romulus, after a forty-year reign, died and was replaced by a Sabine, according to the terms of the original treaty. Rome's second king, Numa Pompilius, also proved to be a man devoted to the interests of his subjects, and after his long reign was deeply mourned by the citizens.

Later kings, there were seven in all, tradition claims, were not so benign however, and life grew more intolerable. Led by a Lucius Junius Brutus in 509 B.C. the people revolted and overthrew the tyrant Tarquin the Proud, an Etruscan who had managed to secure the throne of Rome. This marked the end of the kingdom of Rome and the beginning of the Republic. Brutus' plan called for the government to be a *re* (matter) *publica* (public), that is, one of the people, by the people, and for the people. The king was replaced by two consuls, heading the executive branch, who would be elected to one-year terms, who would have the power of veto over each other, and who would be ineligible for re-election. This was clearly designed to prevent the accumulation of total power in the hands of one man ever again. To diffuse authority even more, there were two other branches of government established, the legislative (senate) and the judicial (courts). It is on the Roman Republic that the United States' system of government is modeled, naturally with variations.

Rome hadn't heard the last of the tyrant Tarquin however. Johnny never tires of the following account, whose setting was the very property on which our apartment building stands. One night in the year 508 B.C. Lars Porsena was encamped with his powerful Etruscan armies, four stories below where I'm typing these words, preparatory to an attack on the heart of Rome, the purpose of which would be to restore his fellow Etruscan to the throne of Rome. The camp fires of the Etruscans danced against the ink-black nocturnal sky and sent shivers through the hearts of the Romans on the opposite bank of the sluggish

Tiber. Looking in horror toward the illuminated Janiculum the Romans invoked the aid of their pagan deities. As it developed, the gods heard and granted their petitions. For the following morning the northerners broke camp, descended the mountain named for Janus, the two-headed god who could look in all directions from our vantage point, by the route now called Viale Giuseppe Garibaldi and clangored toward the only access to the other bank, the *Pons Sublicius,* a wooden bridge erected in the reign of Ancus Martius to connect the city with the Trastevere. A lieutenant in the Roman forces managed, as Kipling exhorts, "to keep his head while all around him were losing theirs." Horatio the One-eyed, so called since the loss of an eye in an earlier battle, volunteered along with two colleagues to stall, if but for a few moments, the invaders at the other end of the bridge. He hastened to the bottleneck to take his heroic stand, the shouting of the men, the screaming of the women and children resounding in his ears. Horatio along with his mates dueled with the first arrivals of the Etruscans. Then he yelled to the troops behind him to cut down the bridge. "Quickly or we'll all perish and Rome with us!"

The deed done, Horatio leaped with his two comrades into the Tiber and amid a hail of spears, stones, and arrows swam to the bank. Rome was spared. There was dancing in the streets. Horatio's name was toasted in every inn across the seven hills and would be forevermore inscribed on the heart of every school boy and on the city's rapidly growing roster of national heroes.

The *Pons Sublicius* of course is gone and so too are several of its early successors. But there stands today on the site another bridge called, in modern Italian, *Ponte Sublicio.* And so we can pinpoint the important spots in this one of Rome's endless legends. In many cases with stories from Rome's past we can do much more than that. We can tread the same stones that felt the feet of Caesar, explore the same catacombs that heard the prayers of Peter, drink from the same aqueducts that quenched the thirst of Marcus Aurelius.

A fantastic attic is Rome and stored there, in beautiful disarray, are tangible reminders of every epoch in her long career — from the period of the kings, the consuls, and the emperors; from early Christian history, the dark ages, the middle ages, the Renaissance, the Baroque, the Risorgimento to our own age.

So the Republic continued, and continued to prosper and expand through wars with nations to the north, then with her southern neighbors. Rome in the course of the next couple of centuries grew to encompass the peninsula of Italy. In subsequent centuries Rome, by necessity, developed into a maritime power and annexed North Africa (the Punic Wars), Spain, Corsica, Sardinia, Greece, Asia Minor. The Romans had the Mediterranean completely encircled and were already calling it *Mare Nostrum* (Our Sea).

In the first century before Christ the brilliant Julius Caesar brought all of Gaul (modern France, Switzerland, Belgium, Holland, Luxembourg) into the Roman fold and the Republic had reached its geographical zenith. While he was busy conquering the transalpine lands, however, the political corruption back home had by now eroded the health of the state to the point where that noble experiment, the Republic, lay moribund.

Caesar in 48 defied the decadent Senate and brought his faithful legions back into Italy and chased the home armies right off the peninsula. The Republic was dead. A dictatorship was established. And this new government came crashing down in four short years, as its architect and leader, on March 15, 44, lay in his own blood in the lobby of Pompey's Theater, having been assassinated by die-hard lovers of the Republic.

A decade and a half of civil war ensued with the result

that Caesar's grandnephew, and hand-picked heir, ascended the throne as Emperor of the Roman Empire. Rome had come full cycle, back to one-man rule. For while the 32-year-old Octavian, to be known as the Emperor Augustus, kept the trappings of a republic, he was in point of fact, the government. In his defense, though, we must point out that his reign was one of peace and prosperity for Rome, the *Pax Romana*. For the first time the arts were allowed to flourish and the Augustan era was also known as the Golden Age of Latin literature. He endeavored to give the militaristic and agrarian Romans a sense of the esthetic and fostered interest in art, philosophy, and architecture. He beautified the city, boasting in his twilight years: "I found Rome a city of brick and left her a city of marble."

His successor, the aged Tiberius, also ruled well although he has always received a bad press from historians. But the next occupant of the throne, Caligula, was a dangerously insane despot from whom Rome was spared within a few years by assassins.

Not long after, another demented ruler plagued Rome, the neurotic Nero. At this juncture in Rome's history, Christianity came to the city in the persons of the Apostles Peter and Paul. Unlike other cults which proved to be ephemeral, this new religion would endure and would in the large be responsible for the fall of the mighty Roman Empire. Nero in order to exculpate himself from charges of burning Rome in 64 A.D. blamed the Christians. This one lie was to launch the pogroms we refer to as the Christian persecutions which lasted for three centuries.

Fortunately for the Empire, decent and gifted leaders thereafter ascended the throne, interrupted now and then by a despot. Vespasian and his son Titus were not too bad, although the Jews of Rome would have much to say, and rightly so, on that score. Together with Vespasian's other son Domitian they made up the Flavian Dynasty in the late second century. This was followed by the Antonine Dynasty, or Good Emperors as some call them. Life in Rome was indeed much improved under Nerva, Trajan, Hadrian, Antoninus Pius, and Marcus Aurelius.

But the last could already see that Rome, because of internal decay — moral, spiritual, political, and social — was on a collision course with catastrophe and he grieved for his country.

Later emperors, like the demagogues Caracalla and Diocletian in the third century, were to inch Rome ever closer to the edge of the abyss. Even the division of the Empire into Eastern and Western branches, each with its own emperor to make it more governable, failed to stem the tide against Rome.

In the fourth century Constantine came to power, freed the Christians from their long oppression, and in fact made Christianity the official religion of the Roman Empire. But the state continued to debilitate while her hungry foes gnawed away at the periphery. The year 410 saw Rome sacked by the fierce Goths. Little more than a half century later in 475 the Senate convened for the last time and the lights went out forever for Imperial Rome. The city was overrun first by this northern tribe, then by that one, then by still others.

Though the city dwindled in prestige, in population, and in every conceivable way, the Lombards thought it still worthwhile to invade her in 568. At about this time the citizens who had not joined the mass exodus from the city turned to Pope Gregory the Great for political as well as spiritual leadership, marking the beginning of papal power. The city was thus saved from oblivion.

The popes enlisted and received the backing of some powerful European leaders, such as Charlemagne, King of the Franks. In a demonstration of unity, he was crowned *Defender of the Church* and *Emperor of the Holy Roman Empire* by Pope Leo III in solemn ceremonies in old St.

Peter's on Christmas Eve in the year 800. After the coronation, Charlemagne prostrated himself before the Holy Father in acknowledgment of Leo's spiritual authority. The round stone of red porphyry upon which Charlemagne knelt may be seen at the beginning, that is the facade end, of the right aisle of the new St. Peter's.

This papal and imperial harmony was to be strained and shattered again and again, however, by vicious discords throughout the middle ages. After the cloudy middle ages came the brilliant glow of the Renaissance, precipitated by the breathtakingly beautiful poetry of Dante Alighieri in the early fourteenth century. This French word meaning rebirth was used to describe the tremendous resurgence of interest in the arts and letters of the classical ages. From the 1400's to the 1600's Rome and Italy were beautified by the painting and sculpture and architecture of the Renaissance masters, preeminent among which was Michelangelo Buonarotti of Florence.

As for civil rule over Rome and the area of Central Italy called the Papal States, it remained in the hands of the popes through the turbulent times of the Protestant Reformation and the sack of Rome by an army under the Emperor Charles V, in which four thousand Romans were killed. The boundless resilience of Rome, or the renewed patronage of Providence, or both, enabled the city to rise once again from the depths to the baroque wonderland we know today.

In 1798 Rome was attacked and occupied by French revolutionary troops and a decade later made part of Napoleon's Empire.

Five years later Pope Pius VII was restored to power. But the temporal sovereignty of the popes was drawing to a close with the movement for the unification of Italy, the brainchild of the visionaries Mazzini, Cavour, and Garibaldi, in the mid-1800's. By 1861 Rome was a political island as all of Italy beyond the Aurelian walls was united under King Victor Emmanuel of Piedmont. Though Pope Pius IX and his supporters managed to hold the city for another decade, Rome was taken on the twentieth of September in 1870 by the King's troops. The Papal States were no more and the Pontiff withdrew behind the Vatican walls after denouncing the King as a usurper, while Rome became the Capital of the Kingdom of Italy.

Rome's streets were darkened once again by intruders in World War II as Nazi occupation forces were dispatched to the seven hills by Hitler to shore up the tottering fascist government of Benito Mussolini. That effort by the German dictator was to prove futile as fascism fell and Hitler's troops were driven from the Holy City by the liberation forces of the Allied Armies.

After the war, in 1946, the country became a republic and Rome added another line to her long list of credentials: Capital of the Republic of Italy. In 1962 Pope John XXIII, successor to Pius XII who saw Rome through the war, convoked the historic Second Vatican Council. Rome, always international in atmosphere, became even more so as the members of the Church hierarchy and representatives of all faiths, from every nation, converged on the city to participate in this convocation aimed at bringing the Church into step with the Space Age and making Her more ecumenical.

Paul VI was elevated to the throne of Peter in 1963 and still reigns. The civil government meanwhile has not enjoyed the stability of the Church leadership. Italy has changed administrations more than thirty times in the thirty years of the *post bellum* era.

This city is truly eternal, I believe, and I have no doubt that some writer living in Rome (and in love with her as am I) 2,728 years from now will be tackling the humanly impossible task of summarizing her long, long history.

Ave atque vale

John Korn pointing to chariot ruts in original paving stones of Via Sacra near the Arch of Titus

II

The Roads

To enter or depart from the Holy City one must eventually take one of the old consular roads (that is, roads originally constructed when Rome was governed by consuls, chief executives similar in their political role to our presidents) all of which, the proverb insists, "lead to Rome." In our work and in our leisure we have driven these historic highways many times over. Most people on a short stay in Rome give a few days over for trips to the many famous places a relatively short drive (an hour or two) beyond the walls. Some of the ennui of a chartered bus ride is alleviated by beautiful scenery along the way, some more by friendly conversation, more still by a probably well-needed snooze. May we suggest, toward this same end, devoting a patch of time to the contemplation of the road's ancient distinction and to imagining the likely events that long ago transpired on these same stones — a legion on the move, farmers' trucks on the way to market, traveling salesmen frequenting the wayside taverns, angry citizens of an Italian town marching *en masse* on the Capital to protest spiraling taxation without representation.

As our motorized tin chariot rolls across the plains between Rome and our destination, we take turns imagining aloud and the ride is, as a result, always more relaxing, entertaining, and informative.

Romans from early on were outstanding road builders. The fabulous network of highways put together by brilliant civil engineers was in very large measure responsible for Rome's rise to, and maintenance of, supremacy over the Mediterranean world. Legions could thunder down the road to nip a budding revolt in one of the provinces, the way Russia today pours her tanks and troops down some modern autostrada in still another gesture of friendly persuasion to Hungary or Czechoslovakia or Poland.

Undisputed queen of all the Roman roads of course is the Via Appia which since 312 B.C. has been handling the flow of traffic between Rome and Capua and even on to Brundisium, the Adriatic port and traditional embarkation point to Greece. Named for the commissioner of roads who authorized its construction, the Via Appia runs straight and level, crossing rivers over great stone bridges, spanning the Pontine Marshes via a viaduct, an awesome feat of engineering three centuries before a virgin gave birth in the province of Judea. Built to "last an eternity," it has a roadbed of stones on which were poured crushed rocks, all fastened permanently in place by a layer of cement. Huge pyramid-shaped paving stones were set in place so perfectly and so tightly together that the road was immune to seepage. This highway has kept a good part of its ancient character and we rarely drive along it without stopping to walk a bit or to translate some epitaphs with the aid of the fastest Latin dictionary in the West, or to picnic beneath a pine, or to take home-movies of these stones "over which two thousand years and more have walked to Rome Eternal," from a Roman army division returning in triumph in the first century B.C. to an Allied Army on its push to liberate Rome in the year of our Lord, 1944.

Via Latina is of this same era and students who survived the third year of high school Latin will tell you that it was this highway Marcus Tullius Cicero traveled on his frequent visits to his childhood home in Arpino. This enters the city through the Porta Latina.

Another of the southern routes is the Via Casilina, which the ancients knew as Via Labicana since it headed southeast to old Labicum. From there it goes, even today, to and through such interesting places as Frosinone and Cassino.

If you are a student of the history of Rome's Republic you may want to follow the Via Prenestina to Palestrina (*Preneste* in antiquity), through lush countryside and over rolling hills to this little town clinging tenaciously to the side of Monte Ginestro. The town and surrounding area enjoyed popularity with the oldtimers. In one ode Horace calls it, "refreshing Preneste." The Latin III scholar could tell you some more about this place. (Remember the First Oration, boys and girls?)

Most Americans coming to Rome in our era will ride the Via Ostiense from the airport into the city. In the excavations of the old seaport of Ostia you may walk upon the original paving stones of the Ostian Highway.

Via Tiburtina, Via Nomentana, and Via Salaria are the great eastern routes. The first leaves the city from in back of the railroad yards at Porta San Lorenzo, passes the basilica outside-the-walls named for the same saint and climbs to Tivoli (*Tibur* in ancient times). Most tourists get to travel this road at least once, for two renowned sites await in Tivoli: Villa d'Este and Villa Adriana. My sons strongly recommend that just a few miles before you arrive in the hilltop town you hold your nose, the better to survive the aroma from the sulfur baths along the road.

The second route takes leave of the city at Porta Pia, heads for old Nomentum, today called Mentana, twelve miles northeast of Rome. Starting out, the road is lined with luxurious villas and their gardens. While the physical features of today's Via Nomentana are modern it still follows the line of the consular road. Six miles outside the gate we come to *Ponte Nomentano* which with its formidable battlements spans the Aniene River. Over the river at this juncture we see the quarter of *Monte Sacro.* To this "sacred hill" retreated the plebian masses in 494 B.C. after their petitions for a stake in the city's prosperity had been ignored for decades. They seceded to form their own new nation. One of their own, Menenius Agrippa, mediated the dispute, convincing both sides by way of a clever allegory to the effect that, "divided we shall all perish."

Via Salaria, one of the oldest Roman roads, got its name from the salt trade Rome carried on with the Sabine nations to which it led. Just beyond Piazza Fiume where Salaria begins we come to the entrance of the Catacombs of Priscilla with their copious second century paintings. The road will also conduct us, if we wish, to the beautiful region of the Abruzzi.

For a northeast route we may take the Via Flaminia which begins where the Corso, one of the city's main drags, leaves off — at the Piazza del Popolo. Opened by the censor Caius Flaminius, this route eventually arrives smack under the Arch to Augustus in Rimini on the Adriatic, up near Venice.

The Via Cassia takes us north inland to medieval Viterbo. While this was roughly cut through to Etruria in early Republican times it was not paved until the consulate of C. Cassius Longinus in 107 B.C. A day in Viterbo and the hamlets surrounding it is one well spent we think. If you get a chance drive out along the Tiber, cross over at Ponte Milvio, bear right at the large white church and you are on the Via Cassia, headed for a pleasant ride through gentle countryside. At the eleventh kilometer marker on your left sits the American Overseas School of Rome, founded after the war by writer Michael Stern and his wife, to provide a place of education for their children and those of other Americans who had suddenly decided they were never leaving. The children of the American Embassy personnel call this, an elementary and a high school, their Alma Mater. The Overseas School, now on a beautiful campus, is a living testimonial to the resourcefulness and optimism of our good friend, Mr. Stern. Read of its one-room schoolhouse beginnings in Mike's best seller, "An American in Rome."

Because of our interest in lovely beaches like Fregene and Santa Severa and Santa Marinella and in fascinating Etruscan cities like Cerveteri and Tarquinia and Civitavecchia, we are regularly on the ancient Via Aurelia. Just up the block from the American Academy is the Porta San Pancrazio which marks the beginning of this western coast-road to the north. The home of some dear friends of ours is also a mile down the Aurelian Way from the gate, bringing us out here even more frequently. There is a really beautiful stretch of the highway about a half hour out of Rome where it passes through a long honor guard of marvelous pines.

Well then, when you are coming in or out of Rome, from now on be a little more conscious of the route you are taking and in the future any reference to such roads in books, programs, movies about ancient Rome will delight you, for you can then say with certitude: "I too once traveled that road."

Omnes viae Romam portant

The Roman Forum

III

The Forum

"In our fair city Jesus and His saints live in the very skies." I once heard this remark by a zealous guide in front of the Basilica of San Giovanni in Laterano. He was pointing to the statues of Jesus and the Apostles, outlined against the peerless blue sky of the Eternal City, that grace the facade of the official Cathedral of Rome. Throughout Rome the guide's poetic line is justified. For breezy angels, mitred cardinals, contemplative doctors of the church, all in marble, peer down at the congested streets of Rome from church rooftops and colonnades, or stare ecstatically in the direction of the heavens.

This celestial population has its ancestors in the Roman Forum of distant centuries where statues of patriots, Roman deities, and emperors, carved in marble or cast in gilded bronze, crowned the pagan temples and imposing basilicas of what some observers have said is, "the most celebrated piece of real estate on this planet."

One must, to appreciate the grandeur and moment of this trapezoidal area today, see, in his mind's eye, statues along with the marble veneers, pavement, and columns, the colorful pageantry of a triumph, the sea of humanity spilling out into the teeming streets of downtown Rome.

Next to our own apartment in the charming quarter of *Monteverde Vecchio,* the Forum is our favorite spot in Rome. Only when one comes here for the first time can the monotonous propaganda of his high school Latin teacher be vindicated. The endless trials with the Ablative, the Pluperfect, the Subjunctive all begin to pay their thrilling dividends when one arrives at the ancient marketplace. And only the student or former student of Latin can grasp the real meaning of the *Forum Romanum.*

In this historical valley between the Palatine, the Capitoline, and the Esquiline, originated the concepts of Roman law which formed the foundations of Western jurisprudence. Here too took place some of the most momentous and far reaching events of the classical era. The fate of mankind was often determined here and the destiny of the world shaped for untold ages to come.

Ancient Rome's family album is the Forum, with souvenirs and visible reminders of her every epoch, from the Etruscan burial ground, to relics of the Monarchy and the Republic, to the handsome ruins of temples and government buildings of the Empire.

If you could have walked along the Via Sacra in 750 B.C., which was then but a sylvan path, you would have witnessed the peace conference of Romulus and Tatius, King of the Sabines.

On November 9, 63 B.C., you would have heard for yourself the fiery eloquence of Marcus Tullius Cicero when he delivered his famous invective, the Second Oration against Catiline, from the great rostrum.

On March 16, 44 B.C., the day after Rome's darkest day, you would have participated in the cremation of Gaius Julius Caesar.

In the year 27 B.C., Augustus' inaugural parade would have thrilled you. In the next century you would have wanted to arrive at the Forum early for a close look at the saintly sovereign, Antoninus Pius.

Later centuries would have excited you with the monumentalization of the eastern end of the Forum via the Basilica of Maxentius and the Rotunda of Romulus.

A great outdoor theatre was the Forum with such varied presentations across the ages as royal funerals, gladiatorial tournaments, triumphal returns, political rallies, raucous protest marches, and bloody riots, assassinations, catastrophic fires, and barbarian invasions.

Another way to describe it as it appears today, I suppose, would be as Imperial Rome's graveyard — a vast grassy, stony, and serene park with a cemetery air to it all, with even the visitors moving about in appropriately solemn silence; a silence sometimes shattered by the gleeful screams of my three sons and their Roman *amici* leaping over fallen columns, through arches, and up and down time-honored flights of stairs in a sacrilegious battle of water pistols.

Camille, undaunted, remains absorbed in a guidebook with a wonderful new device — plastic overlays to present the Forum Romanum in "now" and "then" pictures.

A never ending source of pleasure for me is to take my bride and my brood and the neighborhood *ragazzi* down to the old market place, flightbag slung on one shoulder, containing a light lunch of cheese, fruit and wine for all, a slide camera, clipboard and pens for my *in situ* research. All of us quickly disperse and lose ourselves among the melancholy vestiges of the ages. The kids literally do try to lose themselves in great games of *hide and seek,* in a place that provides an infinity of hiding spots.

Visitors in the summertime do not hold up very well under the heat which, when trapped in the recess of the Forum, turns it into a dusty sauna, and as a result while the other sites of Rome teem with tourists, we have this place to ourselves along with a few other dedicated students of Roman Civilization.

Beautiful in all seasons, even in the gloomy rains of

winter, especially so in the brisk Roman autumn, the Forum is at its most appealing to Camille and me in spring when the ruins are dressed in a necklace of wild flowers and the air is perfumed with mint and other fragrances from the bursting vegetation.

This Forum lies sleeping but her great-great-grandchildren live on, all about the modern city of Rome. For the modern piazza, you see, is a direct descendant of this early neighborhood gathering place. *Fores* is ancient Latin for outdoors, an open space, a meeting place; *fuori* in modern Italian. And these were precisely the original functions of this place.

Inhabitants of the surrounding hills found this recess an excellent, mutually convenient place to exchange goods, crops, and ideas. It remained such for the longest time, resembling very much the noisy but colorful outdoor markets of today's Rome such as the one in Campo dei Fiori, or the Sunday flea market at Porta Portese, until the Emperor Domitian in the first century of our era, deciding that they brought down the dignity of the place, banished the peddlers to other parts of the city.

Other special *fora* developed in central Rome. While there are no tangible remains of any of them we can still locate the sites of four: The Forum Boarium (meat market); Forum Pescarium (fish); Forum Cupedinis (delicacies); and the Forum Holitorium (vegetables).

As Rome grew, so too grew her need for a center of government and bureaucracy and that is how the valley began its career as the political playground of the world. In time the bankers and stock brokers of Rome came here to transact their affairs. Since it was fast becoming the focal point of the Roman citizenry, temples to the gods began to punctuate the Forum too, so that it was to become Wall Street, City Hall, Fifth Avenue, St. Patrick's Cathedral, and Mulberry Street all rolled into one — a place for legislating, banking and investing, politicking and lobbying, worshipping and shopping, pomp and colorful pageantry. Cicero in a letter to Atticus speaks of the political phonies that frequent the place, while Horace writes in complaint of the noise, and the parasites that importune the celebrity up and down the Via Sacra, and how he yearns for the pure serenity of his villa in the Sabines.

Now, after this humble background, be our guest for a few pages on a brisk guided tour of this famous place. Unfortunately, nowadays we cannot enter through the Arch of Titus having first climbed the gentle slope of the Via Sacra, for the entrance to the Forum is on the Via Fori Imperiali at which we must pay an admission of 200 lire (35¢) unless we have one of those M.I.P. (Ministry of Public Instruction) cards good for entrance to archaeological sites and government museums all over Italy. This card is the greatest investment of a dollar during a trip to Rome, I hasten to add. The cards are obtainable back in the states through the Italian Consulate on Park Avenue in New York and in Rome at the Ministry itself on Viale Trastevere.

We pass through the turnstile down a sharp ramp with the impressive Temple of Antoninus and Faustina on our left. Let us proceed at once left on the Via Sacra, a few hundred yards up hill to the Arch of Titus and start all over, following the traditional route of triumphs, imperial corteges, and visiting diplomats.

Standing now on the Sacred Way we admire the flowing lines and bas reliefs of the 30-foot-high arch, erected in 81 A.D., to commemorate Titus' taking of Jerusalem back in 70. The inscription, in some of the most beautiful Latin lettering to be found in Rome, proclaims: *Senatus Populus que Romanus Divi Tito Divi Vespasiani Vespasiano Augusto.* Putting to use our high school knowledge of nominatives, genitives, and datives we translate it to: "The Senate and the Roman People, to the Divine Titus Vespasian Augustus, son of the Divine Vespasian."

On the ceiling and inside walls of the Arch notice the representations of the enslavement of the Jews as they carry their holy tablets, candelabra, and other religious articles. Orthodox Jews of Rome today will not pass through the arch because of its symbolism.

We follow the Via Sacra which descends and twists right for a few yards behind the temple of Venus and Rome, skirting the popular church of Santa Francesca Romana, to the immense halls of the Basilica of Maxentius. The word *basilica* meant law court. Its ecclesiastical use today is due to the early Christian use of the basilical form for church architecture. The basilica style was a hall with a wide center aisle, with two or more side aisles, an apse, in Roman times for the judge's bench, in Christian times for the main altar, with a roof supported by columns. Begun in 306 A.D. by Maxentius, it was completed in 313 in the reign of Constantine and is sometimes referred to by the latter's name.

With its sweeping arches, vaulted and coffered ceiling, and its spacious interior, it served as a model for Renaissance architects. Michelangelo would sit by the hour, by the day, sketchpad in hand, making notes on the dimensions, proportions, material, etc., to help him with his plans for the new St. Peter's.

Adjacent to this ruin is the little rotunda, perfectly intact, called the Temple of Romulus. It honors not the first king but Maxentius' son Romulus Augustulus. The bronze doors are original and, incredibly enough, the lock still works.

There is a long-established policy in Rome never to tear anything down from the past if at all possible. And so for centuries the Romans have built over, under, around, and through, remains of ancient structures. This temple illustrates this practice well for it is now joined to and serves as the sanctuary of the church of Saints Cosmas and Damian the entrance to which is on the Via Fori Imperiali.

I can recommend a visit to this fine church also for the beautiful *Presepio* therein.

Continuing on the Via Sacra we come to the oldest thing in the Forum, established long before the city of Rome in fact. It is a tiny Etruscan cemetery with graves now outlined by grassy patches.

The next stop is my special delight in the Forum, the Temple of Antoninus and Faustina. Dating to 141 A.D., it has its original porch, colonnade and outer walls. The 45-foot high columns, viewed best after ascending a lovely flight of stairs, support an entablature of immense marble stones. Its inscription tells that it was dedicated to the deified wife of Antoninus Pius and in 161, upon the ruler's death, to him too. What delights me most however, is that the eleventh century church of San Lorenzo in Miranda appears to have been dropped from the sky right into the middle of it. So it is possible here to worship inside a Catholic church which is inside a Roman pagan temple.

Crossing the little street through which we entered the Forum we arrive at the skimpy remains of the Basilica Aemilia of 179 B.C. Study the tile floor however to see the green stains from the bronze coins dropped in haste as the people fled from the fire which razed it during the sack of Rome.

An alleyway called the *Argiletum* divided the basilica from the building next door, the *Curia*. The Argiletum was a side exit from the marketplace to the Esquiline section.

The Curia was the Senate chamber where parliamentary proceedings produced the laws that governed the vast empire. Once veneered in marble, the building, finally restored by Diocletian in 283 A.D., owes its remarkable state of preservation to the fact that it became in the 600's a church to St. Hadrian. In the 1930's it was deconsecrated and declared an historic site. The original doors of the Curia can be seen over in San Giovanni in Laterano.

Shakespeare errs when he says Caesar was killed here,

for it is known that the dictator had undertaken a great face-lifting program for Rome's government buildings and that in March of 44 B.C., the senate chamber was full of scaffolding inside and out. As a result senate sessions were being held in the Theatre of Pompey a few blocks away. It is there that Caesar fell, but he likely passed the Curia on his way down from the Palatine that fateful day and checked the progress of the renovation.

In front of the Curia was an area called the *comitium* (meeting place — from which we derive the word committee).

Farther out in front of the Senate near the center of the Forum was the *Rostrum,* or speaker's platform. In this same area we see the steps leading to the *Lapis Niger* (Black Stone), considered the possible grave of Romulus.

The Via Sacra rises here through the Arch of Septimius Severus up the *clivus* (slope) *Capitolinus* to the former site of the huge temple to Jupiter. Halfway up the rise and to the right of it we come to the Mamertine Prison with its horrible Tullianum Dungeon. While we can no longer approach the next few sites of the Forum this way let's pretend so to feel like the old-time *cives Romani.* Actually one must leave the Forum and walk along its edge up at the modern street level to get to where we now want to go. The jail is still intact with the church of St. Joseph the Carpenter standing above it. One flight of steps down from street level brings us into the gruesome *carcere.* Through a grating in the floor, still there, important prisoners were lowered to the hell-hole Tullianum. Down in that cursed place Peter and Paul spent their last earthly hours. A legend on a marble plaque explains how Peter converted the guards assigned to flog him.

In this same room Vercingetorix, the gutsy Gallic chieftain, was executed and here too were strangled the five co-conspirators of Catiline caught the night before with incriminating documents on the *Ponte Milvio.*

Back into the daylight, we turn right and bend with the Via del Carcere Mamertino up to the rubble of the Temple of Concord, erected in 366 B.C., to honor the goddess of harmony on the occasion of the concordat between the patricians and plebians. Next, to the three columns still standing from the Temple of Vespasian from 79 A.D. Both temples backed onto the Tabularium or public archives building of old Rome. Two stories of the hall of records still stand, supporting the current *Palazzo Senatorio,* designed by Michelangelo, which faces the beautiful *Piazza Campidoglio.* From the portico of the Tabularium and from several other vantage points on the Capitoline, one is afforded a breathtaking look at this glorious spot, with the Colosseum peeking over the shoulders of Venus and Rome. Here Gibbon, one day at dusk, derived the inspiration to start his great account of the fall of Rome. On a summer night the view of the floodlit Forum Romanum from the precipice of the Capitoline is also an unforgettable experience. A fragment of the *Porticus Deorum* (entrance of the gods) is adjacent to Vespasian's temple. Heading back toward the heart of the Forum we meet the great ionic colonnade and 30-foot-high porch of the Temple of Saturn, the Roman god of agriculture whose feast was celebrated wildly and merrily in the month of December.

Now we descend deep into the valley again and on our left is the glittering *Milliarium Aureum* (golden milestone) from which were measured, and on which were noted, the distances to all the important places of the Empire. All that remains is a fragment of the column that contained the stone.

And just in front of the milestone looms again the rostrum (Latin for beak; so called because it was ornamented with the decorative beaks of captured enemy ships). From this huge platform the eminent orators of Rome's long and great oratorical history — the greatest being Marcus Tullius Cicero of course — enthralled the populace with their campaign rhetoric and pie-in-the-sky promises.

A few yards out in front of the platform is the youngest of the Forum's monuments, the column of Phocas, who seized the eastern throne. This dates to 608 A.D. and is said to mark the end of the classical world and the commencement of the Middle Ages.

Proceeding back toward the Arch of Titus we pass on our right the Basilica Julia, built in the reign of Julius Caesar and restored by Augustus. This basilica, like the others, had shops, money exchanges, and the like, out in front while inside, courts of all kinds were set up for cases of petty theft, divorce, murder, treason, etc.

Flowing under this courthouse and cutting from south to north beneath the Forum is the *Cloaca Maxima* (great sewer) the gift of the great engineers of Tarquinus Priscus, Rome's fifth king in the 600's B.C. This incredible drain still services that part of Rome and one can see by standing on the *Ponte Palatino* where the Cloaca Maxima spills into the Tiber.

Three columns and the foundation for the porch and the cella are all that remain of the Temple of Castor and Pollux which honored the legendary gemini who helped Rome to victory over the Tarquins. Out in the center of the Forum at this juncture is the relic of the Temple to Julius Caesar and directly behind it — excavation work still goes on here — the *Regia* or home of the *Pontifex Maximus,* chief priest of the pagan religion.

Just south of the Regia we have the lovely rotunda of Vesta, goddess of the fireplace. One temple after another stood on this site to solemnize the primitive custom of having a few women responsible for keeping the community fire going. This was later formalized into the order of the Vestal Virgins, nuns who lived in the convent out back with its cloister. If the fire went out they would be scourged on order of the Pontifex Maximus. Having taken a vow of chastity, the Vestals faced the sentence of being buried alive for violation of the same. Tradition relates that deep below the Tabularium are the vaults of the few unchaste Vestals who entered them, supplied with a portion of bread, a vial of wine and a small lamp, to be sealed into eternity. The virgins spent ten years in study for their religious career, ten years in conducting the sacred rituals of Vesta, and ten in teaching the incoming virgins. After their thirtieth year of service they were free to re-enter the secular life, but few did, for the office of the Vestal Virgin was such a signal honor.

Rising high above us all along this side of the Forum are the Imperial palaces on the Palatine Hill.

Let us then take our leave in the fashion that we entered this most historic place, through the Arch of Titus. And on arriving thither let us turn around and gaze once more on "the most celebrated piece of real estate in the world" and contemplate for a few moments the role it has played in the drama of Western Civilization, and pray that God will grant us the chance to return again and again.

Grazie della tua compagnia

Author on balcony of the dome of St. Peter's — overlooking Rome

IV

The Seven Hills

Rome's unique topography is responsible for much of the city's incomparable beauty. It has rendered Rome a city of hills and valleys and endless *belvederi* (Italian for "beautiful vistas"). It gives the city her marvelous mantle of pink and yellow and violet hues as the sun climbs over one hill and dips behind another.

The hills — none of which are very high (they range from 160 to 180 feet in altitude) but all of which are adorned by nature with the living green of ilex, cypress, and pine, and by man with the grey marble of palaces, villas, and churches — are an integral part of the romance of the city and to know Rome one ought to know her hills.

While the "City of the Seven Hills" is one of the most popular pseudonyms of Rome there are a number of other hills which nestle among these celebrated ones. Whether they are hills in their own right or merely additional summits of the fabled seven depends on one's point of view.

All seven are best viewed together by standing on what the boys and I arrogantly refer to as "Our Hill," i.e. the Janiculum. This elevation is treated in another chapter.

So many people come to Rome and never consciously visit the seven hills for a) they are not aware of this characteristic of Rome or b) it is difficult to distinguish where one hill ends and the other begins. This chapter will resolve both matters, we trust, by giving a historical account of each hill, along with its boundaries, and the landmarks by which it may be recognized.

Yes, the boundaries are discernible. For example. The Via di San Gregorio heading toward the Colosseum passes through the Aventine and then comes to the Palatine on the left, with the Caelian along the right side. The Capitoline slopes up behind the Victor Emmanuel monument from Piazza Venezia. Behind Augustus' Forum rises the Esquiline while the well-traveled Via Nazionale splits the Quirnal from the Viminal.

Two other renowned hills of today's Rome are the Vatican and the Pincian, both described also at some length in other chapters.

Shrouded in legend, this lovely chain of soft, rolling hills pressing in on the Tiber is probably what enticed the Albans to come down from their own mounts to establish a city on the banks of the river in the 8th century before Christ. Some historians though, insist that the site was inhabited long before this and in support of their belief they offer architectural ruins on the Palatine which they claim date from the 1100's.

Livy says that Romulus planted the city's first dwellings here in 753 B.C. but archaeologists insist they have unearthed remains of villages of 1000 B.C., and beyond.

Vergil's account is that Romulus and Remus led their fellow Albans to this area and then debated which of the hills would be the ideal site for a new city. Remus climbed the Aventine to pray for a sign from the gods and while in prayer saw in the sky six vultures, birds of the deities. Romulus having gone to the Palatine indicated that he saw 12 vultures and as a result was given the right to name the new city which he quickly did in honor of himself.

I lean to the theory that it was settled by Evander (in

the 12th century B.C.) son of Hermes from Pallantion in Arcadia, who named the settlement for his native city and that it was expanded by a coalition of Latins, Sabines, and Etruscans three or four centuries later.

Whatever the truth, it is a safe assumption that the original settlers had no idea that their descendants were destined someday to dominate and govern the world from this idyllic and bucolic spot. For the ancient village was very modest in size. Remains of what is popularly called Romulus' wall indicate that the city of the first king — *Roma Quadrata* — was but 24 acres in size.

While I've been daily attending classes or working as a guide, the boys have escorted their mother on many occasions to the Palatine so that she might conduct some *in situ* research whose findings have provided much information for this account. She carries out this scholarship via a simple Italian guidebook on the topic and thereby kills a second bird (i.e. practicing her Italian) with one stone. Camille and our oldest boys are classmates in their Italian studies at a small tutorial school near the main railroad station.

May we conduct you now on a visit to all seven hills starting with the lofty Palatine which is the cradle not only of Rome but of Western civilization.

This hill was significant in each of ancient Rome's three ages — the Kingdom, the Republic, and the Empire. Along with the fragments of his wall have been discovered foundations of Romulus' hut and of the dwellings of his subjects. Large blocks of porous tufa point to the first massive Roman fortifications. These were to serve as the substructure for the Imperial Palaces. A sixth century B.C. cistern has also been found, which gave the primitive city its water supply.

In the Renaissance, the Farnese clan purchased the land and converted it to a sumptuous villa with vineyards and orange groves. In our day the site, wonderfully photogenic, is a large historical park, the Farnese Gardens, where the fragmented marble of Rome's former splendors lies scattered about, half-hidden in wiry grass and wild flowers, with a captivating museum, a quaint but inobtrusive café with outdoor tables, with unforgettable vistas in all directions but especially of *Forum Romanum* in the front and of *Circus Maximus* in the rear.

Centuries unfold for us here on many summer afternoons in the pages of this fantastic living textbook on Roman History. The summit is reached either by the winding road that stretches upward from the Arch of Titus past the picturesque monastery and church of St. Bonaventure, or from the Forum, behind the convent of the Vestals, through the soaring halls of the palatial ruins.

Here was the *Lupercal,* an ancient sanctuary to the Faun Lupercus who defended the sheep from wolves; where licentious rituals were conducted from deep antiquity to (even over the objections of Rome's bishops) the 5th century A.D.

It is here that tradition holds Romulus and Remus were suckled by a she-wolf and discovered by the shepherd Faustulus, a resident of the hilltop hamlet. An Etruscan bronze sculpture commemorating this was erected in the 6th century before Christ. It can now be viewed in the Capitoline Museum.

Though the Kingdom was replaced by the Republic, the Palatine never lost its eminent status; for prosperous lawyers, statesmen and bankers, built fashionable homes here. We know this for certain from their personal correspondence and from contemporary historians. Marcus Tullius Cicero, the recognized leader of the Roman bar and the social lion of his day, constructed a lavish estate above the Forum. This "country bumpkin," as his jealous foes labeled him, had indeed come a long way, from the rural village of Arpinum 60 miles south of the Capital off the Via Latina, having picked his way gingerly through the vicissitudes of the maelstrom of Roman politics. Among his Palatine neighbors were his future antagonists, Catiline and Clodius, and numerous other political luminaries. G. Julius Caesar, however, expediently chose to reside on the Esquiline with *hoi polloi*, whose favor at the ballot box he would soon be seeking.

When the Ciceros first arrived in the Capital (the father had wished the boys Marcus 10 and Quintus 7, to be exposed to the cosmopolitan air of the City and to receive a Roman education) the family lived in a section of the Esquiline called the *Carinae* (keels) for the fronts of buildings there had the shape of a ship because of the peculiar layout of the streets.

When we walk here I always encourage my clan, as *pater familias*, to reconstruct in their minds' eyes the villas with their porticoes, statues, gardens, mosaics, murals, etc., and the snooty dinner parties from which many guests must have staggered in the dark, quite inebriated, down from the Palatine to their homes on other hills.

However, the relics which greet us today are not Republican but rather Imperial. Strolling along to the summer song of a happy bird or the incessant chatter of a shiftless cicada we come upon the ghostly but lovely ruins of the emperors' palace. This place and the Forum have, through the ages, held a spooky fascination for all visitors.

This habitat of kings and consuls became the domain of Augustus, first of the emperors. Born on the Palatine he chose superstitiously and sentimentally to rule from a mansion erected on the site of his birth. Popularly referred to as the House of Livia (Augustus' wife), the place is still preserved enough for one to appreciate its household shrine, its murals, its floor plan. One painting is of a typical street scene of Augustan Rome — houses with balconies, shutters, tile rooftops, apartment buildings with their tiny shops at street level.

While the residence of Augustus was one of moderate

luxury the one of his successor Tiberius was sumptuous. But even this opulence couldn't prevent the elderly sovereign from moving to the island of *Caprea* (Capri) from which he ruled his sprawling dominion by remote control for the last decade of his reign.

His majesty, the demented Caligula, raised a fantastic royal residence between Tiberius' palace and the Forum on the site of Cicero's home (which had been overrun a century earlier by Clodius' gangs after the orator's unjust exile). Of Caligula's place only the substructure now remains. For the gory details of his assassination here on January 24, 41 A.D. in the underground gallery (known in Latin as *cryptoporticus*) you would do well to read Suetonius. Each time we visit the Palatine as a family I must be sure to have a copy of *The Twelve Caesars* with me, for the boys are sure to request, while sitting on fallen columns taking a make-shift lunch, the hair-raising account of this murder.

Most of the palatial ruins visible today are from the House of the Flavians, the dynasty that included Vespasian and his two sons, Titus and Domitian. (The last was also a victim of assassination.) In this royal residence, highly polished marble panels served as mirrors, and works of art abounded. There were spacious throne rooms, banquet halls, and even a vast basilica where the emperor would hear appeals. (Every civis Romanus had the right to appeal to his Caesar.) These palaces, often restored and expanded, were in use as late as the 7th century by the Byzantine emperors.

We like to observe the Forum from this vantage point and, around to the other side, stride out onto the vast terrace or descend to the royal box overlooking the Circus Maximus. On the Palatine too is the battered shell of a sizable stadium whose function still bewilders classical scholars. My suggestion is that it was the scene of many stupendous command performances by the outstanding athletes of the age for the royalty of the age.

The Palatine is a great summer retreat for the Roman and the foreigner both. An ideal place for a walk to contemplate the ancient splendor of it all. And there'd be much more to contemplate if the unthinking lime burners of the middle ages hadn't set up their kilns on the hill to burn the statuary and columns and fountains to lime. When your visit is over go on to the Circus Maximus, cross the valley, ascend the Aventine, and look back for another great perspective of *Mons Palatinus*. (And then come back to the same point at night when the ruins are drenched in the silvery rays of Diana and the fiery glow of orange floodlights. Unreal!)

In the valley of the Palatine and Aventine, Mother Nature provided a race course. All the Romans had to do was to cover the slopes of both hills with tiers of marble seats to create the immense stadium which could seat a quarter of a million people. Now the marble is all gone and Nature has reclaimed her creation.

A gentle ascent from Piazzale Romolo e Remo with its huge monument to the patriot Giuseppe Mazzini — who sits pensively high above the square, eyes closed to the beauties around him — along the walled-in Via di Valle Murcia, will convey you to the summit of the most residential of the seven hills.

Friends inform us that this is the Romans' favorite hill. In fact we were introduced to it on our second night in Rome via a thorough guided tour conducted by our Roman "brother" Mario Tamagnini, his wife Paola and Mamma Tamagnini.

In antiquity the hill was the neighborhood not of the fabulously wealthy, as was the Palatine, but of the financially comfortable (Rome's sparse middle class). They dwelled here in moderate taste and quiet dignity among such landmarks as the Temple of Diana, the Baths of Decian, and fine public parks and gardens.

When the persecutions were lifted, the Christians established wondrous churches and monasteries across the hill. The Aventine is most noted in our age for its many beautiful churches. The music of the hill is that of church bells.

At the top of the street we came in on, is perhaps the loveliest church of them all, the ancient Santa Sabina. Built in the ruins of Diana's temple, this house of worship, completed in 425, honors another virgin who lived in a house on the spot and who was martyred under Hadrian in 124. Its builder was a priest from Ilyria (now Yugoslavia) hence its design is distinct from the Roman architecture of the time. Noteworthy are the cypress doors, with panels of biblical scenes, which date from the early 5th century. Opposite the cypress doors through an aperture in the wall one can catch sight of the little *cortile* with the orange tree that tradition says was planted by St. Dominic. Dominic was a friar here, and so too was St. Thomas Aquinas.

Popes and cardinals through the ages, especially Honorius III in the 13th century, have loved to come here and pray in the Aventine's churches and monasteries.

The tremendous windows have, instead of glass, a material called silenite.

The soaring basilica looks over the shoulders of orange trees and pines in the adjacent park, whose eminence affords another beautiful vista of Rome. From here one can look across to the rooftops of Trastevere, the monument of Garibaldi high upon the Janiculum, and the dome of St. Peter's. To the right appears the graceful bend of the Tiber, the squared alabaster dome of the synagogue, the Victor Emmanuel Monument, and Renaissance bell towers and baroque domes galore. No place more conducive to peace of mind and soul exists in Rome. Peter and Paul evidently thought so, for they came here often to renew their weary spirits while staring blankly out over the city.

Further up the street from Santa Sabina and on the

left is a quaint, gray-walled piazza by Piranesi (which looks like one of his prints come to life). Behind the strong walls and iron gate on the right is the independent territory of the Knights of Malta. The boys are always eager to show our guests the famous keyhole through which can be seen three countries at one time. Try it and you will see the first country — the little territory of the military order with which quite a few nations maintain diplomatic ties, then the rooftops of Trastevere (Italy) and, perfectly framed by a bower of trees, the dome of the Great Basilica (the Vatican, and country number three).

In the same neighborhood we have still another treat, the great Benedictine seminary of Sant' Anselmo, with its pink walls and slender campanile, situated in beautiful gardens. Established in the late 1800's by Leo XIII for scholarly Benedictines from all over the world to have an opportunity to study near the seat of Christendom, the seminary attracts many Romans who still love the old Latin rites of the church. For each day at dusk the voices of the monks at chapel can be heard in the solemnly beautiful and simple chant of the early Church.

Also close by to all this is the 4th century church of Sant' Alessio. Having taken a vow of celibacy and having pledged himself to a life of prayer and solitude, young Alessio fled from his home here on the morning of his wedding day and returned disguised to beg at his parents' door almost two decades later. Approached by a charming courtyard, the church contains relics of the saint and has a well-preserved 10th century Greek icon of the Blessed Virgin.

Largely unknown to and therefore ignored by tourists, the Aventine allows for deep concentration and contemplation. Down the slope toward Viale Aventino is the family's favorite church, favored not especially for its physical qualities as for its rich Christian history. This is Santa Prisca, upon the home of Jewish converts, Aquila and Priscilla (Prisca is a shortened version of the name). When Claudius ordered the deportation from the city of all Jews, the couple, tentmakers by trade, sought asylum in Corinth where they crossed paths with Paul who plied the same trade. It is mentioned in the Acts of the Apostles by St. Luke that they then accompanied Paul to Ephesus. When they were readmitted to the city by Nero they returned to their house on the Aventine where they frequently hosted Peter and Paul. Excavations at the church have turned up parts of the house where the two Apostles often celebrated Holy Mass for the Aventine's Christian community.

Adjacent to Santa Prisca is the romantic inn, Hotel Souvenir, owned by some dear friends of ours. Signora Menciotti takes such a personal interest in the welfare and comfort of her guests that all who stay there leave with almost a filial affection for her. We always recommend the inn for our friends coming from the states and point out to them that they will be awakened each morn by the little bell of Santa Prisca and walk in the very footsteps of the Apostolic Princes.

Where churches there are none, the Aventine is covered with villas of high stone walls, formidable gates, flowered balconies, gardens and vineyards and a great variety of trees. Also to be found are quiet *trattorie* and cafés, free of tourists and in harmony with the gentle Aventine atmosphere.

When energy allows, we enjoy a climb to the top of Little Aventine, across Viale Aventino, to San Saba, an ancient Eastern church. Its reddish glow at sunset is a memorable sight.

Rome's Holy of Holies today, i.e., its most sacred area, is Vatican Hill where the largest church in all Christendom can be found. The *Sancta Sanctorum* of the Ancient City was the Capitoline Hill. On its summit stood the most important temple in all paganism, that of *Jupiter*

Capitolinus, flanked by two other major temples — one to Minerva, the other to *Juno Moneta* (Juno the Warner). In the latter, currency was minted giving English its word — *money.*

From this point the Etruscans dominated the infant city. On the northern summit was the *Arx* (citadel) to which the citizens hastened in time of peril to the city. Southeast is the ridge classicists call the Tarpeian cliff, from which the Vestal Tarpeia was hurled to her death for an act of treason. She lies buried still in the bowels of the hill, the Romans will insist. The early Romans as they passed here would look up in awe and reverence at the hill which they also believed to be the home of the Unknown God who watched over the city's destiny.

In front of Juno's shrine, Augustus erected an altar to another unknown divinity who, so prophesied the Tiburtine Sybil, would someday be honored here and throughout the city. Many believe that this divinity was Christ. From soon after the empire's fall a majestic church, *Ara Coeli* (Latin for Altar of Heaven, a pagan term) has looked out over the center of Rome. A most arresting feature of the church is its wood carving of *Bambino Gesù,* said to have been sculptured from a tree in the Garden of Gethsemane.

During the Republic the inauguration of the consuls took place on this hill with appropriate pomp and circumstance. The Sybilline books, Rome's bible, were enshrined here. This was the terminus for the gala triumphal processions. In 1963, months before his death, President John F. Kennedy addressed the Italian people on this spot.

Fierce Goths in 546 set the Capitol ablaze and erased every trace of the ancient glories.

Yet the hill continued to be held in special reverence by the decimated populace throughout the Middle Ages. The demagogue Cola di Rienzo used it as his base of government.

Then in the early part of the 16th century the master, Michelangelo, was charged with the re-decoration of the Capitoline.

The wondrous beauty of the *Campidoglio* that welcomes us there today is chiefly the work of the prolific Florentine. The *cordonata* we climb to reach the summit is of his creation. Standing as sentries to the great square are the ancient colossal figures of Castor and Pollux, discovered nearby in the Jewish Ghetto among the ruins of their temple. At this point turn left a few paces and lean over the balustrade to see a caged wolf, a living symbolism of the wolf which nursed Romulus and Remus. Proceed along the ornamented tiled pavement to the incomparable centerpiece of the piazza, the ageless tarnished bronze equestrian statue of Marcus Aurelius. Michelangelo requested that this Imperial masterpiece be removed here from its berth in the Lateran. In awe of the great work, he was reluctant to fashion a base for the statue, thinking himself grossly unworthy. He relented and fashioned one out of a pillar from the Temple of Castor and Pollux. While there is no vestige of the Kingdom nor of the Republic on the Capitoline, the philosopher Emperor still rides in stoic determination for the Empire, returning the salute of legions who have been dust for two thousand years.

Michelangelo-designed museums stand to the left (*Museo Capitolino*) and to the right (*Palazzo dei Conservatori*) with the *Palazzo Senatorio* (or City Hall), the restoration work of Michelangelo, straight ahead.

Built into the extensive ruins of the Tabularium of Sulla (79 B.C.) in the 13th century, the Capitol was beautified by the genius touch of the Titan of the Renaissance. Bear left with us at City Hall, down the ramp a bit and, *Voila*! Forum Romanum lies in its stony confusion far below us.

Watch always for special national celebrations such as the Birthday of Rome on April 21. For on such occasions the torches on the facades of the Campidoglio's buildings are lit, rendering a marvelously medieval effect. Climb the staircase to the Palazzo Senatorio, some morning, for then the sun is just right, pause at the top to drink in the *vista indimenticabile* (unforgettable scene).

Upon an autumn night I like to walk with my love on the Campidoglio. Fueled by a decanter or two of Frascati, I seem to see her still; in flowing veils amidst the shadows, wounded, weeping — the tragic Tarpeia. Camille, stone sober, cruelly shatters the reverie with a strident, "You're crazy!" Camille the Incurable Romantic, I call her.

To reach our next hill we must stick close, lest we get irrevocably separated by the swirls of Roman traffic in front of the Victor Emmanuel. Run with us now to the little park by Trajan's Forum and we will proceed back along the Via dei Fori Imperiali past the great screening wall of Augustus whose aim it was to hide the squalid *Subura* (slum district) on the western slope of *Esquilino*. If we make our way to and left beyond the Colosseum we will eventually come upon the *Domus Aurea* of the deranged Nero. The ascent of the Esquiline has begun. This hill, infested during the Empire with thieves, pimps and their commodities, youth gangs, con men and other beautiful people, today has many charms to savor.

A lovely park, scene of many family touch football battles, where once stood the gardens of Maecenas, patron of Horace and Vergil and the boys; the holy basilica of *San Pietro in Vincoli*, home of the chains of Peter and the Moses of Michelangelo; Santa Maria Maggiore in all her magnificence (excavations beneath the Basilica last year turned up the walls of an ancient tavern among whose graffiti was the patriotic palindrome: *Roma Summus Amor*); and let us not leave the Esquiline without a visit to the memorable churches of Madonna dei Monti and Santa Prassede. Paul the Apostle is thought to have resided for a time in this neighborhood.

That's all for the *ine* hills (Palatine, Aventine, Capitoline, Esquiline). We will finish our circuit of the seven hills in a blaze of glory across the Quirinal, Viminal, and Coelian.

Quirinal (oak) is the northernmost hill of Rome. Originally a Sabine settlement it was adorned in later centuries with several important temples and public buildings. Italy's White House, the *Palazzo Quirinale* (formerly the summer residence of Popes) is approached by the long Via Venti Settembre which, as it nears, changes names to Via del Quirinale. Or by the Via Ventiquattro Maggio which climbs from the Piazza Magnanapoli. Let's take this route so we can pass the little chapel of St. Sylvester where Vittoria Colonna would host intellectual rap sessions in the cloister with Michelangelo and others. This approach presents too a better introduction to the great obelisk and the *Dioscuri* (huge statues of two horse tamers with their steeds discovered in the Baths of Constantine) with an *Acqua Felice* fountain at their feet. Ron's campaign pledge when he runs for mayor of Rome will be to close off this street to vehicular traffic, install a snow machine, and presto! . . . the world's most exquisite toboggan run. And he's not even fueled by Frascati!

Another belvedere of Rome is yours for the taking, along the balustrade on the west edge. Get back here some lazy afternoon to witness the ceremonial changing of the guard followed by a free concert of martial music. This never fails to bring out the parade-loving, little boy in everybody passing by. Businessmen, peddlers, even monks and nuns, none immune, stand pleasantly transfixed.

Via del Quirinale climbs to Via Quattro Fontane. On the way we pass some other Quirinal treats — a splendid public park to the right, just before Bernini's own favorite creation, the Church of Sant Andrea Al Quirinale, and right at Quattro Fontane, Borromini's fascinating Church of San Carlino. All strongly warrant your attention.

Via del Quirinale drops sharply now to the Fountain of Moses. Turning right at this juncture we are soon to discover the Viminal. Its landmarks? *Stazione Termini* (Rome's impressive railroad station), the verdant gardens of the Villa Aldobrandini, Teatro dell'Opera (Rome's Opera House) and the *Questura* (Police Headquarters). We enjoy the Latin motto in huge letters on the Questura walls to wit: *Ubi dolor est, ibi est vigilia* (where there is trouble, there is the police). The Romans delight in making the motto into a double entendre, with the cops as the butt.

Two beautiful Viminale churches that come to mind are Santa Caterina da Siena by Soria and S.S. Domenico e Sisto with its cascading baroque staircase. Viminale abounds in good, inexpensive places to eat and lodge.

A trolley ride from here back toward the Aventine would lend romance to a tour of the last of the seven, the *Caelian,* southernmost of them all. Its name honors the Etruscan warrior, Caelius Vibenna.

Like the Aventine this was a fashionable, quiet, residential district in the Empire. Today it is sparsely populated but possesses some fine churches and ruins. There is a lovely park frequented only by the neighbors it seems, the Villa Celimontana.

The fine churches include San Gregorio high upon the ridge opposite the Palatine, the 4th century Santi Quattro Coronati, with its two courtyards, and the mistress of all Rome's churches and the diocese's cathedral, San Giovanni in Laterano, residence of the Popes until the Papal throne shifted to Avignon in Southern France in the 13th century, all of which are discussed in another chapter.

Rome's Seven Hills ask so much of the tourist in terms of energy, attention, and patience but give so much back in terms of beauty, knowledge, and pleasure. We know. We come home from them pleasantly exhausted but enormously edified each day.

Urbs Septimontium

Ronald Korn looks toward the arena floor of the Colosseum

V

The Colosseum

Of all the city's splendid sights the greatest monument to Rome's eternity is the Colosseum.

This stupendous amphitheatre, squatting in the heart of the city, is perhaps the best known structure on earth. While all roads lead to Rome, all streets in Rome, it seems, lead to the Colosseum. Not really. But it is the glorious terminal for the impressive Via dei Fori Imperiali, the Via Labicana, the Via San Giovanni, the Via dei Santi Quattro, the Via Capo d'Africa, the Via Claudia, the Via San Gregorio, the Via del Parco Celio, the Via d'Annibaldi, the Via Nicolo Salvi, the Via Domus Aurea and still others.

Ravaged by time, but more so by unthinking men, the Colosseum today is but a gutted shell of the wondrous stadium the emperors and their subjects knew. Some observers however are convinced it is lovelier by far today, falling into ruin, than when it was young and healthy.

Except for a scattered incident or two Rome, an open city in World War II, was spared bombardment by all combatants. But there's that memorable, comical remark by a young American G.I. upon seeing the arena's ruins from a jeep as the first U.S. forces arrived in convoy on the day Rome was liberated from Nazi occupation: "Gee! I didn't realize how hard the Nazis were bombing this town."

More comical still, I find, is Johnny's reluctance to come to Rome for the first time. The occasion coincided with the summer riots across the United States. Johnny having seen newspaper and television pictures of the riot-torn areas concluded, upon viewing my slides of Rome, that the same thing was going on there, and he was having no part of it.

Neronian Rome had been one of the ugliest eras in the city's eight centuries of existence up to that point. Upon the tyrant's death the citizens rejoiced. Soon after, a Stalin-like purge was launched to turn Nero, or rather his ghost, into a non-person, to divest the town of all reminders of the butcher of Christians.

Vividly recalling the long night of his reign was his Domus Aurea with its expansive lake and gardens. Workmen began to dismantle the palace and the Emperor Vespasian got the idea to drain the lake.

There was growing a need for more sports arenas due to the increasing popularity of the gladiatorial games.

The first record of such games dates to 264 B.C. when the sons of a certain Brutus gave a series of sword bouts in the Forum Boarium as funeral games for their father. By 72 A.D. this activity had developed into the national pastime.

Vespasian having recently returned from his conquest of the province of Judea set to work on the design for a huge stadium an architect by the name of Gaudentius.

We assume this name from an inscription found in the Catacombs of St. Agnese which tells that a certain Gaudentius, had in 72 designed for Vespasian an enormous amphitheatre in the heart of Rome and that this same gentleman was later executed for being a Christian.

Twelve thousand Jewish P.O.W.'s provided a tremendous work force which would make possible the comple-

tion of the mind-boggling project in less than eight years.
Travertine, a yellowish white stone which still changes
hues through the day as Apollo in his chariot runs his relentless course, was quarried in Tivoli and transported the
twenty-five *kilometers* (old Roman miles) to the capital.

With the Jews toiling to save their very lives, great
boulders were hoisted into place with ingenious cranes.
Today we notice two gaping holes in each boulder from the
bronze clamps used to pin them one to another. These
clamps were taken to forge weapons in the middle ages.

Bricks by the million to furnish the superstructure
came in from companies near Ostia.

In the bricks too there are gaps in perfect rows about
every five feet. These are from beams set in on end and
across which were stretched planks to provide scaffolding.
We can draw conclusions here about the average height of
the workmen.

The amphitheatre, built on street level, rose in its
outer walls to a height of 160 feet. Its exterior designed an
ellipse 205 by 170 yards. This outer wall is still whole on
the north side, gone entirely on the south. The facade displayed four stories of different orders of architecture. On
the ground floor we see the Doric order, the Ionic above,
and Corinthian half columns in the two top rungs.

Down on the arena floor the dimensions were 285 by
182 feet. Wooden planks spanning the subterranean superstructure provided the stadium with a floor which in turn
was covered with a heavy layer of sand (in Latin: *arena*) to
absorb the blood of the athletes and animals participating
in the games.

Frank and Ron have long suppressed a burning desire
to get there early some quiet morn, equipped with a bat
and a supply of balls. The plan is for me to distract the attendants just long enough for one of the boys to make the
claim of hitting the first home run in history into the seats.
John thinks it all sacrilegious and I'm with Johnny.

Built on Nero's lake, which had been constructed in a natural bog, the whole theatre is said to float on pilings.

Various estimates are submitted regarding the crowd capacity of the Colosseum from as high as 107,000 to as low as 50,000.

There being no posts, except in the promenade for standing room at the very top, every seat afforded an unobstructed view.

Upon entering the stadium may we advise you to look up to see the Roman numerals over the arches. A ticket system was developed with the number of the arch one was to use stamped on the metal admission plate. Thus a ticketholder knew just where to enter and quickly find his seat in the grandstand.

Note particularly arches numbered XXXVIII and XXXIX for there is an arch between them.

Tradition has it that Titus spent his reign in a palace on the Esquiline, not the Palatine, and had a private underground gallery right to the arena which emerged at just this arcade.

Now *Colosseum* was not the name originally given to the new sports complex. Rather it was called the Flavian Amphitheatre from the family name of Vespasian, who never lived to see its completion.

Dedication of the stadium fell to his son Titus on opening day in the year 80. And what dedication ceremonies they were! One hundred consecutive days of pomp, pageantry, naval battles (the floor could be flooded with water from a passing aqueduct), chariot races, wild animal hunts, and of course the staple — gladiator fights.

In this stretch 5,000 wild beasts were killed. This symptomized already to some observers the decadence, decline, and ultimate fall of Rome.

Juvenal writing at about 100 A.D., would say in disgust about his countrymen: *"Date eis panem et circenses"* (just give them bread and circuses).

The gladiators would enter amidst much panoply. Their colors would indicate their sponsors. In the primitive years of the sport the participants were drawn from Rome's jails, slave population, P.O.W.'s or community of general malefactors. *Gladiator* was a term of contumely then. (Cicero a century earlier had used it as the worst thing he could think to call the hated Catiline.) But the sport caught on with the society crowd too and finally the senators had to be forbidden participation since they were beginning to neglect their duties of office in deference to a good workout with wooden swords.

That the sport gained respectability and acceptance is supported by the discovery in the excavations of Pompeii of a grand gladiator training school with barracks.

And little boys' drawings with names of outstanding gladiators on walls of buildings and gardens indicate that the better athletes enjoyed celebrity status.

Of course all this was in the post-Spartacus era. Conditions for the sword fighters previously had been so intolerable, that the gladiators dared to take on the military might of Republican Rome.

Approaching the imperial box, which surprisingly was situated on about the thirty-yard line, not midfield, the fighters would greet the emperor in chorus with the emotional and fatalistic words: *"Ave Caesar! Morituri te salutamus"* (Hail Caesar! We who are about to die salute you).

We hear of the thumb tradition (*pollice verso*) where the crowd would make a life or death determination for the losing warrior.

Sometimes the crowd would express itself vocally instead with the words *hoc habet!* (He's had it!) And the victor would thrust his blade through his supine opponent's chest.

Indignation by what was left of Rome's humane society rose and pressure was now and then exerted on the emperors to stop the carnage. Constantine was known to have abolished the bloody games for a while, but soon yielded to public demand and reinstated them.

At last, though, in 404 the monk Telemachus stepped before the crowd, now in large part Christian, and asked them, "in the name of Christ," to end the sadism. He was at once stoned to death but his courageous action haunted the conscience of the public, and the Emperor Honorius, not long after, officially decreed the end of the games. Telemachus' memory is celebrated on January 1st.

Well then, the glittering sports palace was baptized in blood to a chilling concert of the agonizing screams of the dying losers wedded to the ecstatic cries of the sadistic throng. It was already and was to remain a theatre of demonic events.

Seating arrangements in the Colosseum were quite regulated. Of course there was the enclosed box for the emperor and a hundred of his parasites. Senators had their own section, their wives another, foreign ambassadors still another. A section was reserved for the esteemed Vestal Virgins, another still on the lower level, for the patricians. The arena wall was 15 feet high and lined with rollers (some say greased) to thwart animals from leaping into the crowd.

The next level of seats was for sons and daughters of the nobility, and for all others with connections, and for the *Equites,* Rome's upper middle class in the imbalanced society. What seats and standing room remained could be enjoyed by the mob.

Vendors hawking hot spiced rolls and cold drinks would singsong their way up and down the aisles. (Some years ago when a snack bar was instituted inside the ruins there was a great public outcry.)

Occasionally the masses would be treated to a free day at the Colosseum by some wealthy candidate, or his backers, currying the favor of the electorate during a vital campaign.

Eighty entrance arcades allowed for the complex to be filled and emptied in minutes. This convenience was necessitated by the horrifying thought of the cream of Roman society and government being trapped inside a stadium during an enemy attack. In fact drills, like our schools' fire drills, were at times conducted. The exit passages were called by the indelicate name of *vomitoria* since through them the arena could suddenly disgorge a capacity crowd.

The best preserved part of the Colosseum faces the slope of the Esquiline hill and it is there that I often like to meet Camille for lunch at the sidewalk café on the corner of Via di Annibaldi and Via San Nicolo.

Camille looks great at any time but her Italian beauty is really enhanced by such a magnificent backdrop.

Facing the Colosseum around the other side is a nice restaurant in the Piazza del Colosseo with the appropriate name *Al Gladiatore*. Alberto, the owner, provides a pleasant atmosphere and good food and his son is a most cordial host who speaks excellent English.

Looking at it thus, one's imagination is called upon to put back the layer of marble, the statuary in all the upper arches, the beams supporting the canvas roof.

Yes, the canvas roof. An ancient *Astrodome*!

Over the windows of the upper story observe the slots for poles for the *velarium*; long strips of canvas pulled together by teams of sailors to form a canopy with an *oculus* in the very middle. This protection from sun and rain was translucent enough not to hurt the lighting of the arena, which was also illuminated by torches.

At the museum of Civiltà Romana in E.U.R. there is a great plastic model of the Imperial City and its monuments. The replica of the Colosseum is excellent and a great aid to the imagination.

To grasp fully the immensity of the whole place one must climb to the upper deck. However the exquisite views from this point up to the early 1800's are gone. It was once possible to look north and see San Pietro in Vincoli or south across the distant plain beyond the pyramid of Cestius to the sublime basilica of St. Paul's Outside the Walls. All this is now blocked from view by the great building program of the last century.

In the reign of Hadrian the marble colossus of Nero as sun god, 110 feet high was transferred by a team of 24 elephants and a crew of a thousand workmen to the piazza adjacent to the stadium. Speculation has it that this proximity to the colossus gave the Flavian Amphitheatre its enduring pseudonym. Hadrian had intended, but never did get around to erecting a companion colossus of Luna in the same square.

Where stood the sun god now stands, at the same height, the graceful campanile of the church of *Santa Francesca Romana.*

Throughout the year 248 Rome's millennium was celebrated with lavish ceremonies in the Colosseum.

In 422 the arena took severe damage from an earthquake but was restored. More earthquakes in the 1200's exacted a heavy toll.

Whether or not Christians suffered martyrdom in the great arena is still debated by classical historians. In any event it became still another site for Christian pilgrimages. Cells with iron grates where the Christians were contained, if they were (and I'm inclined to think thusly from graffiti I have read there), are still viewable.

Pope Gregory the Great, says one legend, when asked for relics would often extend a bag of Colosseum sand. When the recipients frowned in confusion he would squeeze the sack, whereupon it dripped blood.

By the Middle Ages the Colosseum had fallen into disuse, except perhaps as a scene of occasional moonlit seances where zealous necromancers promised to a spellbound, paying crowd that they would resurrect the spirits of Rome's greats of the past; or when it served as the private fortress of the Frangipani family in that turbulent age. And by the 15th century it had been demoted to a public quarry.

Man's toll on the arena has been far greater than Father Time's or Mother Nature's. For the invaders who had swept down on Rome in wave after wave over the centuries had denuded the amphitheatre of its marble and statuary and other trappings.

Popes and nobility in later ages helped themselves through their work crews to enormous amounts of travertine for their churches and palazzi. The Barberini, for example, nephews of Urban VIII, caused the southern side to be razed for material for their lavish palace on the Via Quattro Fontane. This gave birth to the well-known phrase: *Quod non fecerunt Barbari, fecerunt Barberini.* (What the Barbarians didn't do, the Barberinis did.)

Another saying maintains that if all the marble stones of the Colosseum — now scattered in churches and fountains and palazzi across Rome — were suddenly to up and fly back to their original places in the stadium, St. Peter's, San Giovanni, Trevi Fountain, Palazzo Venezia, the Cancelleria and many other famous sites would fall down. "All our buildings are cousins," one Roman put it.

Benedict XIV in 1750, *Deo gratias,* declared the Colosseum sacred property and forbade further despoiling of it. Archaeological excavations continue however and the arena floor in recent decades has been removed to reveal an incredible subterranean network of cells, locker rooms, storage rooms for the elaborate stage props, and dumbwaiters for bringing animals and props up to the arena floor.

In our times the tiers of seats are all gone. The superstructure sprouts weeds of countless varieties. Alley cats roam from the depths to the upper reaches which gives the whole place its unmistakable aroma of feline urine. Which, the Romans point out, is far better than the vermin which would be overrunning the whole area were it not for the ubiquitous cats.

Yet all the majesty of the Emperors' Rome still breathes in the place, and it still kindles awe in the hearts of visitors as it did in every century past.

Stendhal, in his *Roman Journal*, contends that nothing in the world can compare to it. Seen from the air, if you're lucky to come into Fiumicino over the city, it looks like one great fossil.

How many beautiful mornings have I spent there alone in reverie uninterrupted until the arrival of the first busloads of chattering tourists.

The Colosseum is best photographed, basking in the late afternoon sun, from the great vantage point of the ruins of the Temple to Venus and Rome, or through the Arch of Titus right next door.

For a few months recently, in submission to the world energy crisis, the floodlights, that each night drench it in an orange glow, had been turned off. So we had the splendid opportunity to take a late evening horse and carriage ride around the arena and enjoy it the way the sons of Europe's nobility did two centuries ago on their "grand tour," resplendent and romantic in the rays of the moon.

One of the seven wonders of the world it is. And the Venerable Bede had this word of warning for all of us:

"While stands the Colosseum, so stands Rome.
When falls the Colosseum Rome shall fall; and when falls Rome so too shalt the world."
Ave Caesar!

VI

The Walls

Da Vinci and Ciampino are the two airports of Rome. Both are situated about a half-hour from the city, Ciampino — for chartered flights — to the south, Da Vinci — for regularly scheduled commercial flights — to the west and on the coast, at the resort city of Fiumicino.

On Camille's first trip to *Roma Eterna* she arrived with our sons and her folks at Da Vinci. I had preceded them by several weeks to begin my Fulbright year and had secured a splendid flat in Monteverde.

Pacing on the observation deck like the expectant father, which in a sense I really was that day, I could scarcely contain my emotions as that speck in the heavens, T.W.A. Flight 840 from New York, became discernible as a 707 jet, floated to the runway, and rolled smoothly to a halt.

When finally the doors swung open, Frankie was first out (with the complexion of a legal pad). Flying and he had gotten off to a poor relationship. Johnny appeared next and gave me the Nixon greeting, two hands in a V sign over his head; then Ronald and his Pops, both in apparent good shape, followed by my bride and my mother-in-law looking for all the world like returning *Romani* rather than visiting *Americani*.

Passing through customs required just a little less time than the trans-atlantic crossing, or so it seemed, but at last in the lobby we were reunited and at once on our way to the city of the Caesars. All along the Via Ostiense, Nana (Camille's mom, i.e.) could say only: "Frank, I still can't believe where I am."

We had been preparing for this moment for the past year and so the boys, all quite recovered from the crossing now, watched eagerly in competition with each other for the first landmark en route which would be St. Paul's Outside the Walls. Knowing what to expect from all our slide lectures back home they finished in a dead heat with the shout, "San Paolo," as the great mosaic facade came into view above the pines.

The next things to be spotted were the white Pyramid of Cestius, the twin-towered Gate of St. Paul and the red brick Aurelian Wall. Camille won this one and as we neared the futile fortifications thrown around the city in 271 by the Emperor Aurelian (not Marcus Aurelius) we pulled over to the curb to contemplate the whole matter.

Here we were gazing on the pyramid which Paul himself surely observed on the way to his execution in 67 A.D., the massive gate named for the Apostle, and the sixty-foot-high wall which its builder hoped would prolong the already long twilight of the crumbling Empire. In a few minutes we would enter this most historic, almost fairy-tale city, but this little interlude would always be an awesome, never-to-be-forgotten moment in the lives of us all.

It staggers me that when I ask, among other questions, of those who have been to Rome: "What did you think of the wall?" the reply is too often a question itself: "What wall?" The wall is so conspicuous everywhere you go in Rome that I do think it's a *locus classicus* of not being able to see the forest for the trees.

Truly the wall of Rome ranks high among my favorite things of Rome. It, more than any other archaeological

Camille Korn views the wall built by Augustus to screen the slums of Ancient Rome

treasure I think, can transport me back through time and space to the late Empire. I can see the defenders of the city hurling fire and missile down from its heights and through its slots. I can envision the storming of the gates, and the battering rams. I can see the barbarians spilling through and scaling over the barrier to lay waste the aged capital.

Romulus' first public work in 753 B.C. was to enclose the city with a protective wall, built at right angles to form a perfect square around his primitive village on the Palatine to frame what was known as *Roma Quadrata*. Rome has ever since been walled in — next by the Servian Wall, finally by the Aurelian Wall.

If one arrives at Ciampino he will be afforded a better introduction to Rome and her walls. My wife and I, one day soon after she arrived, rode out there on my *Vespa* to welcome some friends coming in with a charter. After the exchange of amenities they boarded their *pullman* (tourist bus) and we our scooter. Up the Via Appia Nuova (as homely as its ancient namesake is beautiful) about 12 kilometers we came to the Via Appia Pignatelli, a spur linking the parallel highways modern and ancient, turned left and sped to the *Regina Viarum,* turned right on the Appian Way toward the Eternal City. The huge paving stones which suffered long under the iron-wheeled chariots of the past were now caressed by the soft tires of our Vespa. Camille, holding on for dear life, her kerchief flapping, skirt billowing, soon caught sight of what we had really come out for in the first place. She was speechless as there stood a few miles ahead, "a many towered Camelot," the walled-in city of Rome. "So this is Rome of which the whole world speaks in such reverence and fear," mused Simon Peter of Galilee upon his first glimpse of her at this juncture. Your time in Rome permitting, get out to the Catacombs of San Callisto, walk halfway up the path to the cemetery, turn and look at Rome from this perspective. You shan't be disappointed, especially in late afternoon.

In any discussion of the walls there arises the need to examine each of them in turn. Romulus' *quadrata* was dedicated to the gods in solicitation of their divine protection. The enclosure was merely the early settlement on the Palatine. Walled-in villages were already commonplace throughout Italy, the Etruscans having imported the practice with them a century earlier. Remus, drunk with resentment over his brother's selection as monarch, defiled the wall thereby committing sacrilege, thereby meeting death at the hands of his twin.

Remains of Romulus' immured hamlet, though scanty, are well worth a visit to the Palatine. For here, as has been said, is the cradle of our own civilization. Along the west foundation of Tiberius' Palace can be seen a wall fragment of tufa boulders.

In the reign of Servius Tullius (578-535 B.C.) the Servian wall rose in protection of what had become by now the *Urbs Septimontium* (City of the Seven Hills). Built of immense blocks of tufa this fortification is often referred to as Republican Rome's Wall because it was rebuilt and enlarged on orders of the Republican Senate in the fourth century, and stretches of it still stand guard in various parts of Rome. One sizable portion remains sticking out of the twentieth century *Stazione Termini* and others near the Baths of Diocletian. On our way to a favorite trattoria, *La Villetta,* (where the fettucini is the best in Rome and the prices very agreeable) on Viale Aventino we pass through two more great portions. A bronze plaque at this point gives an informative account of the wall's story. Thirty feet high, the wall was reinforced by a moat thirty feet deep and earthen ramparts forty feet thick.

But it is the wonderfully preserved Aurelian Wall which lends such sublime distinction to the city we visit today.

With the *Pax Romana* now but a memory, Aurelian in 271 employed tens of thousands of federal troops in the task of walling-in the Imperial Capital, in the vain hope of walling-out Rome's growing list of powerful foes.

Anything of consequential size in its path was incorporated right into the rampart such as the Pyramid of Gaius Cestius. This monument dates from the first century B.C., and the inscription tells us it was erected in less than a year as a sepulcher for the ashes of Cestius, a high public official, who had on a junket to Egypt been so duly impressed with the tombs of the pharaohs. Also incorporated were the Porta Maggiore consisting of two grand arches of the Claudian aqueduct, and the Tomb of Hadrian on the right bank of the Tiber. For the statistic devotee we offer the following numbers. The wall ambled around the hills for 17 miles, had 383 towers, 7,020 battlements, 2,000 windows, more than 5,000 loopholes, and more than 100 rooms serving as guards' quarters.

Walks along the wall, through its corridors, and upon its parapets always make for a great Sunday morning for the kids who, firing through the slots, bravely defend our beloved Roma in her hour of maximum peril. Back in 476 however, the orders were barked in classical Latin, not in Jersey English.

These venerable walls look outward over the rooftops of extramural Rome to the campagna in one direction, the Apennines in another, the sea in a third. Fourteen gates pierce the barrier at the points where the great consular highways depart from the city. The portals themselves make for great sightseeing, with the *Porta San Sebastiano* at the Appian Way, the *Porta Salaria* on the old salt road, the *Porta Aurelia* (now *Porta San Pancrazio*) on the great northern highway, the *Porta San Giovanni* on the new Appian Way, the *Porta San Paola* on Viale Aventino, the *Porta Latina,* the *Porta Flaminia,* and the *Porta Pia* (reworked by Michelangelo), the most distinguished.

A great addition to your slide collection would be one of you entering or exiting the city by any of these gates.

At one point the wall is referred to as the *Muro Torto* (twisted wall), near the Piazzale Flaminio. Peculiarly irregular and looking about to fall, it nevertheless slouches on with no help from restoration projects, for an old legend has it that Peter himself is pledged to watch over and save this particular portion.

For avid wall watchers Rome offers still more delights. There is for example the Janiculum Wall of Urban VIII, from 1642, up on the hill named for the city's janitor. This was the site of Garibaldi's confrontation with Marshal Quindinot's French forces in 1849. This *Muro Gianicolense,* as the Italians call it, also encompasses the pretty public gardens of the Villa Sciarra.

Within the walled-in city of Rome is the walled-in Vatican City. Pope Leo IV in 848 surrounded the entire Vatican district with a massive, clay-colored wall for defense against the Saracens. It is still known as the Leonine Wall, and "The Leonine City" is another appellation for the Vatican.

My favorite Pope, Pius XII, grew up as the frail but scholarly Eugenio Pacelli within the very shadows of these walls.

Rome abounds in walls not only of the defensive type but of the functional and ornamental as well, walls that shore up parts of the hills, the walls that Augustus commissioned to screen out the squalor of the Subura.

The Augustan Wall to hide Rome's shame, which could be seen by foreign dignitaries walking in the dazzling white and opulent beauty of the Forum, served one other purpose. Wooden tenements of the *subura* were wretched fire traps and the threat of conflagration, to the Forum as well, was all too real. Fires were a way of life on the Esquiline. Therefore, a fireproof stone, *peperino,* (Frankie and Ronnie call it *pepperoni*) was used in the building of the wall to safeguard the nerve center of the Roman Empire.

There are vine covered garden walls, walls of villas

and embassies bedecked with plants, or statues, or flags, or all three; walls that stand as the sole surviving portions of splendid temples and sumptuous palaces of another time.

Whatever, enjoy them all. They are another of Rome's distinguishing features.

"The very stones of Rome's walls
are worthy of reverence." — Dante Alighieri

VII

The Antiquities

As this account begins to take shape in my mind we lunch, the family and I, in an obscure trattoria just off the Largo Argentina, my thoughts in the distant past while I gaze at the travertine remnants of four Republican temples just a football field away. These shrines belong not to the G.O.P. but rather to the period between Rome's early days as a monarchy and her twilight as an empire.

Frankie's thoughts however, and Ron's too, are strictly in the present for yesterday was the annual Major League All Star Game back home and they are as jittery as junior prommers, waiting for today's edition of the *Daily American* to hit the streets. Twenty-four hours ago they would have gladly traded the glamor of life in Rome for a seat next to America's Number One baseball fan, Grandpa Korn, in front of his color TV set in Elizabeth, New Jersey.

John is trying to throw a half-nelson around some elusive strands of spaghetti and my wife is chatting with the proprietor's angelic five-year-old daughter.

The thought occurs to me that so many of Rome's splendid ruins go unvisited, unphotographed, and even unnoticed by the ordinary tourist. In some cases it is a lack of time; in others, I sense, a lack of awareness.

Whatever, allow me to introduce you to some of Rome's archaeological attractions of which I'm especially fond.

Of course the city has two fabulous ruins familiar to every last person on earth — the Forum and the Colosseum. Here the focus will be on less fabled — but nonetheless, impressive and interesting — leftovers from Old Rome.

Archaeology derives from two Greek words meaning the study of old things. Since time immemorial men have been scrutinizing the past in order to understand more fully the present to prepare better for the future. There is in each of us, I suspect, a yearning to know what transpired in the world before we arrived here. Tangible remains of ages past enable us to envision more vividly the activities and talents and life styles and outlooks of our distant forebears in Western Civilization.

Thornton Wilder, who once took archaeological studies at the American Academy in Rome, expressed it this way: "Once you have swung a pickax to reveal a street four thousand years covered over, which was once a busy highway, you are never quite the same again."

If you'll just wait while I pay the bill, leave a tip for Tonino Ferroni, Rome's most likable waiter, and gather my gang, I'll take you around on a peripatetic lesson in Roman archaeology. *"Tonino, il conto per favore."* (He'll insist I have a *sambuca* on the house but today I'll decline so that we can get started. I have to sip sambuca very slowly. Were I to down it fast I'd see Rome upside down.)

"Vuol una sambuca, Signor Korn?"

(What did I tell you?) *"Oggi no, grazie, Tonino. Arrivederci e auguri alla Signora ed i bambini."* Ah, the paper's out, I see. And I can tell you from here that the National League won, for Ronnie's teeth are all showing while Frankie's lower lip is near the pavement.

In this frenzied place, a beehive of bus activity, since

Camille inspects ancient weaponry on roof of Castel Sant'Angelo (Hadrian's Tomb)

this is a main terminal, we see a fenced-in sunken area, twenty feet below the modern street level. Discovered by accident when some buildings obscuring that beautiful eighteenth century concert hall across the square, the *Teatro Argentina,* were being torn down, the site was fully excavated by order of Mussolini in 1934. The theatre, now the scene of concerts by the Academy of Saint Cecelia, and occasional operas, stands on the site of the lobby of Pompey's theatre where Caesar was assassinated.

Il Duce incidentally, however many his faults, was a great patron of archaeology. His patronage was not so altruistic though, for he fancied himself Caesar reincarnated — in less grandiose moments only a direct descendant — and hoped to resurrect the ancient empire. His contributions to archaeology then, were aimed at lathering up the Romans about the city's former glory so that they would help him to achieve his dream. The discovery of this site and many others were the happy by-products of urban renewal between the world wars. In 1928 much scientific excavation had been carried out at such places as the Palatine, the Circus Maximus and the Baths of Diocletian.

Later in the 1930's Mussolini cleared the slums in the Forum area to create the Via dei Fori Imperiali, the fine boulevard from the Victor Emmanuel to the Colosseum which dissects Rome's most important archaeological zone.

But for many scholars this spot at which we stand is the pearl of all ruins, containing houses of pagan worship from as early as the fourth century before Christ. It is possible — if you can get the attention of the caretaker in that medieval tower who has the keys — to descend into the pit and walk beneath the pines and among the foundations, walls, columns, and altars. The temples, all orientated to the east, are now — as you see — overrun by cats. A compassionate old lady comes by each day to walk among the animals distributing scraps of food and filling their pie tins with water. John (and everybody else for that matter) calls her *Catwoman* and the two have had some pleasant conversations since he is also a fancier of the feline species.

From here we will proceed toward the Forum on which the long shadows of two and a half millennia of history now play but which until the birth of antiquarian interest in the 18th century lay under many feet of refuse. So deeply was the place buried that the tops of the three arches of the monument of Septimius Severus were barely visible.

Throughout the Middle Ages this historic place was demoted to a cow pasture. *Campo Vaccino* they called it. Today we can enter the Curia or Senate Chamber from which the vast territory of Rome with 6,000 miles of frontier was administered. We can sit at the reflecting pond behind the Temple of Vesta where the holy virgins meditated and relaxed.

Back across Via dei Fori Imperiali are all of the later annexes to Forum Romanum. Julius Caesar, his grand-nephew Augustus, Nerva, Vespasian, and Trajan all extended the Forum when the increasing bureaucracy called for more offices, courts, and departments.

Of these annexes, my wife finds Trajan's the most fascinating, and I'm in total accord. Trajan's column right before us soars 100 feet into the blue velvet of Rome's sky. Commemorating his victory over the Dacians (now Rumania), it is ornamented with spiraling bas reliefs which depict the most important events of the war. From this marble photo album we can learn much about such things as uniforms, weapons, strategy, etc. of the Trajanic era. It would be good to have along a powerful pair of binoculars for this.

Look, up there at the top. It's a statue of St. Peter where once stood an image of the Emperor, facing the Colosseum, the Forum, the Circus — surveying the grandeur of his dominion.

Notice where the Prince of Apostles is looking. He has his back contemptuously on old Rome and is gazing out over the rooftops to the glittering dome of the Vatican, silently proclaiming: "Pagan Rome is dead! Look at her crumbling! Long live Christian Rome!"

An almost identical column to Marcus Aurelius still stands in Piazza Colonna. This one is crowned by Paul also with back turned on Rome and eyes toward the seat of Christianity. If you can afford it some evening dine in the *Ristorante Ulpia* (Trajan's family name) adjacent to the ruins and look out across this remarkable place which offered to the Roman populace two libraries, one Greek, the other Latin, and a sprawling merchandise mart where in the second century of our era the shopper could meet all his needs under one roof. Antiquity's answer to the Space Age shopping mall.

In your guide books you will find this listed as Trajan's Markets. And what a shopping center! To this mall, for which huge portions of the Esquiline Hill were removed by Trajan's engineers, came goods imported from all over the known world. The remains are extensive, reaching six stories in some places. A small admission charge lets you walk the paved streets lined with shops which once sold food, clothing, hardware, oil, wine. Here too were restaurants and banks. The whole complex was roofed and the ancient Chamber of Commerce provided esthetics via potted plants, sculpture, exotic birds, splashing fountains and wandering musicians. Erected between 98 and 110 this shopping arcade was a bustling place during what Tacitus describes as "a happy and prosperous time" in Rome.

Down the street left of the Colosseum we'll come upon the skeleton of Nero's Domus Aurea, center of pagan debauchery, sadism, and bestiality. To envision the shameful luxury of the deranged tyrant — at the edge of Rome's Subura where people were starving — let your mind's eye panel the walls with gold as we tour the remains. Let it cover the expanse of grounds with lakes, forests, vineyards.

Let it restore the hideous colossus of the glutton in the immense vestibule. The complex of palaces and gardens reached from the Palatine to the Caelian to the Appian. Tacitus drily observed that there were "a few parts of Rome unobstructed by Nero's home."

The madman's succinct observation upon moving into this humble abode was: "At last I can begin to live like a man." Those of us, in other words, who have less of a dwelling are little more than beasts.

He had his banquet halls equipped with a sprinkling system which would spray a fine mist of perfume upon his parasitic guests.

It was among these ruins, mostly subterranean now, that the renowned sculpture, the *Laocoon Group,* was found.

Weary of Nero's excesses, we'll go now to the Baths to relax. On the way we pass *through* on foot (*around* by car) the triumphal Arch of Constantine which after 1700 years doesn't look a day over a hundred. Erected soon after his smashing victory over Maxentius in 312 when the Emperor publicly embraced Christianity, it contains medallions and reliefs taken from Trajanic monuments.

Its inscription in giant Latin letters translates in part to: To the Emperor Caesar Flavius Constantine, Who by Divine Inspiration Freed Rome from Oppression.

South of the Colosseum and just inside the Aurelian Walls we come upon the Baths of Caracalla, along Via Terme di Caracalla. This amalgam of our Y M.C.A., health club, swim club, and turkish bath was opened in 216 during the reign of the Emperor by the same name. Built largely of brick and used as late as the sixth century, the baths had facilities for 1600 bathers and for their pleasure offered libraries, lecture halls, restaurants, theaters, stadia, and gyms. In the gardens were shaded promenades where businessmen, after the baths and a luncheon, could discuss deals with each other, where politicians could line up support for the coming campaign, and where gossips could give their restless tongues a vigorous workout.

These were truly public baths where the working class could fraternize with the bluebloods. Some of the plebians who could not suffer the condescension of the wealthy patrons of the baths chose to swim in the Tiber or go unwashed making the aroma of Imperial Rome uh — not too appealing.

At one stage there were more than eight hundred bathing establishments in the city ranging from very small private clubs with a capacity of twenty or thirty to the Baths of Diocletian which could accommodate 3,200. The baths of Titus and of Nero, nothing of which is left, were the most luxurious of all. Other prominent ones were those of Agrippa, Constantine and Trajan. At the public baths there was an admission charge but it was nominal. Politicians would now and then throw free days at the baths trying to romance the electorate into support at the ballot box.

Women incidentally were granted the use of the baths only on certain hours of certain days and they had to pay a double fee.

The men would be out here every day from one to four. Later historians would pin some of the blame for the indolence that afflicted the Roman, and for the decadence and ultimate fall of Rome, on the baths.

The procedure for the bather went like this. He would go into the *apoditerium* to undress. Attendants would be stationed there to watch the clothes.

Next stop would be the *tepidarium* where he would begin to perspire. Now his system would not be overly shocked by the tremendous heat of the *calidarium* beneath which were huge furnaces, stoked by slaves, which radiated heat through a network of *terracotta* pipes. After this sweat bath our friend would go into the adjoining *frigidarium* to plunge into a gigantic pool of cold water. This would close his pores and complete the cleansing. At Caracalla and the other large establishments the frigidarium was set in a richly decorated hall with vaulted ceilings, wonderful murals, and copious statuary. The *Belvedere Torso* now on display in the Vatican Museum was salvaged from these ruins.

After the cold dip the bather often opted for a rubdown in oils then falling sound asleep to the rhythmic slapping of the masseur's hands.

Do not pass through Rome — if it is summer — without spending one night at the outdoor opera here. You'll never forget the evening under the stars and pines of Rome when you watched and listened to the beauty of Verdi's *Aida* set on a vast stage in the venerable ruins of Caracalla. You'll enjoy the blend of high culture and a ball park atmosphere (with the vendors hawking soft drinks and potato chips, coffee and pastry) in the bleacher section.

On the other side of Rome are the extensive remains of the Baths of Diocletian built in 305 by ten thousand enslaved Christians during the most violent of the persecutions, all of whom were executed when their job was done.

These baths covered thirty-two acres and included shops and cloistered gardens. Mosaic floors and walls of Capadoccian marble beautified the various halls. In such grandeur could the citizens tend to their personal cleanliness.

Today we never fail to be awed by the immensity of the ruins. Diocletian must have turned over in his urn when in the 1560's Michelangelo miraculously transformed his Tepidarium into the huge Church of Santa Maria degli Angeli.

Enough bathing? Let me take you now to what I like to call Hadrian's Rome. Among the emperors he is a favorite of mine for I find him so versatile, so enigmatic, so downright fascinating. I believe he never wanted to rule, that his first love was architecture. The fact that he spent fully one-half of his twenty-year reign traveling across his empire sketching all the buildings and monuments that impressed him reaffirms my belief. His major ambition it seems was to return to the Capital and erect facsimiles of these architectural splendors in one private estate. He did just this and the place is intact enough to view today. One of the most delightful sightseeing ventures of a Roman holiday is a trip to Hadrian's Villa in Tivoli, one half hour by motor from the city.

Hadrian's Rome is best exemplified by the huge rotunda in the Campus Martius which is known as the Pantheon. Undoubtedly the finest relic of antiquity anywhere in the world, the Pantheon gives the best idea of the architectural genius of the Empire.

We pass through the magnificent portico of sixteen Corinthian columns. Above the entrance to the frieze reads: *M. Agrippa L. F. Cos. Tertium Fecit* (Marcus Agrippa made this in his third consulship).

Originally erected in 26 B.C. by Agrippa, Augustus' man for all seasons, it was restored, after a fire, by Hadrian who added the great dome. Now we enter through the original towering bronze doors and view the interior still very much the same as what Hadrian saw.

We are overwhelmed by the coffered dome with its huge hole at the top, by the rare and costly yellow Corinthian columns reaching to it, by the staggering dimensions of a perfect sphere (which is what it would be if the curve continued to the floor) 142 feet in diameter and height.

Pantheon is Greek for "All the Gods" and this temple honored the entire Olympic Council, with a colossus of Jupiter occupying the great apse. The *oculus* or eye in the center of the dome (27 feet across) was designed to let the gods into this windowless temple. It is thrilling to stand here on a showery day and watch the rain come through in one great shaft resembling a fluted column. The drains and the convex floor prevent puddling.

The Pantheon is perfectly intact. Emperor Theodosius in 382 A.D., proclaimed Christianity as the state religion and shut down all pagan temples. The Pantheon remained closed for two centuries until in 608 it was given by the Emperor Phocas to Pope Boniface who promptly consecrated it as the Church of Santa Maria ad Martyres. The Pope had twenty-eight carts full of the martyrs' bones removed from the Catacombs and entombed near the high altar which displaced Jupiter in the apse. The statues of the pagan deities in all the alcoves were replaced by Christian altars. Once a shrine to all the pagan gods, it stands today as a church in honor of all the Christian saints. Incidentally Holy Mass is celebrated here on but one day a year, All Saints Day, completing the irony.

If he's on duty I'll slip the organist a couple of hundred lire and have him play Shubert's *Ave Maria* for you. The sound, having nowhere to go but around and around in this big ball, is extra rich. Thus you may think you are at the threshold of Paradise, and start looking for a Choir of Angels to appear.

Raphael of Urbino so loved the Pantheon that his wish to be entombed here was granted. He left a fund for Masses to be offered for the repose of his soul. The fund is still being drawn upon for that purpose.

"Pride of Rome," Byron called it, and here too Victor Emmanuel II, and his assassinated son, King Umberto I, with his Queen Margherita, sleep the eternal sleep.

Pope Urban VIII had Bernini remove the bronze exterior and interior of the dome, melt it down and recast it for the canopy, with its twisted columns, over the high altar in St. Peter's.

As we leave we walk out onto the pavement of Rome, while Hadrian had to descend a long flight of steps to reach street level. It is hard to believe that the surface of Rome has risen so much through the ages.

Walking now in the direction of Piazza Navona we will soon pass the *Borsa Valori* (Stock Exchange) whose facade is the colonnaded wall of an Augustan temple to Neptune.

For more of Hadrian's Rome we must continue toward the river and turn left on Lungotevere toward St. Peter's. One bridge down from the *Palazzo Giustizia* we come to the Hadrianic bridge called *Pons Aelius* in the Emperor's day. Decorated with statues of angels by Bernini it is now the romantic Bridge of the Angels.

Across this bridge is the site that Hadrian selected for the imperial sepulcher. Following the cue of Augustus who devoted much attention to the construction of his own mausoleum, Hadrian designed his final resting place — that huge, drum-like structure with the fortress top on the opposite bank. While it is one of the most popular subjects for postcards, travel folders, and pictorial guidebooks on Rome, many visitors remain ignorant of its checkered history.

To protect his remains from desecration Hadrian made the interior of the tomb labyrinthine. Nevertheless his urn and those of his wife Sabina and of his successors, Antoninus Pius, Marcus Aurelius, Commodus, and Septimius Severus and their families, were confiscated and emptied of their contents by the invading Goths.

Originally the tomb had a roof garden of cypresses punctuated by towering effigies of the rulers.

In the course of time the mausoleum would serve as a fortress, a mint, a prison (from which Benvenuto Cellini, for one, escaped), and a papal residence. It was as this last that its upper chambers came to be lavishly decorated with murals, tapestries, and other regal trappings. From the elegant but simple loggia of Pope Julius II one gets a bird's eye view of the Bridge of the Angels and the curving Tiber.

The papal terrace around back looks straight up Via della Conciliazione to the Basilica and the walls of the Vatican. Don't get caught up here without a camera. You shan't forgive yourself, especially if the itinerary permits only this one visit.

Around the base of the great tomb you see a lovely park. A confusing tour of the mausoleum will turn up some lovely courtyards, one with old Roman heavy artillery, another with piles of marble balls for the catapult — a snack bar, and a museum. A spiral gallery takes you down to the original resting place of Hadrian's ashes. These halls which one day long ago heard the melancholy chants at Hadrian's funeral now resound to the music of the opera *Tosca,* whose story is set in this antiquity, and performances of which are given here a few times a year. Poor Hadrian. He had gone down to the sunny clime of the Bay of Naples hoping to recover there from a serious illness, but in vain. His cortege took several days, solemnly crawling up through the campagna, to reach the great tomb.

We have yet to mention the contemporary name of this place. Almost all who do know this structure refer to it as the *Castel Sant' Angelo.*

A.D. 590 was a year that saw Rome beset with a plague which had wiped out nearly half the city's population. One night Pope Gregory the Great led a candlelight procession of prayer through the streets from the Colosseum to the Vatican. As he reached the old bridge he had an apparition of Michael the Archangel standing high atop the mausoleum. The angel was returning his bloody sword to its sheath. That night the death toll was low. Within another day the plague had lifted. Gregory, concluding that the angel had been sent by God to kill the menace, ordered a statue to be placed above the tomb and renamed the Emperor's sepulcher, Castle of the Holy Angel.

One more interesting feature of the place is the fortified passage which runs from here to the Vatican to provide an escape route for the pontiff in time of peril. More than one pope has taken refuge here by fleeing along the passage and at this hour there stands a Swiss Guard, with the only key to the escape route, at the Vatican end of it.

Archaeology buffs will also want to see the moated tomb of Augustus back in the Campus Martius and the *Ara Pacis* nearby. This Altar of Peace Monument was ordained by the Senate in 13 B.C. to honor Augustus for the Pax Romana or long period free of war that he achieved. It stands there in its own protective pavilion, its bas reliefs illuminating Augustus' accomplishments.

Archaeology in Rome is not confined merely to these pagan antiquities we've been exploring. There is too the field of Sacred Archaeology. Of all their archaeological experiences, our sons cherish the most their trips to the excavations beneath St. Peter's.

In his reign, Pius XII wished to enlarge the crypt of St. Peter's to make room for the tomb of Pius XI. During the effort workmen came upon a pagan mausoleum and after years of digging reached a point directly below the high altar where they found a little tomb. It was recalled that Constantine ordered the first St. Peter's Basilica built over the tomb of the Apostolic Prince. But the tomb was empty except for a few bone fragments.

Some time earlier, unskilled Vatican diggers had transferred bones, from a small marble niche in a wall close to this tomb, in a box, to a storeroom. An expert in Greek and Roman calligraphy, Margherita Guarducci, was called in as the excitement mounted. She worked on the deciphering of wall inscriptions in the area of the tomb.

Her interest was arrested by the marble niche with its fragments and inscriptions. By chance she heard of the transferral of the niche's contents and began a minute investigation of them — with the help of a research team from Rome University.

The skeletal remains proved beyond question to be those of a heavy set, old man which describes Peter well. Threads from garments indicated the type of vestment early bishops were known to wear. One lucky day a fragment of an inscription was found with the name *Petrus* which jigsawed perfectly with the two words above the niche: *Est Hic.* (Peter is Here!)

To foil grave robbers in the post-Constantinian era, some of the faithful or one of the popes must have exhumed the bones of Peter from their original tomb to place them in the secret cache. Pius XII, in light of the evidence, then proclaimed to the world that the bones of his Galilean predecessor had indeed been found and would be returned to the tomb.

Immediately over this humble sepulcher is a tiny chapel where Mass is celebrated. My pastor back in Jersey, Father Edward Hennessey, maintains that the highlight of his priesthood will forever be the time he offered the Holy Sacrifice here upon Peter's grave.

Excavation has continued beneath the Basilica turning up whole streets of pagan mausolea from the cemetery that shared the Vatican Hill with the Circus of Nero. A complete tour requires several hours and must be arranged well in advance, but the spiritual rewards will well redeem your efforts.

If you are going to be in Rome for some time and you get on to an archaeology kick you might go north a few days and investigate what's left of the civilization of those pre-Roman inhabitants of Italy, the mysterious but talented Etruscans.

Just an hour by car from the city you arrive in Etruria with its ancient cities of Cerveteri, Tarquinia, and many others, with their tombs from eight hundred years before Christ and with their outstanding modern museums.

I like to walk the beach at San Nicola with my dear friend Alberto Faustini, a self-taught expert in Etruscology. While Camille and her mother play cards with his wife Lucia back at his condominium and Grandpa Gatto supervises all the kids in the pool, he lectures and I listen, spellbound.

Alberto ought to be lecturing on his expertise at the leading universities of Europe. But he tends bar at his place in Rome. His father died when Alberto was a boy and when he soon after came of age he inherited the duty of running the family bar. When I'm with him I recall Seneca's words: *"Sibi dat mores; ministeria casus assignat."* (Each man gives to himself his character; fate assigns him his job.)

We love to go a little farther up into Etruria now and then with our friends Aldo and Cadia Miralli to Bagnaia where their parents live. The elder Miralli, for six years a P.O.W. under the British in Africa in W.W. II, has a farm outside this tiny walled-in village where he's constantly unearthing Etruscan pottery with his plow. Cadia's dad, a retired Carabinieri, tends to his peaceful vineyards close by and he also enjoys discussions of the ancient people of this area over a generous glass of wine.

For a whole town full of antiquities we recommend enthusiastically Ostia Antica, the seaport of the Empire, reached by a pleasant train or car ride within a half hour from Rome.

Now if all this tramping around crumbling buildings and fallen columns has stirred you the way it affected Thornton Wilder, get to bed early tonight and get up very early tomorrow and we'll hit the autostrada for Naples before the traffic. For in the next chapter we are going to the Archaeologist's Paradise — Pompeii.

Buona notte!

VIII

The Excavated Cities

A time machine? How often in our youth did we long for such a contraption that could transport us back through time and space to the awesome Egypt of the Pharoahs, the legendary Camelot of Arthur, the turbulent France of Napoleon?

Or, if we chose to, we might sit in the groves of Academe enthralled by Plato's lectures, walk the Via Dolorosa with Christ, witness the great fire of London, or stand in the rear of the Virginia House chamber for Patrick Henry's thunderous exhortation.

While we have seen Buck Rogers and the world of outer space elevated from the comic strips to the front pages, I fear we shan't see, in our lifetime at least, such success for the time machine.

However, there is a way for us to go back through two millennia to the glorious world of Ancient Rome. We can in our own day, visit two Roman cities, walk their streets, enter their homes and shops, drink from their fountains, pray in their temples.

Just outside of modern Naples, Pompeii and Herculaneum, the smaller town that shared her awful destiny, await us.

These are the two towns that almost 19 centuries ago were both devastated, and yet preserved, by a volcanic eruption.

Pompeii, situated five miles southeast of the volcano Mount Vesuvius, was a bustling seaside resort, 125 miles south of Rome. The Roman jet-set frequented it in season. Rome's political luminaries had summer retreats there. Cicero was especially fond of his Pompeian villa. The Riviera of its day, it was a city of fashionable shops, first-class hotels, prominent banks, high-priced brothels, and handsome villas overlooking the bay. Its population was somewhere from 20,000 to 25,000.

Less than five miles from the mountain on the shore of the Bay of Naples lay Herculaneum. It was only one-sixth the size of Pompeii and had a far less flamboyant life style than its neighbor. Herculaneum was a tranquil, intimate, residential suburb of *Neapolis* (Naples). Garden apartments, boarding houses, small but elegant villas, and a tiny shopping district constituted its real estate character.

Of the two seaside municipalities it was Pompeii then for night life and a smashing time, and Herculaneum for serenity and relaxation.

As day broke August 24th, in the year 79 A.D., Pompeiians and Herculaneans were already engaged in their daily commitments. The clatter of wooden shutters opening, the bustle of the peddlers setting up their stands in the open air market, the delivery men rambling down the narrow streets in their iron-wheeled vehicles, small clusters of men here and there in animated Latin conversation, the aroma of meat sizzling over a charcoal fire, the waitresses readying their outdoor tables, the laughter of children, the barking of dogs all greeted the visitor to either of the two towns on what was to be their last day of life.

Under an unblemished blue sky ships from every nation sat in the harbor and a babel of foreign languages emanated from them.

Author in a street of excavated Herculaneum

The verdant slopes of enormous Vesuvius reaching heavenward provided the backdrop for this magnificent stage.

But catastrophe was approaching. Under the mountain's calm countenance a monstrous fury was struggling to break its chains. None of the local gentry had any notion of the violent potential deep in the bowels of Vesuvius, though some had wondered about the mountain since the awful earthquake of 63. That Pompeii's forum is in ruins is due not to her burial by Vesuvius but rather to the earthquake 16 years earlier. The Pompeiians were just now getting around to the reconstruction of its government buildings and temples.

Then soon after midday, a horrible thunderclap resounded from the mountain, the top of the mountain blew off, the earth rocked, the sea heaved mightily, birds dropped dead in midflight, animals went berserk, and an internecine rain of four days' duration commenced.

Midday metamorphosed in an instant to midnight, for the dreadful cloud of smoke, which Pliny likened to a massive umbrella pine tree, completely shut out the sun, rendering flight to safety nigh impossible.

Pumice stones, or *lapilli,* poured down on Pompeii, clogging the streets, pelting the houses. After a few hours, the strange shower continued, now along with hot ashes. Deadly volcanic gases contributed to the death toll which was to climb to 16,000 before Vesuvius was through with her fit. When three more days had passed Pompeii was transformed; as archaeologist Amedeo Maiuri describes it "from a thriving port into a huge burial vault." The flood of rock and ash had risen far above even the highest rooftops.

Herculaneum, during all of this, was suffering a different death. Where Pompeii was eventually covered with a rain of fiery ash and pumice borne by the wind, on the other side of the volcano water had condensed, caused by the heat of the eruption. Mixing with ashes it rolled down with incredible speed as a river of mud and lava upon the hapless town. Within hours the community was drowned in this turgid cascade and Herculaneum too belonged to the ages.

Because of the constant humidity in its volcanic envelope, Herculaneum has been singularly fortunate in the preservation of its buildings and the wooden furniture of its houses.

Since there have been relatively few human remains found in the excavations here, it can be assumed that most of the populace had the time, and the good sense, to flee.

And so two cities died. Years passed, then decades. Pompeii and Herculaneum became vague memories and eventually not even that.

Centuries marched on, the two vast graves disguised now as grassy fields.

In 1709 an Austrian prince digging a well in the woods near Vesuvius struck the walls of a theatre and later realized he had found Herculaneum, whose tragic end had been recorded by eyewitnesses.

Organized excavations did not begin until 1738, however. Through documents and books found in Herculaneum it was learned that another city, Pompeii, was in the vicinity.

After a decade of probing the region the searchers failed to find Pompeii. Its discovery, also to be accidental, was made by canal diggers.

Formal digging began there April 1, 1748. The work was rather easy since Pompeii lay under soft pumice. Excavations at Herculaneum were extremely difficult however, because of her cover of rock-hard lava.

Excavation has continued to this day, with Pompeii about four-fifths exhumed and Herculaneum two-thirds. There is now reason to believe that other smaller Roman towns lie sleeping in graves around the foot of Vesuvius, and archaeologists are drawn to the area like bees to honey.

So the misfortune of Vesuvius' victims was the good fortune of all historically and archaeologically-minded people of today.

For we can now swing open the covers of another massive history book and walk through its pages. A visitor to Pompeii or Herculaneum can see first-hand what life was like in the world of the Caesars. He can stroll the cobblestoned streets, duck in and out of the plethora of shops, pay a visit to a private home, climb the stairs to the second floor and step out on the balcony, drop in at a neighborhood tavern, sit in the sundrenched theater, stop at a public bathhouse, be entertained by the traditional and outrageous political promises of the campaign billboards, or read the endless graffiti on the walls.

There are such profound messages as "Romula loves Staphyclus," and "Anyone could as well stop the winds blowing, and the waters from flowing, as stop lovers from loving." While one wry boy scribbled: "Everyone writes on the walls except me." One Pompeiian drew a last-minute parallel to the destruction of two towns by fire and brimstone with: *"Sodoma e Gomorra."*

The visitor can be impressed by the majestic architecture of the temples and government edifices and just as impressed by the mundane appearance of the average home where inside he will find the furniture, statuettes, toys, pots, utensils and even loaves of bread, exactly as they were abandoned by their owners in their furious, but in thousands of cases, futile, flight from death.

The victims of 79 still denounce Vesuvius from their graves while we of 1975 stand deeply in her debt for the sort of time machine she fashioned for us.

De Profundis

IX

The Fountains of Rome

In the misty depths of yesteryear I can see and hear the fabulous fountains of Roma Antica. Ever since the censor Appius Claudius had his civil engineers, in the late fourth century before Christ, convey the waters of the Castelli Romani to the Capital via great aqueducts, the city's inhabitants have been enamored of the sights and sounds of architectural fountains.

Books by the score have been written about the fountains of Rome and here I am taking on such a goliath of a topic with the mere slingshot of a short essay. Wish me luck!

No city anywhere has so many fountains as does Bella Roma. As the central feature of a piazza, a courtyard, a public park; as the facade of a government edifice or private palazzo; as the setting for an ancient Egyptian obelisk or some other monument, the architectural fountain is as much a part of the landscape of Rome as the archaeological ruin, the imposing basilica, the umbrella pine.

The fountains freshen the air of Rome and one can hear their murmur throughout the city. Murmur? Nay, the fountains' melodies are the very folk music of the Holy City.

With their splendid Latin lettering, huge travertine stones and their population of nymphs, gods, heroes, birds, and beasts they soar into the Roman heavens, as inspiring as the very cathedrals of Rome.

While the Romans' love for these watery showpieces is rooted in antiquity it was Greece, Rome's sister nation in classical civilization, that gave the world this art. An old proverb maintains that when Rome conquered Greece she was in fact conquered by Greece. That is to say that the Romans, heretofore agrarian and militaristic, upon their march into Athens and the other Greek cities were so impressed with the Hellenic life style, they began at once to adopt much of the culture of the Aegean.

In Athens, the earliest architectural fountain on record was the Enneacrunus fountain which had nine bronze lions' heads spouting water into a basin.

Superstitions soon arose about the healing powers of the fountain's waters and other such fountains began to grace the streets of the old city. Now we have accounts too of splendid fountains in Egypt and Antioch.

Water pressure was achieved by ingenious combinations of pipes of varying diameters. And with the help of compressed air, water would flow through pipes and sound the horns of marble or bronze trumpeters, or warble through the mouths of carved eagles and otherwise perform an incredible repertoire of hydraulic tricks.

As far back as the era of the kings the Romans have enjoyed the fountain. One tradition tells of a sacred spring, watched over by water nymphs called the Camenae near the Porta Capena, which culminated in a fountain near the same gate. To this site each evening would come Numa Pompilius, successor of Romulus, to imbibe the sacred waters and to carry on his love affair with Egeria, one of the nymphs.

Water has long been symbolic of power, life, and eternity to the people of Rome and they have always demand-

John steadies himself before slaking his thirst at one of Rome's fountains

ed constant reminders of it in their city besides the one
Mother Nature provides, i.e. the Tiber.

During the censorship of Appius, the first aqueduct —
named the *Aqua Appia* for its patron — rerouted water
over the span of ten miles from the hills to the east into the
southern quarter of the city.

Eleven more aqueducts, ranging from ten to sixty
miles in length, were engineered in the next few centuries
supplying Rome with an abundance of water for not only
her public fountains but also for running water in her private homes and for her sumptuous country club establishments known as the Baths.

Some of these water conveyors were overland, some
underground, and some combined both of these features.

Overland, the aqueducts are characterized by serpentine, bridge-like structures with conduits above their endless arches. They would sometimes crisscross on their journey toward the Capital.

At the peak of the Empire some 200 bathing institutions and 1,000 fountains drank insatiably from the dozen
aqueducts.

These rippling ribbons of brick radiated out from the
hills across the lovely campagna to, and through, or over,
the walls of Rome.

So big did the water business become that the Water
Department was headed by a director with cabinet status.
Marcus Agrippa, of Pantheon fame, was the most distin-
guished of Rome's long list of *"Stationes Aquarum."* The
department's sprawling office complex was adjacent to the
Forum.

Water bills were headaches for Roman property
owners but they paid willingly for the luxury which they
considered themselves lucky to get. Martial in one of his
letters complains of getting a run around from the department when he sought a water grant for a pipeline to his
land.

A job in the department was not the usual political sinecure. The engineers were kept busy all hours of the day and night with complaints of pressure failure. They would not infrequently trace the problem to a leak out in the campagna where some farmer had drilled a hole in the span as it crossed his fields.

More woes were caused by the periodic necessity of shutting off the pipelines in order to clean them of lime deposits. This still goes on in Rome where each quarter has its specific day of the week when it must go waterless for a good part of the day. In fact, on the second day of my first trip to Rome I was made painfully aware of the practice when the faucets of the little inn where I was staying suddenly dried up.

Each aqueduct then, as each of the modern ones now, was terminated in an extravagant architectural fountain. Then the Latin inscription eulogized the censor, or the emperor while today's pays tribute to the pope who commissioned the whole project.

Often the fountain would be named for the sculptured figures involved. The Fountain of Prometheus and Fountain of the Fishes as well as many others in antiquity are still known to us.

There are but two fundamental types of fountains — cascades and geysers, that is, waters which fall and waters which rise. And every fountain regardless of its spectacle has to be but another variation on one of those two themes.

They were, and are, multi-purpose creations, these fountains. They are functional. One can fill his bucket or slake his thirst at the site. They are esthetic. Beautiful merely to behold or listen to. They are inspirational, conducive to meditation, to poetry, to romance; soothing to the nerves, psychologically cooling in the sultry summers of the Eternal City.

Strange isn't it, that the human mind which can't bear

a tiny drip from a bathroom faucet can thrill to the deafening roar of a powerful fountain, such as the great cascade in the Villa D'Este?

Fountain lovers the world over protested vigorously, but in vain, when Mussolini decided to remove the stumpy ruins of the *Meta Sudans* (Sweating Goalpost), an imperial fountain, next to the Arch of Constantine, in order to ease the flow of traffic through the area. Today a circle on the pavement there indicates where the Meta Sudans stood — for almost two millennia — and once quenched the awful thirst of gladiators coming from the Colosseum.

With the advent of the Middle Ages and the invasions of barbaric hordes, the aqueducts went the way of all other Roman structures. They were smashed to choke off the city from its water supply. This measure soon rendered Rome a ghost town.

The population went from 2,000,000 to less than 20,000 in the ensuing era. As for the Fountains of Rome, the Middle Ages were to be the Dry Ages.

As the Renaissance dawned, ancient manuscripts describing Imperial Rome's aqueducts were found in the Benedictine Abbey at Monte Cassino, enabling the popes' engineers to get some of the old conduits rolling again and to design newer, improved ones.

Water was about to make a glamorous comeback on the breathtaking stage of Rome Eternal.

In 1453 the *Acqua Vergine Antica* led the way. This aqueduct was followed by the *Acqua Felice* in 1586 and the *Acqua Paola* in 1611. It was not until 1870 that a fourth, the *Acqua Pia Antica Marcia*, was added, to be followed in the next century by two more, the *Acqua Vergine Nuova*, opened in 1937 and the *Acqua Peschiera* in 1949.

Thus far this has been an essay more on aqueducts than on fountains but I thought the background information well-warranted. Knowing all this, the visitor to Rome will be appreciative of, and interested in, the fountains.

Each aqueduct nurses a brood of fountains with one pet child, the *mostra* (or showpiece) as its terminus.

For example the Acqua Vergine finishes in the watery fireworks of Fontana di Trevi. You'll remember Trevi well from such films as "Roman Holiday" and "Three Coins in A Fountain."

The largest of the city, this fountain is admired for her grandeur and originality. Erected under the patronage of Clement XII in 1735 with blocks of travertine from the tomb of Cecilia Metella on the Appian Way, Trevi is a cascade fountain with an abundance of sculpture including a colossal Neptune, two sea horses, the goddesses Health and Abundance, and some tritons.

Her charm is mainly in the legend that if a visitor tosses a coin into her immense basin his swift return to Rome is ensured. Her charm for Johnny however is in the fact that the souvenir vendors at Trevi constantly gift him with key chains, pen knives, statuettes, rings, bracelets, guide books, for they find him irresistibly cute. On our very first night in Rome, John cons us into a trip to Trevi where he's sure to get a rousing welcome back.

Camille's favorite fountain, *La Fontana di Trevi* is the big sister of the fountain centerpiece of Piazza del Popolo, the Pantheon fountain, the fountain in Piazza Cononna, and *La Barcaccia* in Piazza di Spagna. The last, designed by Bernini's father, is Johnny's choice too because he can expend some of his nervous energy running along its decks and gangways (it has the form of a sailing vessel). The Barcaccia represents a boat that, having saved many lives in a Tiber flood in the 1500's, was stranded on this spot by the receding waters. People come from blocks around to draw its water, which they say is of a superior quality. Artichokes, zucchini, whatever you're cooking, turn out better prepared in these waters they insist.

Also related to Trevi is *Il Facchino* on the Via Lata and the little known *Il Babuino* (the Baboon) on the Via

Babuino. But of all Trevi's siblings and in fact of all the fountains of Rome, the little Fountain of the Tortoises gets my blue ribbon. Perhaps it is because of the four exquisitely carved youths, each gracefully boosting a cute little turtle into the basin for a sip of Acqua Vergine — perhaps it's because of the gentle music of her spray — perhaps it is her incomparable setting in the miniature *Piazza Mattei* in the bosom of the Jewish Ghetto.

Acqua Felice races to and through the city appropriately to the Happy Waters Fountain also known as the Fountain of Moses. The name first arises from the fountain's uniquely sweet water which descends to Rome from the Alban Hills. Since its creation this fountain has been the target of derision because of the ungainly statue of Moses in its central arch. The young sculptor, Prospero Bresciano, was so distraught over the poor reviews his work received upon its unveiling that he committed suicide by flinging himself into the Tiber. I am the only person alive I suspect who actually finds the fountain attractive, though in a spooky kind of way. My first encounter with it was late at night while returning alone on foot to my quarters. Out of the corner of my eye I caught sight of Moses, looked up, and it scared hell out of me!

Perhaps the homeliness of the Moses fountain is offset by one of its sisters, Bernini's fine Triton with its tall jet and beautiful bees in Piazza Barberini dating from 1642.

Also in the Acqua Felice family are the magnificent *Dioscuri* of Monte Cavallo, a spur of the Quirinale. This fantasy in water is the vista that greets the President of Italy each morning when he peers through the shutters of the Presidential Palace across the piazza.

The fountains of the area of the Capitol, among them the twin cascades at the base of the Victor Emmanuel Monument, the cute font in Piazza d'Ara Coeli, and the splendid Capitoline fountain of the Danube and the Nile are also part of the family, as is the splendid baroque piece in Piazza Bocca della Verità, and the basin fountains in Viale della Trinita dei Monti and in front of Santa Maria Maggiore.

For my part however the stars of the Felice clan are the little quadruplets — the *Quattro Fontane* at the intersection with four incomparable vistas: to the Esquiline in one direction, and to the Pincio in another; eastward to the Porta Pia, to the Quirinale in the west.

Acqua Paola probably mothers more truly beautiful and spectacular fountains than all the other *mostre*. Its showpiece is virtually unknown to tourists for it perches on a promontory of the Janiculum, which is the domain of the Romans themselves for tour directors don't care to nag their bus drivers up the city's highest hill.

Fontana Paolina, so called for Pope Paul V of the Borghese family, has adorned the hill of Janus since 1612. It is fed by water from Lake Bracciano, 35 miles away, brought to the city by an aqueduct which is actually a restoration of the one built by Trajan in the first century.

Paolina is the work of the architect Fontana. So by a fascinating coincidence its name accidentally honors both patron and creator. A cascade with an enormous lake fronting it, this fountain is really an oasis in Rome's oppressive heat. Just how much of an oasis it is I never realized until one blistering day in the summer of '73 I was standing at the edge giving a commentary on the fountain to a small tourist group. Up rolls one of those little three-wheeled trucks so ubiquitous in Rome. Out jumps the driver, a middle-aged guy, sinewy, with jet black hair, a dashing Valentino type. Unabashedly he strips to his undershorts, takes a running start, and executes a beautiful horizontal dive which ends in a classic belly whop to the great amusement of the startled visitors. After a few minutes of doggy paddling, floating supinely, and swimming underwater, our hero exits from his private pool, re-dresses and drives off into the setting sun.

I struggled to maintain my composure and my lecture throughout and I could see that the tourist folks were impressed with my aplomb toward such shenanigans.

When I got home that night, however, I betrayed my own touristy side when I could hardly wait to tell the family about the whole scene.

Paolina's kid sisters are no less glamorous. The most distinguished among them would be the Bernini masterpiece of the Four Rivers in Piazza Navona.

Married to an old Egyptian obelisk (as are five other Roman fountains) found in the ruins of the circus of Romulus in the Appian Way, the Fountain of the Four Rivers, a cascade, has four colossal figures personifying the Ganges, Danube, Nile and Rio Della Plata.

This unforgettable fountain, a gathering place for lovers, bohemians, priests, cops, hustlers, the young, the old, has two children, one at either end of the great square, in which water plays over from or around a titanic Moor, a huge dolphin, tritons, porpoises, eagles, and griffins. The whole complex makes for the most stupendous of all the city's water shows. The Four Rivers is the swim club not of truck drivers but of neighborhood kids who dive for tourists' coins, with one always on sentry duty to scream "*Polizia!*" if one of Rome's finest approaches.

A captivating anecdote about Bernini and this fountain is covered in the chapter on Rome's piazzas.

Acqua Paola's other dependents are the fountains of Ponte Sisto, Sant'Andrea della Valle, Santa Maria in Trastevere, the Prisoner in Trastevere, all of the Vatican's fountains, and the two big bathtubs in Piazza Farnese.

In Via Giulia there is one more, the Fountain of the *Mascherone* (big Mask).

Young Frank, if you asked his opinion on fountains, would no doubt escort you to Piazza dell'Esedra to gasp at the voluptuous maidens of the beautiful Fountain of the Naiads. He and Ron are at just about the perfect age to appreciate these busty girls in their "Why don't you come up and see me some time?" poses.

The fountain celebrates the arrival in Rome of the waters of Pius IX through the Acqua Pia Marcia. A powerful jet of water from a large fish in the mighty arms of the sea god reaches heavenward while softer jets spray water outward onto the reclining beauties and inward to an immense basin. When the nymphs were added to the fountain it became a *cause celebre* and was called scandalous by the town council, the Vatican, and the schools.

We like the place as a family because on our tight budget we can while away a hot summer evening sitting on its edge, slurping watermelon, at eight cents a big slice, while enjoying the free concert of Italian folk music on the outdoor stage of the *Café Grande Italia* across the street.

All this nocturnal gaiety agrees with the maidens too for they are night people, at their most beautiful when illuminated by powerful underwater flood lamps.

To meet some other Acqua Pia fountains one must visit the Borghese gardens' *Cavalli Marini* (sea horses), *La Terrina* in the Piazza della Chiese Nuova, and the two fountains in the Park of the Orange Trees on the Aventine.

From the terrace of the Pincian hill, at just about the site of Gnaeus Pompey's luxurious villa, fall the waters of Acqua Vergine Nuova.

And in the Piazzale degli Eroi we see the worthy mostra of Rome's youngest aqueduct, the Acqua Peschiera.

In the reign of Augustus the city was divided into 14 regions (*rioni* in Italian). Today ten of these districts have a rione fountain which represents the medieval character of the area.

For example the wine-loving trademark of the Trasteverini is evident in that quarter's rione fountain in the Via della Cisterna. It is a vat and a barrel from which the water spouts. Try your hand someday at finding the other nine *rioni*.

One need never suffer thirst too long in Rome for in addition to all these wonders we've been herein discussing there is the mundane corner fountain, with all the architectural splendor of a tall, battleship-grey, fire hydrant. A great drink, good for you, and free. When the boys finish a vigorous game of *calcio* with Daniela and Paola Guarnaccia, Roberto Pannetta and his kid brother Maurizio, and Massimo, Mario and Maurizio Faustini in the street, our corner fountain looks far more beautiful to them than Trevi and all the rest.

On Via Monte Brianzo along the river there are two more fountains I should like to commend to your attention before we start bringing this chapter to a close. Across from No. 74 is a font where water flows from a bear (*orso*) representing the noble clan of the Orsini whose property it once was; and in the courtyard of the same number a Medusa fountain.

We love the fountains of Rome, Camille especially so, and we enjoy the quiz game as we stroll the aged streets, of telling the family background of each fountain we pass.

Camille and I pride ourselves on being so "native" and so "untouristy" but we are just touristy enough to make a visit to Trevi on the eve of each departure and toss coins over our left shoulders into the basin.

The legend may be just that but we're not taking any chances. It has been working quite well in our case, I must say.

One day when the boys were quite small they had taken to frolicking in Trevi's waters. Whereupon I quickly snapped them with my camera. On the resulting photograph which I mailed to my dad I couldn't resist captioning the scene with the obvious and unforgivable pun:

Three Korns in a Fountain

X

The Piazza

When in Rome be sure to become a connoisseur not only of the *pizza* but also of the *piazza* — that marvelous descendant of the ancient fora — a vast, open space where the community may gather for shopping, banking, promenading, sipping and gossipping. Or for practicing that old Roman craze of *dolce far niente* (the sweetness of doing nothing).

Piazze are everywhere in Rome — of varying degrees of celebrity, importance, magnitude — and consequently too numerous for all to be discussed or merely mentioned in even the most thorough of guide books. With your indulgence though, we would enjoy taking you to the most glamorous, and to some (I was about to say, "off the beaten trail" but in this city that measures time by millennia there's not a trail left that hasn't been beaten) not so dazzling but nonetheless dear to us.

A few squares, such as the queen of them all, *San Pietro,* we visit at some length elsewhere on these pages.

The piazza is fed by a number of streets and one of the esthetic effects of this is, after picking your way down a labyrinth of dark, narrow, twisting streets (many of which in American cities would be called alleys) you are greeted by a tremendous blossom of light and space and marble and water and churches and restaurants. Uncelebrated small neighborhood piazzas are adorned instead by an *alimentaria* (grocery), a *macellaio* (butcher shop) and perhaps a *farmacia* (drug store). Even if you've been to Piazza del Popolo countless times, the effect, if you have an ounce of poetry in your blood, is always the same. Breathtaking surprise!

It was the destruction of this very aspect of the piazza that caused such an outcry when Mussolini carted the broad boulevard, *Via della Conciliazione,* right through the old *Borgo.* Find some old prints (pre-1929) of St. Peter's Square looking from the dome toward the Tiber and imagine how the thrill you now get upon entering the mighty square, having seen it all the way up the modern avenue, would have been magnified by coming into the arms of Bernini's colonnade from out of the alley of the Borgo.

And this effect runs a broad range of human emotions from being overwhelmed by *Piazza del Popolo,* enchanted by *Navona,* charmed by *di Spagna,* inspired by *San Pietro,* saddened by *Cenci,* and then pleasantly surprised by *Esedra.* Unfortunately, as I write, Esedra, Bernini, and other fine squares are a mess due to construction of Rome's new subway. *Rotunda* is torn up by restoration work on its leaning obelisk. Unfortunately too, too many of Rome's proud piazzas have yielded to the exigencies of the city's automobile population explosion and have gone into the parking lot business. *Che peccato!*

Find some more old prints — I like the Piranesi works that show many of the piazzas in infancy — or merely some *ante-bellum* (i.e., W.W.II) photographs of Bernini, del Popolo, di Spagna, *et al* before they were smothered by Henry Ford's iron creature. "The Bicycle Thief," filmed in Rome soon after the war, might give you an idea of the piazza's former purity and charm.

Surrounded by cafés and churches the squares are

Piazza Esedra at night

often centerpieced by those colossal granite needles from Egypt, the obelisks. They are to be found across the city, 14 in all I believe, so be alert for them, appreciate them, and you might even measure your coverage of the city by counting them. Study them, for you may be gazing upon things that the eyes of Moses and his fleeing followers saw along the muddy Nile. Born and raised in Egypt these monuments were already ancient, some more than a thousand years old, when Cleopatra came on the scene.

The emperors had them, amazingly, dismantled from their bases in the Middle East, floated on the Nile out into the Sea to Ostia and upstream on the Tiber to Rome. In circuses, on tombs, in courtyards, they stood as trophies of victories over Egypt. One pope, Sixtus V, was especially fascinated by them and with the genius of Fontana moved them from Imperial sites to embellish modern piazzas.

Sixtus planned a sequence of five streets reaching out in the form of a star from the Pincian Hill with each street finishing in a square centered by an obelisk. These obelisks incidentally, many of which witnessed Christian slaughters, are now crowned with crosses.

Someone has called the soaring obelisk in St. Peter's square, "the world's most stately exclamation point!" And how it does so beautifully punctuate the splendor of the place.

Many times the centerpiece obelisk is wedded to an architectural fountain, enhancing the appeal of it. *Allora*, back to the original subject of the piazza. How shall we proceed? Alphabetically would be as appropriate as any other way don't you think? Well then, here is your scouting report on Rome's public squares.

From Via Nazionale, a street almost every visitor comes to know well, let us ascend on foot, Via Quattro Fontane. (Let us not ascend by car for it is one way coming at us and driving in Rome is chancy enough going in the *proper* direction.) Regal Palazzo Barberini will soon appear on our right and from this height it is but a short drop to Piazza Barberini. No obelisk, but at least a great Bernini fountain hails us. With his gold hue, a Triton squats with his head tossed back and a great conch shell raised to his lips through which he spouts a lofty jet of Acqua Felice. Before the war it was more park-like here, a very fashionable square with far more trees and benches, with the music of horse-drawn carriages playing on its weary old cobblestones. We still enjoy it nonetheless and would recommend your attention to the little Fountain of the Bees by Bernini for Pope Urban VIII at the foot of Via Veneto. Bees were prominent in Urban's family (the Barberini) coat of arms. The Barberini liked the symbolism because of the industry and productivity associated with bees. That the Barberini themselves were industrious and productive there can be no dispute. You might take in a movie at the Cinema in the square and when you decide to take your leave, leave by the Via Sistina for some expensive shopping, or by Via Veneto for some expensive drinking, or by Via Barberini for some expensive plane tickets (most airlines have an office along here).

It is my judgment that Piazza della Bocca della Verità, one of the least appreciated squares, has the most things to see and photograph. On the Tiber side is a quaint park in which are situated two incredibly well preserved pre-Christian temples — one (which always reminds me of a mini *Maison Cairee* of Nimes, France) to the goddess Fortuna Virilis and the other to Vesta. Perhaps the former is the one Pliny says housed a statue of Fortuna clothed in a woolen toga which had not worn out in 500 years. But these two names are in constant dispute among archaeologists. However we do know that both temples were used as Christian churches in the medieval period and this accounts largely for their good health. In the same park, amidst lush shrubbery and colorful plants we find another splashing Acqua Felice fountain from 1717.

Across from the two temples is an open area with the brooding *Arcus Quadrifrons* (Arch of the Four Fronts also called the Arch of Janus since it looks in all directions) of the Constantinian era. Sprouting vegetation, its niches emptied of their statues, it's still impressive. In antiquity, here was the *Forum Boarium* or cattle market, and that little arch you see by the church was erected by the cattle dealers in tribute to Septimius Severus.

Two very old (sixth century) churches with bell towers, complete the piazza's beauty. To the rear of the arch is *San Giorgio in Velabro* with its 12th century campanile. Around to the front, across from the fountain, is *Santa Maria in Cosmedin* with its seven-story Romanesque belltower. As with the piazza, develop an eye for these campanili too, which embellish the peerless skyline of Rome. In the portico of the church we see the intriguing Mouth of Truth (*Bocca della Verità*) from which the piazza gets its name. This large, round, marble well cover with the grotesque face and open mouth, legend says, was the original lie detector. The story goes that people suspected of lying were taken to this and had to thrust a hand into the mouth, which hand would be swiftly bitten off if the accused were indeed lying. The legend and the mouth are not as laughable as might be thought however. Last July we picked up the paper one day to read of a smart-aleck tourist who for a gag photograph plunged his hand into the *bocca* and immediately let out a blood chilling scream. A spider nesting inside had not taken kindly to the intruder and took a quick bite.

Down in the Jewish Ghetto close by are the forgotten Piazza Cenci and Piazza Mattei. These are visited in the lines on that historic old quarter. And Piazze Campidoglio and Quirinale we examined in the Seven Hills selection.

Cross town is the vast but mutilated Piazza dei Cinquecento with its obelisk of the Pharaoh Rameses. It is named to honor the 500 Italian soldiers who died in battle in 1887 at Dogali. When the subway work is done perhaps it will be restored to its parklike charm, a sanctuary for weary pilgrims recently come by train to the Stazione Termini across the street.

Back across to Via del Corso where a right turn will shortly bring us to Piazza Colonna with its soft rose colors, its second century column of Marcus Aurelius and its gently murmuring fountain of Acqua Vergine.

The column with bas reliefs commemorating the philosopher-emperor's successes over Germanic tribes is like an upright photo album (anyone have those binoculars?) which tells us much about military uniforms, weapons and techniques of the ancient Romans and their northern foes. The emperor's statue at the top has been supplanted — reminiscent of Trajan's bow to Peter on his column — by one of the Apostle Paul.

Notice the familiar letters S.P.Q.R. (*Senatus Populus Que Romae* — the Senate and People of Rome) on the base. This initialed motto was engraved on buildings, monuments, helmets, documents of the Empire and has been retained as the city's slogan. Today it appears on buses, street signs, manhole covers, and what not. The irreverent poet of Trastevere, G. G. Belli — not especially fond of Papal domination, insisted the letters represented *Solamente preti qui regnono* (only priests rule here).

In Piazza Colonna is the headquarters of Italy's Democratic Socialist Party. Let's not fail to examine the portico of 16 Etruscan columns on the Palazzo Wedekind. But it is the landmark just across the Corso that we enjoy, the *Galleria,* which is actually two interesting streets with a glass roof. It is lined with shops and eateries of all kinds and is much like those in Milan and Naples. It affords the best of both worlds, being outdoors with the sun shining and the fresh air sweeping through the arcade while still enjoying the protection of indoors. Café Berardo with its garden of little tables enclosed by stands of potted plants is the scene of free nightly concerts (free if you don't mind standing on the periphery of said stands).

Back on Via del Corso toward the immense Victor Emmanuel Monument, left at Piazza Venezia and (wiggling with the road) we will soon find ourselves climbing the busy Via Nazionale. What is that geyser we see on the summit? Why that's the jet of the scandalous fountain of the nude sea nymphs, Fontana Naiade. Here we are in this great square, which is geometrically rather a circle, called Piazza dell'Esedra (nobody calls it by its new name — Della Repubblica; does anyone really call New York's 6th Avenue, *Avenue of the Americas*?). *Exedra* was a Homeric Greek term for outdoor area enclosed by a semi-circular wall. Two huge, awe-inspiring palaces by Gaetano Koch, ingeniously curve with their giant porticoes halfway around the piazza, following the contours of the exedra of the Baths of Diocletian, the enormous health spa whose extensive pink remains grace the opposite end of the square. And in whose lecture hall Michelangelo fashioned the Church of Santa Maria degli Angeli when he was 88 years old.

There are free nightly concerts here also in July and August at Café Grande Italia, the place incessantly throbs with vehicular (like Demolition Derby) and pedestrian (the Boston Marathon) traffic and is a great extravaganza at night with the fountain wonderfully illuminated. There's also a man who scissors your silhouette out of black paper, for a half dollar, and mounts it on white cardboard, while you wait. In the neighborhood are Stazione Termini, The Opera House, and an extensive shopping district.

Now if we will retrace our steps down Via Nazionale through Piazza Venezia onto Corso Vittorio Emmanuele we will shortly see signs pointing left for Campo dei Fiori. Through the narrow ancient streets we find our way across the outdoor market to our next square, Piazza Farnese. Straight ahead of you is the elegant Palazzo begun for Cardinal Farnese by the noted Sangallo and completed by the master Michelangelo. The top floor and entablature are the latter's. The French Embassy is currently housed here. Let your eyes back up now to the twin tub fountains, each carved from a single block of Egyptian granite and adorned with lions' heads. These came from the Baths of Caracalla. Such charming little Renaissance buildings in this quiet piazza! Talk about burnt siena — look at the color of that slender structure on the west end! Now to the right, a few blocks, in Piazza della Cancelleria with its awesome wedge-shaped Renaissance palazzo. This is the Chancery office of the Diocese of Rome and since it belongs to the Pope it is extraterritorial Vatican. The Cardinal Vicar of Rome resides here.

Piazza Navona is probably the choice of most piazza lovers. This immense oval rose on the site and contours of the Stadium of Domitian (50,000 seats). Foundations, pilasters, and seating sections of the old chariot track are still visible in the cellars of today's buildings. One well-preserved arch can be viewed at the rounded end in Piazza Tor Sanguigna. Some of the basement bars offer the patrons a chance to sit in the seats of Domitian with a small table for their drinks and club sandwiches. Everyday is party day here and the night is no different — in fact it's better.

During the persecutions poor Agnese was dragged before the howling throng and ordered to denounce her Christ. Refusing, she was stripped of her garments whereupon her hair suddenly flared to veil her from the mob. The square's name is a corruption of St. Agnes in Her Agony (St. Agnesse in Agone — N'Agonu — Navona) and is the site of the lovely, rich baroque church of St. Agnese by Borromini. It surely warrants a visit, and then another, and another.

Enriching the square are three stupendous fountains. On the southern end one of the two smaller fountains, this by Bernini, is called the Fountain of the Moor. Gian Lorenzo Bernini, Neapolitan by birth (1598-1679), was a most prolific architect and sculptor. On guided tours it seems everything in Rome — this church, that statue, those fountains are "by Bernini." He has been credited by some over-enthusiastic and underinformed guides with almost every edifice in Rome but the Colosseum. His father Pietro is responsible for the boat fountain in Piazza di Spagna. At the other extremity is *La Fontana de Nettuno* by Della Bitta and Zappala.

There in the center though, where people have clustered and flashbulbs are popping, there is where that tireless artist out-Berninied himself. Staggering! Don't try to grasp the magnificence or the magnitude of this masterpiece all at once. It's no use. Regardless of how pressed for time you are — you are esthetically obligated to return and to gaze upon it several more times.

Water cascading from everywhere, horses champing to burst forth, a towering obelisk confiscated from the Circus of Romulus on Via Appia dwarfing everything around it, and four colossal, finely carved men representing the four rivers, Danube, Ganges, Nile and Plate, in turn representing the four continents, Europe, Asia, Africa and America, in various poses of fear. Fear? Some say that the African shielding his eyes as he shrinks back in horror, his companions, one about to swoon, the other covering his head with a shawl, the last pulling up anchor to get the blazes out of there, are all Bernini's way of paying eternal insult in marble to his hated rival Borromini and his church facing the fountain. "Your damn church is about to fall down!" Bernini is shouting through his sculpture.

Ultra chic it is to have an apartment overlooking the scene, in any of the endless yellow buildings with their green shutters, flowered balconies and terraced roofs. Brazil's Embassy to Italy has its base in the fantastic Palazzo Pamphili to the left of the church. What great duty for a

young, lively bachelor Brazilian foreign service officer!
Sit, stretch your legs, and savor the beehive of activity
from any of the square's elegant but not exorbitant *ris-
toranti* — Panzironi, Mastrostefano, and — this family's
pick, *Tre Scalini* (so named because of the three little steps
you must negotiate to enter). Specialty of the last house is
Tartufo, chocolate ice cream in a chocolate shell with a
brandied cherry center. (re: ice cream — we found a place
off the square, two blocks in back of Tre Scalini, with towering cones for 50 lire, or eight cents). Little Johnny staggers at first under the weight of one but always comes back
in the late rounds for a knockout victory.

Honey-colored by day, apricot-hued by evening, simply dreamy by night the cobblestoned piazza — closed to
vehicular traffic — is the city's playground. Navona knows
no generation gap, nor social strata, nor ethnic divisions.
Frankie, Ronnie and Johnny have friends, from the vicinity, of every age and gender, and Camille and I will often
deposit them here in this wild-life sanctuary, confident of
their safety, and return hours later to find their disposi-
tions and their Italian much improved. (They all know
how to get home from here if Camille dallies too long in
the shops.) For, as in old Ebbets Field, there's never a dull
day at Navona. Frisbee matches, soaring mechanical birds,
while-you-wait artists, impromptu rock concerts or sere-
nading by begging waifs whose parents wait in the wings,
tricycle races, governesses whacking their mischievous
charges, TV commercials being filmed, cops hauling kids
in their shorts out of the Four Rivers, hippies hawking
their tin jewelry, two oldtimers engrossed in chess throughout the beautifully orchestrated mayhem. That's Navona!
In addition, our sons have recently introduced that grand
old game from the sidewalks of New York — pitching
coins.

Then I think of Belli's verses about this place: *Questa
nun è una piazza, è una campagna, un teatro, una fiera, un*

allegria. (This is not a square, it's the countryside, a theater, a fair, a fantasy.)

Turn the clock back a century and a half at this point, if you will. It is Saturday night in July (or August) and from every nook and cranny of the Campus Martius people and kids (they're people too) are excitedly converging on Navona. We've arrived at last huffing and puffing but what a show! Piazza Navona has been flooded by order of His Holiness for the weekly regatta. What pomp and panoply! The emperors' ashes must be turning green with envy for surely they've been out-spectacled this time. Now if only we could turn the clock forward a century and a half for a Kodak Instamatic to snap this unforgettable show.

Oh to be in Rome when Christmas is there! Navona is lined with stalls vending toys, sweets, Christmas ornaments, mangers and figurines. Down from the Alban Hills are the shepherds in their sheepskin jackets, their bagpipes squealing. *La Befana* (the good witch) is rewarding all the bambini who were good all year with little favors, and the naughty with lumps of coal. I've witnessed the scene *molte volte* but never have I seen any shrimpie get a piece of coal.

And Easter Vigil (Holy Saturday night) is so inspiring with a candlelight procession, to the music of Rome's 2,000 church bells, through the piazza into the lavishly decorated church for Mass.

One never gets enough of Piazza Navona it seems but surely the reader has had quite enough of my attempts to capture it in words.

Would you care to go with us now to two really charming squares? We will have to violate the alphabet at this point for I consider Navona part of a trilogy with little-known *Piazza San Eustachio* and well-known *Piazza della Rotunda.* For whenever we make one stop we usually make all three.

Eustachio, though miniscule, has much to recommend

it. Using the twirled ice cream cone top of the church of Sant'Ivo as our star of Bethlehem wc grope our way along shadowy *Via dei Sediari* (street of the chairmakers) into the square. Some pleasant old buildings enclose it along with the back of the Senate building. The piazza is named for that ninth century church there across the tiny area. Its brick campanile is from the twelfth century. The relics of Eustace and his family, all martyred in the Colosseum by being roasted alive in a brazed bull, are enshrined in the sanctuary.

Over the portico of the church we see a head of a deer. One of Trajan's generals, the legend relates, had a vision of a deer's head which spoke to him of Christ. Whereupon he embraced Christianity, changing his name to Eustachius. Soon after he, like the biblical Job, suffered every kind of perdition and ultimately lost his life for the faith.

Tucked away in this obscure back alley of Rome is *Café San Eustachio* with simply the best cappuccino in all Rome, ergo in all the world. Let's sample it and see if we agree. Don't be surprised if we stand at the bar elbow to elbow with luminaries of Italy's stage or screen. For this is a great esoteric spot, popular among the socially chic of Rome, yet a place where plebe and patrician are at ease in each other's company.

I always offer to buy the establishment's huge cardboard reproduction of a great oil painting of Piazza San Eustachio. I'm always gently refused as you will see for yourself shortly.

Via del Seminario takes us from here to Piazza della Rotunda, where we find ourselves face-to-face with the oldest building in the world that's still in actual use, the Panthcon. The huge pagan temple, pride and joy of its architect, the Emperor Hadrian, is a rotunda. Hence the square's name.

Such a romantic little spot! An obelisk fountain (restoration work upsets the square at this writing to right the

leaning obelisk), a quaint café, *Bar Antonelli* is opposite
the pagan temple, and next to that an excellent restaurant,
Tempio d'Agrippa. But the Trattoria Pantheon with its
tempting smorgasbord is often our choice for a brown bag
lunch which we take along with a drink to the steps of the
fountain, setting up our own outdoor restaurant. Try the
cold fried potatoes and the cold Sicilian pizza, or a heated
sandwich of *proscuitto e formaggio*. What vittles!

Camille is always charmed by the cute little buildings
which shove each other about for a small place in the
square. The pink facade on your right, looking from the
portico of the Pantheon, belongs to the Albergo del Sole.
(But this Hotel of the Sun is really an inexpensive inn and
what an *in* place to stay during one's sojourn in Rome.)

One day Ronald wandered off from a fountainside
lunch here and some minutes later came flying back with:
"I just discovered a midget piazza a block away!" He led
us one short block behind Antonelli's to Rome's tiniest
square, Piazza Rondanini. Cute as a button with its fruit
store, its church and its sidewalk café, Rondanini is often a
rendezvous point for a mid-afternoon wine and cheese session for the wife and me.

Back to the alphabet for Piazza Minerva which fortunately is just behind the Pantheon. The yellow church on
your left is *Santa Maria Sopra Minerva* where under the
high altar lies in eternal rest the beloved St. Catherine of
Siena, whose body is still incorrupt. Also noteworthy are
the sculpture of *Christ with the Cross* by Michelangelo, the
room where Catherine died, and the tombs of five popes
and sixty cardinals.

The name of the church has a triple symbolism. First
the church stands on the ruins of a temple to Minerva. Second it looms out over the square of Minerva and lastly it
boasts of Mary's victory over the pagan deity in the hearts
of the Roman people. St. Mary over Minerva.

Andiamo sempre diritto (Let's keep walking straight

ahead). *Ecco, Piazza di Monte Citorio* with its pink palace of Italy's Chamber of Deputies (the lower house in the Parliament) and its tremendous obelisk. This was transported back to Rome by Octavian as a trophy of his successes versus Anthony and Cleopatra. We will find too the buildings of two of the country's leading newspapers, *Il Tempo* and *Il Mondo*.

Out onto the Corso and if the heat is oppressive a lemon ice at any bar along the way to Piazza del Popolo will help.

Dead ahead we can discern the grand Porta del Popolo with the Via Flaminia taking off from the city for the blue beyond, and the thirteenth century B.C., obelisk of red granite erected here in 1589. This, likely the oldest thing in Rome, once graced the *spina* (dividing island) of the Circus Maximus.

Upon arrival in this vast open space, often called the Lobby of Rome for this was where most visitors from the north first entered the city, we are overwhelmed by the remarkable symmetry of identical twin 17th century churches to Santa Maria, by semi-circular walls adorned with statues to our left and right, by the Café Canova on one side looking across to Rosati's on the other, by the gardens of Ristorante Bolognese and the overhanging lush vegetation of the Borghese gardens, the terrace of the Pincio (the Balcony of Rome), the waterfall fountain. As *Il Tramonto* (sundown) nears, you will see the terrace fill up with humanity eager to watch the fiery red ball drop from Rome's copper sky behind the dome of San Pietro in the distance. Nothing can quite compare to this and the natives never weary of it. They have a saying about it: "If one has not seen the sunset from the Pincio one has not been to Rome."

If you like ghost stories this is the place. Every Roman has his own version of how Nero's ghost (the church near the gate, Santa Maria del Popolo 1099, rests upon the Emperor's tomb site) plagues the enormous square each night. And if you like to watch the *Intelligentsia* at play, stay here and gape at the brainy set which frequents Rosati's and Canova's.

At times the alphabet works out fine in a piazza tour. Piazza di Spagna is next in spelling and in proximity, just down Via del Babuino a few blocks. If it's not too late we will look in at the Lion Book Shop, the only English language book store in the city, with some great buys on secondhand stuff.

Sooner or later all Americans staying in the Holy City for any length of time come to di Spagna and its American Express office. The chief features of the piazza of course are its rococo staircase, its pink, hilltop church of Trinità dei Monti, its Bernini (the father Pietro) fountain.

Just outside the square proper is the lofty monument to the Immaculate Conception. Piazza di Spagna wakes up early and doesn't completely retire until past three on a summer eve. It is a raucous place of indescribable beauty and color.

Piazza Venezia can be reached quite simply from here. As we walk along Via Condotti, window-shop — but for the sake of your wallet never, but never, shop — unless you are in Jackie Onassis's economic class. Incidentally, this is one of her beats when in Rome. Condotti ends at the Corso and we go left some blocks looking at a chopped-off picture of the Victor Emmanuel Monument all the while. The Corso spills us into Piazza Venezia. On the left the fort-like building of the Venezia Insurance Company. On the right the fort-like Palazzo Venezia built for a cardinal in 1455 (magnificent inner courtyard!), which headquartered the Fascists in the 1920's and 1930's. From the balcony over the central door Mussolini in his hollow glory was wont to harangue the throng, often hastily assembled on orders of the demagogue. Shouts of *"Viva Il Duce"* would ring off the brown fortress when he strode into view.

Rome's rulers through the ages have put to extensive use that Roman architectural device, the balcony, for their public appearances. From the consuls on the terrace of their *Domus Publica,* to the emperors on their perch upon the Palatine, to the Middle Ages with Cola de Rienzo at the Capitoline, to the popes from the Loggia of Benedictions above the center doors of St. Peter's, whence the Holy Father delivers on solemn occasions his *Urbi et Orbi* (to the city and the world) blessing, to Benito Mussolini over Piazza Venezia.

The square, a putrid open burial pit in Caesar's day, is fed by the Vie del Corso, del Teatro di Marcello, del Plebiscito, and dei Fori Imperiali. It is considered the center of the city, so this is where you're heading whenever you pick up the yellow metal signs of, *Il Centro.*

Now the Victor Emmanuel Monument. All of us will want to be photographed on the steps of this *wedding cake* (as the Roman *cognoscenti* mock it) for the home folks.

Symbol of the unification of Italy, it is less than a century old. It is named for Victor Emmanuel II, first king of Italy. It is his effigy that sits astride that great steed looking down, in disgust I'm sure, at the daily despoliation of the piazza by the automobile.

Twin fountains at the base of the monument represent Italy's two seas, the Tyrhennian and the Adriatic. On the first landing is the nation's Tomb of the Unknown Soldier flanked by eternal flames and two sentries, who change off every half hour in a brief ceremony. The various armed services provide the sentries on a rotating basis.

Though the whole does not give an impression of height but rather an illusion of squatness, it is indeed very high (over 200 feet) and from the rear of its magnificent loggia the Colosseum can be beautifully photographed — particularly in late afternoon. Also known as the *Vittoriano* the monument houses a worthwhile museum.

Piazza San Silvestro is rather homely with its bus station but very useful for its telegram and telephone offices. An innocuous looking little church stands off to one side of the telegram office but it is a most worthy place. The church of San Silvestro has its chief claim to fame in the enshrinement of the head of John the Baptist but it is beyond that a lovely, most historic site originating in 258 on the site of Aurelian's Temple of the Sun. The rose colored courtyard is a personal favorite.

Piazza Santa Maria in Trastevere will be our last piazza on this tour but it might well turn out to be one of the most interesting. The church is one of the oldest of the city, anterior even to Constantine. A splendid basilica with a mosaic facade a la St. Paul's Outside the Walls, the current building was consecrated in 1198 by Pope Innocent III. Its great bell tower rings out the hour, and each quarter, over the piazza and its vicinity. Rather an immense open air theatre with the local gentry in the main roles, the piazza is not especially frequented by tourists and so a visit here will afford a candid look at daily life in one of the most colorful, flamboyant, vibrant, quarters of all Rome.

Two good restaurants, Galeassi (great *cannelloni*) and Alfredo's, two bars with outdoor tables, a baroque fountain, a Renaissance palazzo, picturesque apartment buildings with gardens on high surround us here.

As Piazza Navona is the city's playground, Santa Maria in Trastevere is the city's amusement center of transpontine Rome. The Trasteverini boast that they are the real Romans, that only *their* roots, of all the modern inhabitants, go back to the Empire and before. Indeed, they say that their neighborhod dialect is more Latin than what is heard in the rest of the city.

Let's sit here awhile and watch the human drama unfold. With acquiescent wallets we may take a table under one of Galeassi's gigantic umbrellas and order a light meal. Otherwise a seat at one of the bars, or even a completely free one on the steps of the fountain will do.

The parade has already begun — a husband and wife in hot debate, the neighborhood Little League (soccer, that is) in a vigorous workout, a priest from Santa Maria engrossed in his breviary, a winetruck making a delivery, a man setting up shop to sell shirts, transistor radios, and religious medals, two soldiers on furlough playing a tennis type game with a small sponge ball and two bongo drum paddles, a pair of white-uniformed traffic cops playing the more popular game of watching everything feminine, and much more, and set to music too; to the pop tunes of the vendor's transistors, to the Neapolitan favorites on an over-volumed stereo on one of the terraces, to a spontaneous serenader, to the faithful Bells of St. Mary's. Perhaps it out-navonas Navona.

Whatever. You are now a full-fledged and foot-weary member of the S.R.P.L. (Society of Roman Piazza Lovers).

Congratulazioni!

Camille, John, and the author in the courtyard of the Villa D'Este

XI

The Courtyards

Just as the piazza is a descendant of an old Roman concept, so too is her kid sister, the courtyard. The Imperial Roman of means built his house around an open area instead of with a backyard. As a number of streets feed into a piazza, many rooms opened onto this area, known then as a *peristylum*. This peristyle, or courtyard, actually a Greek invention adopted and adapted by their conquerors, usually consisted of a roofed, colonnaded walkway enclosing a colorful garden with fountains or birdbaths, some statuary and marble benches. As the neighborhood congregates in the piazza for relaxation and companionship, the family gathered here.

The Roman was in the habit of walking off his noonday meal here, protected by the colonnade from the heat or rain. Here too he would consult with clients and business associates, chat with his children, take the sun, relax over wine and cheese with his wife and their friends. Because it was enclosed by the dwelling it gave the desired effect of country villa living in the center of the bustling city.

Should you get to Pompeii or Herculaneum you will see some fine examples of the peristylum in the excavations.

This *peristyle* was left behind after the Empire passed into history in the forms of the *atrio* (atrium) which often fronts a Roman church, the *chiostro* (cloister) of the convents and monasteries of Rome. The atrium, or colonnaded front yard of the church, was a place for the early Christians to wash their hands and arms and face in a symbolic cleansing before entering the Church. Its modern descendant is the holy water basin at the doors of churches around the world.

Though it is so characteristic of Rome, far too many visitors to the city are unaware of the courtyard's inherent charm and historical significance and as a result miss one of the city's great visual treats. Walter Hagen, the famous American golfer, was fond of exhorting those around him:

"Life is a path we travel but once. So take time out and smell the roses!"

Courtyards are among Rome's roses. Stop and enjoy them, now and then. On all of your walking tours of the city glance constantly left and right through the portals of all the palazzi to find these charming little oases of vegetation and sculpture and serenity. Occasionally ask the *portiere* (gatekeeper) if you might visit the *cortile* a while. You'll be afforded the customary Roman hospitality with a quick *Prego* ("please, go right ahead").

Our little dissertation here will give you a start with a review of some courtyards we cherish. But you are charged with adding to this list a few of your own discovery.

If this tour should begin at our apartment we can all set out by passing through our own peanut-sized but beloved cortile of orange stucco walls, decrepit gray statuary and verdant plants.

Hard by our humble abode in the Monteverde quarter there is the Sant Onofrio on the ascent of the Janiculum Hill. The solitude and the vistas here are without peer. Another nearby courtyard is the one at my Alma Mater, the American Academy, with its whispering cypresses and central fountain and its whispered conversations of classical scholars from the states.

My other Alma Mater, the Istituto Dante Alighieri down in the Campus Martius is also built around a pleasant court. 'Tis a nice way to start and finish the school day, discussing (or lamenting) the assignments with classmates in the beauty and tranquillity of a courtyard.

Descending the Janiculum we cross Viale Trastevere to the foot of Mount Aventine. The ascent of this hill by courtyard hunters is richly rewarded by the orange tree cloister of Santa Sabina and the Renaissance court, with its ancient columns, of Sant Alessio.

On a tour of the Vatican be sure to watch for the many courtyards of the Papal city but especially for the two huge courts (larger than many piazzas), the *Belvedere* and the *San Damaso* and regret with us their conversion to parking lots. Passing through the unending corridors to the Sistine Chapel pause occasionally to look down upon the Vatican courtyards from this unique vantage point.

Over in the Lateran (extraterritoral Vatican) visit first the great Basilica of St. John, the Cathedral of Rome. At the end of the left aisle take the door to the impressive cloister. Regrettably it has lost much of its mosaic adornment but we still enjoy what's left, along with the fragments of ancient sculpture and sarcophagi.

St. Paul's Outside the Walls offers another lovely cloister. Enhanced by the apricot shade of the basilica's rear wall this court has a handsome colonnade of twisted columns inlaid with mosaic tiles, early Christian sarcophagi, fragments of Christian epitaphs cemented to the walls, a perfectly symmetrical garden centered by a pond of *pesci rossi* (Rome's gold fish are red fish) and palm trees. If you've had high school Latin you will enjoy the mosaic legend on the colonnade's facade which tells of the courtyard's role in monastic life — a place of meditation, exercise, study, and relaxation for the taciturn monks.

When you stop at Piazza Navona save a little energy and interest for a short walk to and through two charming courtyards — the exquisite 15th century, two level, arcaded cloister of *San Salvatore in Lauro* (which is followed by another tiny court with a run-down, but appealing, fountain) and the dignified Renaissance courtyard of Santa Maria della Pace by Bramante, which has been welcoming the Faithful to Mass for nearly five centuries.

Palazzo Borghese in the Piazza of the same name (also in the vicinity of Navona) surrounds the handsome cortile and rich garden of the Borghese Pope, Paul V of the 17th century.

Anytime you are near the Colosseum consider a stop at old San Clemente with its cobblestoned cloister, ancient colonnade, murmuring fountain and four pathetically skinny palm trees. Walk around the colonnade several times in meditation or in contemplation of the sufferings of St. Peter's good friend and third successor as Supreme Pontiff, St. Clement, who established a church at his house on this very property.

From San Clemente a short walk will take you to the double courtyards of the Church of *Santi Quattro Coronati* (the Four Holy Crowned Ones).

At the corner of Quattro Fontane (Four Fountains) is San Carlo (also called San Carlino) with the cutest two-tiered cloister in Rome, at least in the opinion of my good friend, Ken Schnall, fellow Romaphile, and self-appointed courtyard expert. A fine painter, Ken, who spent a recent summer in the city's artists' quarter on Via Margutta, first opened our eyes to the appeal of courtyards and we've been fanciers since.

San Carlino is open only from 9 to 12 mornings and 4 to 6 P.M., unless you can convince the old portiere to admit you at other times. I've never succeeded, even with bribes of a thousand lire or more, in getting him to interrupt his siesta. That part of the Roman's day is, it seems, inviolate even vis-à-vis the chance to make some money. We can again heartily recommend to you also, the incredibly pink, tiny courtyard of the Church of *San Silvestro in Capite* in Piazza San Silvestro. Broken statuary, pieces of epitaphs embedded in the walls, enhance the yard which is, sadly, a little neglected as of the moment.

Piazza Campidoglio's museums each have a splendid center yard. My sons always enjoy the one to the right, Palazzo dei Conservatori, with its broken colossus of Constantine. Ron will show you the hand of the "Liberator of the Christians" with one finger raised in the, "We're number one" sign of triumphant American athletes. Frank gets a kick out of the size 314 foot. And John will gladly climb up to and nestle in the biceps, flexing his own for a great mug shot. The orange shades tone up the place.

Michelangelo created a beautiful cloister within the Baths of Diocletian. With its hundred columns, stately cypresses and lush shrubs, broken tomb stones and sarcophagi (and the two basalt feet of Nero's colossus) the courtyard is a most scenic place to refresh oneself during a taxing day of sight seeing.

One last favorite we should like to bring to your attention: the 18th century, ivy-covered, courtyard of Sant' Agata dei Goti just off Via Cavour.

This is a very modest listing of the Courtyards of Rome for there are almost as many *cortili* as there are *palazzi*. But after sampling them, you may become so enamored of this aspect of Rome that your first impulse upon returning to the States will be to pave your backyard, tear down its chain-link fence and enclose it with a cinder block wall topped with plants and covered with stucco, painted burnt ochre. Add some statuary (plaster if you can't afford marble), a bird bath, and some stone benches and — *che meravglioso!* — a secluded courtyard in place of an open backyard. Check your local ordinances first.

Buona Fortuna!

John scans the bend in the Tiber and the Old Synagogue

XII

The Tiber and Its Bridges

If Rome is truly the Mother of the Western World perhaps the venerable River Tiber is, to continue the metaphor, the Grandmother. For it was most likely the attraction that caused the inhabitants of the Sabine and the Alban and the other chains of hills encircling Rome to abandon their settlements and swoop down upon the future site of Rome. Hills they already had plenty of but a river to link them with the Sea they had not.

Even Vergilian and Livian legends would support the grandmother theory, for thanks to the acquiescent Tiber the twins Romulus and Remus did not drown but were spared in order to found a city on the Palatine above.

Called the *Albula* in very deep antiquity, it received its current name from Tiberinus, a king of Alba Longa who drowned in its raging flood waters.

While not attractive like the Seine, nor graceful as the Danube, nor grand like the Rhine, the Tiber enjoys the affection of the Romans who quickly note that no other can hold a candle to its historical importance and of course they are correct. They concede though that it is, "too large to be harmless, too small to be useful."

Harmless indeed the Tiber is not! It has a long list of

indictments for flood damage to the Forum, to villas and churches along its banks, and even for malaria (*mal aria* — or foul air) over its long, spotty career.

Particularly after heavy spring rains would the Tiber go berserk. One area down by the Circus Maximus was and is still called *Velabrum* (lake) for the huge body of water the Tiber would leave behind there after a flood. A beautiful ancient church in that area is called *San Giorgio in Velabro*. But lofty marble quays of the last century have tamed the river at last.

As a greenish stream flowing down from the Apennines, laden with a heavy cargo of alluvial silt, the Tiber was always the city's natural northern fortification. It was later aided in this role by an extension of Aurelian's wall.

While it is Italy's second largest river it sees very little traffic anymore; there are no glass-topped tourist barges to be sure. Still it is a pretty thing, I feel, as it picks its serpentine way through Urbs Aeterna to Ostia on the Tyrhennian fifteen miles west. My wife and I find that a walk up and down its banks rejuvenates the romance in us. We and other lovers can on a lazy Sunday afternoon often be found whispering sweet nothings under one of the endless trees which lean precariously over the quays in a futile attempt to slake their relentless thirst.

Caligula once had thousands of plebes thrown into the river while he sat and howled with delight on the right bank. He explained later that he was bored and wanted to witness something unusual.

When the great state funeral of the hated Tiberius wended its way along the left bank a frenzied mob rushed the cortege shouting "Tiberius in Tiberim! Tiberius in Tiberim" and damned near succeeded in committing the old boy's mortal remains to the deep. The Praetorian Guard or Secret Service was hard put to maintain control.

Centuries later a similar incident occurred, at the funeral of a pope no less. Pius IX, it seems, had in life incurred the political enmity of some of the populace and now they hoped to retaliate if only in death.

Tarquinius Priscus, the city's fourth king first bridged the river with the Pons Sublicius of Horatio fame. When other bridges followed in later centuries a transpontine Rome developed. *Tevere* the river is called in Italian, and one of Rome's most delightful quarters is the one across the Tiber from the Aventine, the *Trastevere.*

We would like to take you now on a walk along the Tiber. Imagine that it's a balmy Sunday afternoon in November, the tourists have evacuated, all is peaceful and we have just come from a favorite trattoria on the Aventine, full as ticks. What better way at this time is there to aid the digestion and the waistline than *fare una passeggiata nell'aria autunnale lungo il Tevere.*

Let's start at the base of the Aventine across from Porta Portese and stop to consider the many bridges that span the Tiber. Some ancient, graceful, historic and architectural; others modern, nondescript, homely and mundane.

Our first bridge is the plain Ponte Sublicio, known also as Aventino, spanning the river at the same point of the Pons Sublicius which Horatio the One-eyed ordered demolished to deny the Etruscans entry into Rome.

Ponte Palatino, an old marble structure with iron railing, not exactly known for a *bella figura,* is next. Johnny is an informal member of an informal fishing society which congregates here daily with their long makeshift rods and five-and-ten-cent reels in a futile attempt to extract some living creatures from the polluted waters far below. The society knows no age limits, nor membership restrictions of any kind. John enjoys the company of ancient mariners, shopkeepers, university students, lawyers, and occasionally a couple of nuns.

From this span the quaint Tiber Island can be beautifully photographed or sketched. Just ahead is the single remaining beautiful arch of the *Ponte Rotto* (broken bridge, or the Pons Aemilius of 181 B.C.).

Two bridges link the island to either side of the city. Ponte Fabricio has changed little since Veningetarix gazed on it while he walked across it in chains on his way to incarceration and eventual execution in the awful Mamertine.

Ponte Cestio, its companion, is also pre-Christian and ties the island to the right bank.

Ponte Garibaldi is not much to look at except in late July when it is adorned with wreaths and lights for the colorful festival of *Noi Antri* (We Others) in Trastevere. It is also redeemed by the area of the Arenula with its cafés, fruit stands, flower and book stalls giving the place a distinctly European flavor.

In 1473 Pope Sixtus IV had the next bridge built, the Ponte Sisto, in preparation for the heavy pilgrim traffic of the Holy Year of 1475.

Let us give the next two, Ponte Mazzini and Ponte Principe Amedeo, a bye to reach the beautiful architectural Ponte Vittorio Emmanuele II with its quadruplet of colossal Angels of Victory outlined regally against the azure Roman sky. This is always a feast for my poetic eyes and yet I suspect it goes largely unappreciated by untrained tourists. A perfect place to catch our breath and enjoy the scenery is that corner café with its awninged tables. We must try the great chocolate cream puffs here with the rather good cappuccino. Look at the constant flow of pedestrian traffic on its eager way to Via della Conciliazione and on to St. Peter's.

Refreshed now? Good, because we have miles to go before we sleep. All cameras ready for wonderful photographs of ourselves with the incomparable backdrop of the bridge's sculpture, Hadrian's Tomb, the Bridge of the Angels, and the Palace of Justice.

From here it's but a couple of hundred yards to the

pièce de résistance of all the Tiber's bridges, Hadrian's Pons Aelius of 135 A.D., decorated in the 1600's with breezy marble angels by Bernini's students and sentried by the Apostolic Princes Peter, always with his keys, and Paul, the scholar and fighter, never without his book and sword. By day or night the Ponte Sant'Angelo, as it is known today, is easily the most singularly romantic spot on this planet and the holder of the world's marriage proposal record. In either direction the view is gorgeous. Toward St. Peter's or over the other rail to Palazzo Giustizia, on to the fortress capped rubble of Hadrian's mausoleum (now the Castel Sant'Angelo) or back to the narrow, twisting Via Paola peeking into the Corso Vittorio Emmanuele.

At nightfall as the lights of the bridge and the silhouette of the Castel glisten in the historic waters one wishes he could spend eternity here as did Hadrian.

What distinguishes the next span, Ponte Umberto Primo, is its climax at the immense Palazzo Giustizia, Italy's Supreme Court, with its galaxy of great Roman jurists of every age, starting with Cicero, standing around out in front of the courthouse.

Ponte Cavour brings the Corso to the Prati district, Ponte Regina Margherita conveys the traffic from Piazza del Popolo in the direction of the Vatican and Ponte Matteotti links up with the consular highway to the northeast, Via Flaminia Vecchia, where my author friend Michael Stern ("American in Rome") lives.

I know you're weary now but push on with us — we'll work up a powerful appetite for the evening meal — past the Ponte Risorgimento and the Ponte Duca d'Aosta. (Take a quick look across the latter to the Foro Italico with its modern obelisk engraved vertically, *Mussolini Dux.*)

At last we stand on the Ponte Milvio where Constantine beheld, in the copper sky of the late afternoon, a fiery cross with the huge caption: *In Hoc Signo Vinces* (In this sign thou shalt conquer). On his way to the critical battle with Maxentius for the throne of Rome he had his soldiers decorate their shields and helmets with this Christian symbol. Thence he went on to a smashing victory and to embrace the beleaguered Church.

It was at this spot that Cicero beautifully set up the conspirators of Catiline, where on the blustery night of December 2, 63 B.C. they were arrested with incriminating documents. Anyone who survived to the third year of Latin in his high school days could elaborate on the incident and its gory aftermath.

If we cross this bridge to the Piazzale Ponte Milvio and bear right at the beautiful white church we will be on our way up the old Via Cassia to Viterbo and Siena.

Well I should think we have all by now walked off the *fettucine*, the *pollo arrosto*, and the *pane e burro* and the *gelato* of the mid-day meal. A public bus ride back along the right bank will feel great. Tonight, delightfully exhausted, we will feast and rejuvenate in Trastevere; and be conveyed home beneath the stars via horse and carriage.

Buon Appetito!

XIII

The Tiber Island

Should you, on some *bella giornata*, find yourself on the Lungotevere (street along the Tiber) between Ponte Garibaldi and Ponte Palatino, visit the romantic Island in the Tiber (*Isola Tiberina* or *Isola di San Bartolomeo*).

From the left bank, right in front of the neo-Babylonian synagogue, cross over the Ponte Fabricio of 62 B.C. The oldest bridge in Rome, it was named for the Censor and Commissioner of Roads and Bridges, Fabricius. Use the Ponte Cestio, just a mite younger than its colleague, from the Trastevere.

If you like tradition you'll want to know that the Tarquins, in their hasty retreat from Rome threw tons of their belongings and grain and whatnot into that part of the Tiber in order to walk across. This man-made island eventually metamorphosed into a genuine one. Tradition aside, the island is by all means thoroughly natural, its geological nature being identical to the rest of the city.

Ovid tells us that a plague in the early third century B.C., prompted the consuls to dispatch a delegation to Greece to bring back that nation's god of medicine. As Aesculapius was being transported upstream to the city from Ostia a snake, his mascot and symbol, raced ahead of the ship, crawled upon the island and nestled on a rock at the far end. This site was thus selected for Aesculapius' hospital where he cared for the victims of the plague, and conducted a medical school for aspiring physicians.

Isola Tiberina was an ideal place to isolate the sick and the island has an unbroken history of hospital service to Rome. Today a hospital complex occupies the upper half of the tiny island and is run by the Brothers of St. John of God. The Romans call them the *Fatebene fratelli* (the do good brothers). They treat in particular the sick poor and the aged from the ghetto.

Adjacent to the hospital is the cute church of St. John the Calybite, a 5th century monk. Though it is usually closed don't be discouraged. Ask one of the friars at the main desk and there'll be a flurry of activity to accommodate you.

St. John's is overshadowed by the imposing church of the Apostle Bartholomew, whose remains rest beneath the high altar. In its millennium of existence St. Bartholomew's has been ravaged again and again by floods, especially in 1557, but it maintains its mystic beauty. Inside there are some fine paintings and 14 ancient columns. The church is enhanced by a fine Romanesque bell tower and a little piazza with a monument to the First Vatican Council in 1870.

In the 1200's Rohere, jester of King Henry II, while on a pilgrimage to the Holy City, was stricken with malaria, for the water and the air of that part of Rome were badly contaminated. While convalescing on the island under the tender care of monks he prayed to the Apostle and vowed to build a church back home in his honor if cured. Thus London's famed "St. Bart's" has its roots on this island.

Some very photogenic scenes present themselves to the visitor of the island. The exotic facade and squared alabaster dome of the synagogue rise majestically above the

Castel Sant' Angelo on island in the Tiber

trees on the left bank. The massive tree-lined quays have a great European look to them. A fruit peddler at her stand near the Ponte Fabricio affords a quaint picture. Pines on the distant Aventine give a biblical backdrop to it all.

But come down the steps to the river edge with us and take a walk around the entire island. At the base of the first pier of Ponte Cestio is a great spot for watching the deafening rapids. The boys used to give Camille *agita* here when they would lean over the raging Tiber to start their popsickle stick kayaks on their stormy course to Ostia and the sea. How pleasant it is of a hot summer day to sit on that ledge, armed with a book, taking advantage of the shade of the bridge and the cooling effects of the rushing waters.

Walk to the western tip for a look at the mouth of the *Cloaca Maxima*, and the single arched *Ponte Rotto* (broken bridge). This restoration of the 2nd century Pons Aemilius was condemned as unsafe by Michelangelo just a few days before most of it was swept away by one of the Tiber's classic rampages.

About face at this point and, if the sun is right, the enchanting mass of ochre-tinted medieval buildings with their tiled roofs will thrill you. The ancient Romans decorated the island architecturally as a boat and at this point, too, some of the old travertine stern can be seen forming a foundation for these buildings.

We approach now the base of the Ponte Fabricio also called Ponte Quattro Capi for the four-headed marble hermae on the two entrance pillars, badly eroded by wind and rain and sun. Rounding the upper tip of Isola Tiberina we behold another biblical scene produced by the beautiful foliage of the court at the back of the hospital.

Climb the stairs back to St. Bartholomew's and if you're not too weary we'll go over to the Jewish Ghetto.

Venga!

XIV

The Jewish Ghetto

A most fascinating place is the Jewish quarter called the Ghetto — and yet it manages to escape the attention of all but a handful of the tourists, even those of Jewish ancestry, who pour into Rome year after year. It is easy enough to find, extending from the ancient Theater of Marcellus to the Via Arenula, from just beyond the Porticus Octavia — that imposing monument by Augustus in honor of his sister — to the Tiber. From many points in the city the neighborhood's landmark, the majestic square-domed Synagogue, can be seen and used as a beacon to lead the way to the Ghetto.

It is a district cluttered with little shops on the ground floors of old palazzos on tiny streets that dart off in every direction. Rundown medieval and Renaissance dwellings, peddlers with decrepit pushcarts, dimly lit restaurants — one with a menu written partly in Latin, can you imagine? — dark skinned, dark-eyed bambini playing and shrieking gleefully among Roman ruins and Christian churches also characterize *Il Ghetto*.

Then there is the moody facade of Palazzo Cenci presiding over the eerie atmosphere of the piazza by the same name. A family, the Cenci, notorious for its bizarre crimes

of incest and rape, sadism and murder, inhabited the place
centuries ago and left an indelible stain on palace and
square alike.

We live not too far across the Tiber from here so we
have come to know and love the Ghetto well — first for its
good and gentle people, secondly for its little stores and
places to eat, and for its archaelogical ruins, and for its
miniature piazzas especially Piazza Mattei, with one of the
most adorable fountains anywhere, the Fountain of the
Tortoises.

For porcelain or crystal and for our hardware needs
we often see Signor Limentani; for antiques we roam the
little alleys finding new shops each time; for good buys on
fruits and vegetables we come too.

Historically, the Ghetto ranks high among Rome's
districts for a Jewish community had been established in
the very area even before the days of Julius Caesar. And
since its inception the community has been a victim of
hardship, of injustice, of bloody persecution. An inexplicable but virulent hatred for the Jews developed early on
among the pagans. We see clear evidence of this in the literature of Republican and Imperial Rome. Cicero gripes in
one letter written in 56 B.C. about certain privileges extended to "those Jews and Syrians, races themselves born
to be slaves." By Cicero's time however the Jews already
constituted a sizable and important ethnic group among
the plebes in a squalid, congested city — perhaps as many
as ten thousand — and the Senate had to reckon with
them.

Perhaps it was their unusual form of worship that
bewildered and even infuriated the libertine masses of
Rome. That they would observe their holidays as Holy
Days and in abstention from ordinary activities, from certain tasty foods the year round, struck the Romans as the
essence of unreason. Other early writings often allude to
them as those *Judaei superstitiosi*. One needs little Latin to

Author at the Old Synagogue in the Jewish Quarter of Rome

interpret this slur. The poet Horace whenever he heard a fish story would advise the teller — *Credat Judaeus Apella* (Tell it to the Jew, Apella). They were ridiculed for their worship and for their code of ethics, and for actually believing their traditions to be accurate accounts of what really happened, when the Romans considered their own myths to be fascinating, beautiful but irrelevant little stories and nothing more. Jewish observance of a Sabbath — that every seventh day must be given back to God — and the rite of circumcision also came under heavy fire. One of Horace's characters is reluctant "to offend the circumcised Jews on their sabbath."

Nevertheless under the administration of Julius Caesar the Jewish community had begun to gain better living conditions. The dictator established absolute freedom of religion in Rome and made it a particular point to defend that freedom for the Jews who as a result of this and other humane measures held him in esteem. At Caesar's death the whole community was understandably grief stricken. Friends of ours here have told us that a similarly profound grief resulted at the passing of Pope John over a decade ago. "He was the Jews' Pope too," they say.

Under Augustus, Caesar's heir, the Jews continued to make progress. Such sensitivity did the young Emperor demonstrate that he even shifted the day for the grain distribution to the poor from the Jewish sabbath to a different day of the week lest they be inconvenienced or offended. At this time the Jews were vigorously proselytizing for converts and the spread of Judaism in the Augustan City was rapid. For we know of the existence of several synagogues, three by name: *Augustenses, Volumnienses,* and *Agrippenses.* Excavation of the old seaport at Ostia in 1961 uncovered still another synagogue from this period. Jewish catacombs or underground cemeteries were being dug during these times also, a large one on Via Appia, another along Via Nomentana.

Then Tiberius, following the lead of his predecessor, worked energetically to restore the ancient rituals and put the now all but abandoned pagan religion back on its feet. The government had hoped to use religion to keep the restless rabble in check by inferring that any act of disobedience to or defiance of the authorities would incur the wrath of the gods. The growth of Judaism was an obstruction to this plan for as Juvenal complained, "They despise the laws of Rome and revere only the Law of the Jews." Alarmed at this state of affairs old Tiberius sent four thousand male Jews off to fight in Sardinia and ordered the rest to renounce their "eccentric and dangerous" rituals, embrace paganism, or leave Italy before a fixed date, which date is lost to us.

Things began to deteriorate more under the next ruler, the obnoxious yet pathetic paranoiac, Caligula. He insisted on being deified and had effigies of himself set up toward that end in public buildings, temples and shrines throughout the world of Rome. The tyrant soon got a taste of Jewish spunk however — he had mistakenly assumed them to be as docile as all his other subjects — when he had his statue placed in the great and holy temple at Jerusalem. A revolt ensued and after it was quelled the Jews still steadfastly refused to pay homage to the Emperor. Caligula's advisors wisely convinced him that the Jews' "fanaticism" was unimportant and the matter was laid to rest.

Trouble erupted again the next reign when Claudius ordered another expulsion, blaming the community for all the unrest in the city. Documentary proof of this is provided by Acts 18:1-2 of the New Testament which in referring to Paul's meeting with Aquila in Corinth reads: "(Paul) found a certain Jew born in Pontus lately come from Italy with his wife Priscilla because that Claudius had directed all Jews to depart from Rome." Gradually the emotion-charged situation calmed down, the ban was lifted, and the Jews returned. Another eruption was brewing after the

Christian community was indicted for the burning of Rome, since the pagans and their rulers considered the Christians to be merely a heretical Jewish sect and made little more distinction between the two groups. The fact that some Jews had set up their own synagogues or *ecclesiae*, apart from the established ones, for the new worship, fostered this lack of distinction. Eventually a clarification was made and matters again grew calm for the harried Jews of Rome. They took now to behaving more like their pagan neighbors in dress, in speech, in outlook in order to get into the mainstream of the city's life and out of the awful glare of unfavorable publicity. Many began to refer to Rome as their *Patria* — or fatherland. But they were destined to suffer terribly again and again — under Vespasian, Domitian, Caracalla and others. Rome fell in 476 A.D. The city became a ghost town, the population dwindled to but a few thousand, but the Jews stayed on. During the ensuing dark ages life for Jews in Rome was no less nor no more wretched than for any other inhabitants. But the fact that the community did hang on uninterruptedly down through the centuries to our day means that Rome today truly belongs to the people of this Ghetto as much as to anyone.

Such claims to seniority of residence were to be of small help and of no comfort to them however, when in the 1400's they began again without cause to be subjected to indescribable sufferings and persecutions, this time by cruel Christian leaders who were now enjoying civil power as well, and into whose hands from time to time Holy Mother Church is allowed to fall by the Holy Spirit for some mysterious reason. Jews were now subjected to curfews and other restrictions and Christians were forbidden under threat of excommunication to fraternize with them. At carnival time the men were forced to run almost naked in races on Via del Corso. In the 1500's one moody pope ordered all Jews to wear yellow — for the men, hats, for the women, veils — so they could be easily recognized. A ghetto was marked off with pipes and chains. (The *Albergo della Catena*, Hotel of the Chain, commemorates those dark times.) The residents were forbidden to exit from the area before sunrise and had to be back in before sundown. They were kept out of guilds, the only route to decent employment, and forced to trade in junk and practice usury to survive. Some later popes would lift the restrictions while some would reimpose them. Jews were always being charged without proof of unspeakable crimes. Ironic wasn't it that this crop of Christians whose spiritual ancestors had fought the good fight against religious persecution, in this very city, were now the perpetrators of such mindless activity. Finally, the Jews were rounded up each Saturday and compelled to attend Mass and listen to a sermon by a Dominican Monk in the old church of *Sant'Angelo in Pescheria* established in the pontificate of Stephen III, which you may visit in the ruins of Octavia's portico. Throughout the service the captive audience would finger the *mazuze* around their necks and cough, sneeze, wheeze, blow their noses in order to drown out the words of the preacher. But the humiliation continued until in 1848 Pius IX abolished all restrictions and promised to deal severely in the future with anyone guilty of harassment of the weary Ghetto dwellers.

In 1904 two great architects of the day, Armani and Costa, finished work on the magnificent synagogue called *Tempio Maggiore*. Perched proudly on the left bank of the Tiber, just across from the island in the river, the synagogue of Babylonian architecture soars triumphantly over the treetops. Within are two altars from previous temples on the same site flanking the stunning central altar. One dates back three centuries, the other five. The square dome of the finest alabaster, and translucent, and the star-frescoed ceiling are inspiring. My family and I love the synagogue, visit it often, and never fail to bring our friends, passing through Rome, to see it. The people there have befriended us and we are often invited to their Bar Mitzvahs and weddings. At our first wedding there (the boys and I and Grandpa Gatto having donned yamulkas, and Camille and Nana Gatto black veils) we were deeply moved by the beauty and solemnity of the ceremony. We recall particularly the point at which the bridal couple, both sets of parents, and the three rabbi celebrants huddled under one small canopy while chanting a long series of prayers.

Another note of irony that suddenly strikes me is that opposite this holy edifice is another, the little church of Madonna della Pieta on whose facade is a painting of the Crucifixion with this text from Isaiah in both Latin and Hebrew lettering: "All day I have extended my hands to a disloyal nation."

Hell broke loose again for the Jewish quarter during the Nazi occupation in 1943. Hitler had insisted that Mussolini implement the same racist laws that were in effect in other parts of Europe. When the real picture of the northern labor camps and their sequel was painted for him by his aides, the Duce was rightly appalled. He directed his staff to make a show of compliance with Hitler's wishes but to make every effort to avoid actually doing so.

Fear was etched in every face and every heart stopped as, in September of that year, gruesome Nazi tanks and trucks followed by menacing, goose-stepping troops rumbled menacingly day after day through the quaint streets of the picturesque quarter. Later that same month Jewish community leaders were summoned to Gestapo headquarters on the Via Tasso and told that the Jews of Rome would be wiped out for their hatred of the German people unless they paid a ransom of one hundred pounds of gold within the next forty-eight hours. Cherished rings, watches, dinnerware, family heirlooms were reluctantly and at the same time eagerly relinquished in the interest of survival. The reigning Pope, Pius XII opened the Vatican treasury of gold to the Jews in order to meet their needs. With little to spare in their race against the merciless sands of time the Jews bought off their annihilation, the ransom was paid. October 16th soon arrived and with it came the Nazi betrayal of the agreement, as the troops smashed into the synagogue, destroyed whatever sacred objects had not been secreted away, loaded the men onto trucks, blocked off all exits from the Ghetto. A proscription of all adult males for deportation to the labor camps was instituted.

Many managed to flee — some by daringly leaping over alleyways from rooftop to rooftop, others by hiding for several heart-pounding hours until they could crawl out of the designated area under the cloak of night. Among the fugitives from Nazi "justice" was Angelo Zolli, Chief Rabbi of Rome, who made his way miraculously to the Vatican where the Holy Father granted him, and scores of others who later made it, sanctuary. Hundreds more made it to convents, monasteries, and churches throughout the fallen city where the Catholic clergy concealed them at great personal peril. One man told us quite seriously that it was his high school Latin that saved him. He had gone to a monastery which had no good, safe hiding places. So he donned the robes of the monks, was tonsured, and when the police barged in from time to time during services he was always singing the Latin hymns as proficiently as the others and was not detected when the police studied each face looking for imposters.

Though great numbers of the male population were now living in monastic calm, terror continued to pace the alleys of the poor Ghetto. Shattered families sitting down to the evening meal never quite adjusted to that inevitable awful knock on the door, the long interrogation that always followed the knock in a frenzied but futile quest for information on the whereabouts of certain family members.

Rumors, well founded, began to circulate about Nazi intentions to raze the beloved synagogue. A desperate plea for help was sent to the Vatican and Pius responded by declaring that the temple was now under the holy jurisdiction of the Church. Staking his hope on the Nazi agreement that all such property was inviolate, the Pontiff had all the doors of the synagogue marked with a symbolic Vatican seal, silently telling the intruders from the Rhine — "hands off!" Guides at the temple will, upon request, draw back the curtains at all the doors to show some remnants of the seals of red wax. The war came to an end and this trial, as with all the others for God's chosen people through the ages, had passed and the vitality of the Ghetto, sapped by the nightmare, began to return. Rabbi Zolli and some other Vatican stowaways converted to Catholicism, a move that scandalized the community at first. But U.S. Brigadier General Edgar Hume later told of how he happened to be in the Vatican soon after the liberation of the Eternal City when a delegation of several hundred Jews arrived to thank the Holy Father for his gallant fight on behalf of the oppressed Jewish people of Rome.

So the Ghetto on the Tiber along with the rest of Europe, indeed with the rest of the world, learned slowly but surely how to smile again. But the Ghetto will always be, for me and my family at least, synonymous with human suffering. Perhaps this is why we come here almost daily — to walk its streets, to feel its wonderful vibrancy in the hope that by association with them we will acquire at least a small measure of the boundless courage and inner strength and longanimity of these dear people.

Shalom

XV

The Ardeatine Caves

Rome in her long, dramatic history has seen many dark hours and many armed foreign troops in her streets. In September, 1943 Nazi forces of Adolf Hitler entered the Eternal City and entered Rome's already bulging log of barbaric intruders such as the Gauls and Goths, the Arabs and Byzantines, and the latter-day Gauls, the French.

The Holy City of churches and church bells, of gaiety and song, of history and art, with its peace-loving population, was transformed in a flash to a soul-wrenching, ugly grey, police state.

Where stood, just days before, clusters of Romans, nattily attired as always, in animated conversation, there now stood bands of Nazi soldiers, helmeted and bayoneted, in somber vigilance.

Vatican City was now ringed not only by medieval-clad, innocuously ceremonial Swiss Guards but by dead-serious, deadly Wermacht troops. The beloved romantic *carrozze* (horse-drawn carriages) so endemic to Piazza San Pietro were now replaced by tanks and jeeps.

Some of Rome's most fashionable hotels were now Nazi command posts. The peerless Excelsior on the Via Veneto suffered such a fate. No longer did her lobby echo to the excited chatter of the continent's aristocracy but to the ominously clicking heels of the low-breed, goose-stepping collection of misfits of German society known as Hitler's storm troopers.

Travel throughout the city was restricted. The buses and trolleys ran irregularly, and when they did run, people feared to ride them for the Nazi police were in the practice of stopping them at random, and conscripting the riders to be sent off to forced labor camps. To be caught in the streets without special identification papers was tantamount to being caught in the act of some high crime. Bicycles were outlawed. Food was rationed and Rome's cat and dog population would suffer as a consequence. An awful winter of gloom had come early to Rome.

At No. 145 Via Tasso a building was converted into a Gestapo prison to handle any Romans who might prove a thorn in the Nazi side. A Fascist torture chamber on the Via Principe Amedeo was already in the same business. The Roman people, perhaps the happiest anywhere on earth, with the greatest zest for life, had become docile. For while they lacked not the courage they simply hadn't the heart for confrontation in a city which had suffered more than her fair share of it over the ages.

Some of Rome's citizens were having none of this docility however. The Nazi occupation was giving rise to *La Resistenza* (the Resistance), an underground anti-Fascist and anti-Nazi movement particularly attractive to communist-leaning university students.

Throughout the autumn and winter the Resistance was to cause the occupiers some anxious moments but the overall effect was that of a fly on an elephant's back — a nuisance but no real threat. There were snipings, grenade attacks on jeeps and tanks, fire bombings of precinct headquarters. Undaunted by the Nazi promise to bring the perpetrators to Nazi justice, the movement was planning a more meaningful attack. If they could demonstrate a ca-

Author with group at entrance to the cemetery at the Ardea-
tine Caves

pacity for serious damage and threat to the Nazi position in the city perhaps their ranks would swell and the fever of liberty would spread until all Romans were fighting as one the foe from the north, whose ancestors had been repelled twenty centuries earlier by Marius, uncle of Julius Caesar.

While I had been to Rome three times previous to my Fulbright year, I had never heard of the *Fosse Ardeatine*, a series of caves on the Via Ardeatina which forks from the Via Appia Antica at the Church of Quo Vadis. One day, while returning from our field studies in the Alban Hills, our professor asked the class if we would like to visit a most unusual though little-known site of Rome.

Since my fellow scholars and I were always ready for something new regarding Rome the proposal received a ringing endorsement. The prof directed our busdriver, Renzo (who drove with both hands on the wheel and both eyes on the girls in our class) to the caves and while en route he briefed us on the tragedy that took place there in the closing months of the Nazi occupation. The stop was to be one of the most moving experiences of my life and evidently for the rest of the group too, for the ride back to the American Academy was a strangely silent one for such a garrulous gang as ours. Each of us preferred to be alone with his thoughts for awhile. I've been back many times since that day. While it can never be considered a pleasant tourist attraction in the ordinary sense of the term, it is, I believe, a site that ought to be seen by every visitor to Rome. For the place preaches an eloquently unforgettable and solemnly moving — though eerily silent — sermon on the horrors of war, on the barbarism of Hitler, and on man's eternal inhumanity to man. Camille and the boys and I insist on showing the caves to all our visitors from the states and all of us never fail to take away a profoundly spiritual experience from each visit.

In the ensuing pages I shall do my best to explain to you the events leading up to it, the tragedy itself, and the

aftermath of it all. It would be good if while you were reading you might have a street map of the city before you, to
help you reconstruct vicariously those fateful 48 hours.

It was 1944 and the winter having spent itself, Rome's
trees and shrubs were dressing for spring. Members of the
Resistance were eager for a major attack on the hated foe,
and an idea had recently come forth. The Nazis were in the
habit of parading through the center of the city each day at
2 P.M. as a vivid reminder to the populace of just who was
in control. Normally, the parade route was down the Via
Flaminia through the grey-brown stones of the Porta del
Popolo into and through the Piazza del Popolo, left of the
twin churches down Via del Babuino, through Piazza di
Spagna, onto Via del Traforo, left up the sloping but nondescript Via Rasella, right onto Via Quattro Fontane to
Via Venti Novembre, and onto Nazi Headquarters at Via
Tasso. The column of troopers numbered 156, marching
three abreast to the beat of a drum.

The route of the parade had been scouted in the minutest detail by some of the partisans. They now knew just
how many steps were required from one designated point
to another, how many seconds it would take walking in
normal fashion to get from the scene of the planned attack
to the various proposed escape routes.

Via Rasella was selected because of its tranquillity and
lack of pedestrian traffic particularly during the siesta
hours. This street begins at the Via del Traforo and climbs
two blocks — Via Boccaccio intersecting it halfway up —
to the Palazzo Barberini on Via Quattro Fontane. It is
lined with shops — barbers, tailors, artists et al — and
paved with cobblestones. At No. 156 there is the Palazzo
Tittoni, the elegant town house of Senator Tittoni who had
died in 1931, still inhabited by the widow.

Volunteers were needed, thirteen in all for this daring
mission. The two lead roles went to Rosario Bentivegna,
21 and a pre-med student and Carla Capponi his fiancee. A

powerful bomb had been readied by the group's explosives expert, and a fuse of sixty-seconds' duration had been attached. A grey-blue sanitation worker's uniform had been secured and a garbage can pushcart stolen from the city yards near the Colosseum.

On the appointed day, Thursday, March 23, 1944, at one o'clock, Rosario pushed the cart onto the Via Claudia. The other 12 were already at or on their way to their stations near the Via Rasella. Carla, who some weeks earlier had daringly and singlehandedly blown up a truck and 2,500 gallons of gasoline at a Nazi depot, was headed for the top of the appointed street equipped with a pistol in her purse and a man's raincoat over one arm. At one point during the nerve-tingling wait she attracted the attention of Nazi detectives who wanted to know if she had her papers with her and why she was carrying a man's raincoat on a balmy, cloudless day. Only the arrival of an old friend of her mother's saved her from further investigation. She had all she could do not to betray herself, to keep her limbs from trembling vehemently.

Rosario pushed the cart around the ruined stadium — straining because of the excessive weight of the cart's cargo but straining too, not to show it — onto the Via dei Fori Imperiali through Piazza Venezia. Years later when asked in an interview what his thoughts had been on the way, he related that while flirting with death only one recurrent thought played on his mind and that was: "Rome is truly beautiful and I may never see her again." I now suspect that for all Romans, when faced with death, this is the most tormenting thought of all.

He continued the strenuous climb up the Quininale Hill, now past the Presidential Palace down the long Via Venti Settembre to San Carlo at the Four Fountains. Turning left here it was but two short blocks uphill to the battleground. Left again he turned and eased his cart down Via Rasella to Tittoni's. Along the way he had several

close calls of being exposed. Once by two genuine street
cleaners and on the Via Rasella itself by another. Many
times the temptation to call off the whole thing and run
was near overwhelming. Projecting the insouciant air of
the ordinary street cleaner required, under such mind-
boggling pressure, an Oscar-winning performance. But a
more agonizing pressure was to come. For arriving there at
ten minutes of two he had, without realizing it at the time,
not ten minutes to wait but nearly an hour and a half for,
inexplicably, the punctual Nazis were late that day.

Nervously he swept the street around him again and
again. Carla paced anxiously at the top of the slope. The
other 11 fidgeted while fighting panic. At about 3:10 a
comrade brushed past the cart and mumbled: "If they
don't show in 10 minutes it's all off." This was the worst
prospect of all, with the mere thought of criss-crossing the
city again with the incriminating material enough to give
anyone a stroke.

Suddenly in the distance could be heard a muffled
drum and chanting of many male voices. "Here they
come!" Now they were before the deserted Spanish Steps
with the weeping Trinita dei Monti looking down at
Rome's latest humiliation.

Louder grew the drums and the boots on the pavement and the singing voices and the beating of Rosario's
and Carla's hearts — hearts which beat as one in love.
Carla braced herself in the doorway of No. 158 Quattro
Fontane. With the front ranks already at Via Boccacio,
Rosario received the signal to light the fuse. Trembling he
touched his pipe to the stem, checked to hear if it had ignit-
ed and abandoned the hissing device — drowned out by
the clangor of the doomed men — and walked — not too
briskly lest he arouse interest — to the corner and to the
safety of Carla's arms and the raincoat she helped him to
don. The two walked away from the impending
catastrophe arm-in-arm, like the lovers they really were.

Now when several lines had passed Palazzo Tittoni, the fuse had spent itself and triggered the bomb which went off with such incredible fury that it shook the surrounding area as bodies and parts of same flew through the air, facades of buildings cracked, cornices and windowpanes dislodged themselves and rained down upon the bomb's victims: 33 dead, and countless others maimed beyond recovery. Mains burst and water mingled with blood in a gruesome cascade down over the cobblestones into Via del Traforo whose tunnel had provided an escape route for some of the partisans.

At the bottom of Rasella other partisans tossed in some grenades. The rear ranks of the parade turned and opened fire at the windows of buildings behind them. Walk down the Via Rasella today and you will see that the pockmarks caused by Nazi machine guns have never been filled in. This partisan act — which to our own day is viewed with mixed emotions by the Roman populace ("Stupid!" some call it; "Heroic!" others feel) was to precipitate a slaughter the likes of which even the worst days of pagan Rome never knew.

High German officials — in the case of General Kurt Malzer the alcoholic "King of Rome" *very* high — arrived on the scene in moments. While Col. Eugene Dollman, head of the SS in Rome, Col. Herbert Kappler, Malzer's *aide de camp*, and the head of the German Embassy, Consul E. F. Mollhausen tried calmly to get a handle on the whole incident, Malzer, in a drunken stupor as usual, became hysterical. He ordered the entire block blown sky high along with its inhabitants. He was bundled off to his lair to sleep it off and to get him out of the hair of Kappler who saw himself as the most competent Nazi officer to deal with the matter. Kappler loved Rome as a second home — fancied himself as a scholar of her art, a connoisseur of her wine, a bon vivant with the Italian signorine.

All the residents of the street were taken from their

homes — the old, the young, the infirm — and forced to stand hands over heads for hours of terrifying and menacing and often physical interrogation. This was judged to be such a serious act as to merit the attention and assessment of the Führer himself. Reached at his headquarters in East Prussia, Hitler ordered 10 Romans killed for every Nazi fatality. This was less drastic than Henrich Himmler's order from Berlin to deport the entire male adult population of Rome to concentration camps in the north.

Kappler reluctantly yielded to Hitler's edict which specifically called for the reprisal to be completed within 24 hours.

Kappler decided to use all political prisoners sentenced to death. When informed that they numbered less than 100, he resolved to use all political prisoners. Failing even then by far to meet the awful quota, he called for an indiscriminate roundup of Roman males, with concentration on the long-suffering Jewish Ghetto. Some families suffered multiple losses. One Jewish family, the De Consiglios, lost five males: the grandfather; two sons; and two grandsons. The lady from whom we rent our apartment lost her handyman and good friend, Alfredo Mosca. Men from all walks of life, ages ranging from 15 to 80, including one priest, comprised the group.

Our Roman Mamma's father barely escaped the roundup. Over the underground radio a Jewish shopkeeper on Via Tritone heard the Nazi plan, saw him walking past the shop, reached out and hauled him in — shushing his objections — pulled down the iron grating and concealed him in a closet. Less than two minutes later the hunters rumbled past in an open-back truck. By this courageous act, at great peril to himself, the shopkeeper won Mamma's undying love and devotion to the whole Jewish race, whereupon she joined an organization of Catholic and Jewish women whose *raison d'être* was to alleviate the plight of Rome's Jews. Mamma is still active in it.

An execution site had to be selected. While the aim was to teach the Romans a dramatic and traumatic lesson in the swiftness and ferocity of Nazi justice, a massacre of innocent people before the very eyes of the Romans might precipitate a revolt that even the Nazi war machine in the city could not handle. Kappler was informed of a labyrinth of caves just outside the walls and he declared it ideal. The innocents were tied back-to-back in clusters of three and trucked to the site. They were led into the caves and each was murdered by one pistol shot through the back of the head. The task took many hours but the butcher's deadline was met. Witnessing the carnage from behind some pines at the Catacombs of San Callisto, across the street where he served as a guide, was Father Bruno Brunori, by whom word was filtered back to the families of some of the slain.

Nazi authorities warned Father to stop intruding and he quickly complied — not from cowardice but because he was hiding hundreds of political enemies of the regime in the subterranean cemeteries of the martyrs. On March 25, Saturday, mines were detonated to seal off the entrances to the caves. They remained sealed until the Americans liberated Rome and Michael Stern, the celebrated columnist and author, went out to the caves at the behest of Father Brunori.

A massive exhumation and identification of the bodies was soon undertaken. Eventually they were entombed in separate sepulchers but in one great mausoleum under one massive tombstone. This, perhaps Europe's most impressive war cemetery, was opened in 1949 to the public. It is particularly touching to see on Sundays the families of the victims coming to pray, to think, to decorate the graves with flowers.

Each of the tombs has a photo of the victim with an inscription of his name, age and occupation. One is marked simply: *Ignoto* (unknown). At the entrance to the indoor cemetery (the sensation is one of being at a massive, unending wake) is a huge monument by the sculptor F. Coccia in 1950 of three men, one a mere boy, tied together with a look of bone-chilling fright in their faces.

Today all is serene at Fosse Ardeatine. In the caves themselves are memorial chapels — one Jewish, the other Catholic. In back of the cemetery there is a museum with grim reminders of the war and of that spring day 30 years ago. Birds play tag and make love on the branches of the stately cypresses that grace the landscape.

What has become of the central characters in this tragedy? Many of the partisans are still active in politics, most with the Communist party. Rosario Bentivegna is a doctor in Rome. Carla, his wife, served in the Italian Parliament. The partisans were sued years later by families of some victims for "an irresponsible act which caused the deaths of innocent Romans." Suit was denied on the grounds that it was a legitimate act of war on the part of the people against their oppressors.

At war's end the slaughterers were brought to trial. Malzer, tried in Rome in 1946, has since died in prison. Kappler also tried here, is serving his life sentence in a cell at the prison in Gaeta.

It is altogether fitting, I think, that the martyrs of Fosse Ardeatine sleep eternally in the immediate area of the catacombs, the area made holy by the bodies of Jewish and Christian martyrs of another mindless savagery of another day. . . .

Requiescant in Pace

Camille on the eminence of the hill, the Janiculum, with Rome in the background

XVI

The Janiculum

"*Gianicolo*" the yellow metal signs say, pointing in the direction of the hill named for Rome's mythological janitor — Janus the two-faced god of beginnings and endings. (So too is January, the doorway to the year, named.)

High above the city she sits, on the Vatican side of the Tiber. Reached from St. Peter's by the climbing, immured Via delle Fornaci or from Trastevere by the Passeggiata del Gianicolo or from the Ponte Principe Amedeo by the Via del Gianicolo, the hill is the best vantage point from which to view the whole of Rome. Far below it spread the seven hills, in the distance like a massive amphitheatre designed by that greatest of architects, God the Father, sparkle the Roman Castelli or hill towns, to the left the snowcapped Apennines. It is a world apart, yet within the old Aurelian walls which stretched from Porta Portese in the Trastevere over to the Vatican. Its own imposing walls are the gift of Pope Urban VIII who raised them as insurance for the area's defense during the Thirty Years War.

Up here Lars Porsena paused with his Etruscan warriors before the futile storming of Roma (futile, thanks to Horatio Cocles). Up here Cleopatra relaxed at a magnificent villa during her sojourn in Rome. Up here the Korn family of Kenilworth, New Jersey, U.S.A. lives one-fourth of each year. (Don't be surprised if the last fact doesn't appear in all of the guide books.)

The approach from Trastevere, on foot up a flight of steps near the old fountain on the Via Manili, will take you through a path flanked with ceramic Stations of the Cross and to the 15th century church of San Pietro in Montorio (the *Hill of Gold* so named for its golden sands; in Latin: *Mons Aureus*).

Even from this level the vistas will take your breath away. We never fail to linger here if we are guiding a group, for the church holds many surprises. Behind its simple Renaissance facade are many famous frescoes, especially the *Whipping of Christ* by Sebastiano del Piombo, the *Madonna of the Letter* by Pomerarcio, and the *St. Francis in Ecstasy* sculpture by Baratta.

From here we always go to the adjacent courtyard. Generally unfamiliar to tourists it always offers welcome relief from the chaos of the city. In its center reigns the *Tempietto* (Little Temple) of Bramante which marks a traditional site of Peter's crucifixion, though it is fairly indisputable that the Prince of the Apostles breathed his last in Nero's Circus on *Mons Vaticanus*.

This adorable work by a Renaissance giant in 1502 houses two chapels, one above the other. The interior of the dome was later frescoed by Bernini with scenes from the life of Peter. In its sanctuary lie entombed two Irish noblemen. It must be photographed in early morning hours from just outside the courtyard's portal.

For the first-time visitor to the summit, however, we would recommend strongly the approach on the other side of the hill along Via del Gianicolo. In this way we will pass the grounds of the North American College where American Roman Catholic Seminarians of great academic and ecclesiastical promise are sent to prepare for ordination.

Twisting with the road we soon arrive at the fabled

stump of Torquato Tasso's Oak in the former shade of which the poet of the late 1500's (*Jerusalem Delivered*) would meditate and dreamily contemplate the Eternal City below. Just beneath Tasso's oak is a sarcophagus fountain.

Up ahead, the 15th century monastery and church of Sant Onofrio await. It was to this monastery that poor Tasso retired, terminally ill. His last words are most touching and inspiring: "In Manus Tuas, Domine."

Sant Onofrio ranks very high with the lovers of Rome's churches. With its idyllic setting, its beautiful 15th century cloister and splashing fountain, its incomparable views, Sant Onofrio is truly a place of the soul and the intellect.

Another landmark awaits just beyond on our left. This light house, a gift in 1911 to Rome from the Italian settlement in Argentina on the occasion of the fiftieth anniversary of Italy's unification, flashes out over the city by night Italy's colors — green, white, and then red.

We reach now the lower level of the Janiculum, furnished with a fine snack bar with plenty of tables out on the terrace where Chiesco Tasso (the name's a coincidence) and his staff always provide a friendly reception. A brief stop here will prove heavenly. Try the spyglass for ten lire. If you succeed in focusing it before the time runs out, your eyes will be amply rewarded with whatever sight you shoot. A word of caution with the bambini. Keep their little hands off of the swivel. Johnny's forefinger was almost unceremoniously sheared off in this tiny guillotine.

There is still quite a climb left but it's rendered painless by the sight of so many swaying palms, stately umbrella pines, and stone walls. We must stay alert for out of the right will come riding the fiery Anita Garibaldi in a 1932 monument by Rutelli. Holding her infant son Menotti in her left arm while brandishing a pistol in her right hand, she charges to the fore alongside her beloved Giuseppe until she collapses and dies of hunger and exhaustion. The monument's base contains the heroine's ashes and is bas-reliefed with scenes of her life. Our friends from the states, Harry and Sharon Carr, favored this of all Rome's count-less monuments and whenever we meet, whether here or back home, their request is for the legend of Anita.

Now the road becomes lined with the busts of patriots of the new Roman Republic as the Piazzale del Gianicolo comes into view.

Dominated by the tremendous equestrian statue of Giuseppe Garibaldi — who gazes majestically across the skyline of his Capital — the square grants of all the bel-vederi of the city, the greatest. The monument incidentally is the 1895 work of Gallori the Florentine.

In late afternoon the ochre-toned *rosso di Roma* from this vantage point can, and often does, bring tears of joy to these old sentimental eyes. On the other side of the piazza take a different view, for one from *above* it, of the Dome of St. Peter's. And then look north to the floral designs and lush vegetation of the expansive Villa Doria Pamphili.

The view of the city provides us all the chance to show off in front of visitors our familiarity with Rome's land-marks, pointing out the great attractions: the gray-domed Pantheon, the twin-spired Trinita dei Monti, the statues of San Giovanni, the bell-towered Santa Maria Maggiore, dazzling-white Palazzo Giustizia, sober-brown Castel Sant'Angelo, ad infinitum.

If we are wise we will bring a picnic lunch with us, gathering all the fix'ins down in the *alimentarie* of Tras-tevere before we ascend, for there is a well-stocked bar in the piazza and the top of the square's wall provides the world's longest outdoor table. Don't have a drink in your hand precisely at high noon, however, or the cannon perched just under all this will send some flying with its daily mid-day boom. This ear-splitting, man-made thunder will immediately be followed by the gentle Angelus bells of the surrounding churches.

What a festive atmosphere prevails here at any time of day! There's the singing peddler, the man who sells the musical plastic tubes (giving a free concert all the livelong day), the puppet show where the *dramatis personae* knock each other's bloody brains out, impromptu frisbee tournaments, beetles and lizards having a ball along with everyone else, motorcycled lovers, horseback *carabinieri*. Yes, even the Janiculum's beetle and lizard communities get into the spirit of things.

Camille has always had carte blanche from me to buy whatever mementoes of our adopted home town she wishes. But up to last summer she was simply obsessed with getting one of those ubiquitous tin *gelati* signs that adorn all the bars and cafés of Rome. These unfortunately are not for sale, but August last the poor guy at the Bar in Parco Gianicolense finally succumbed to her entreaties and we now have a gelati sign in our rec room back in the states.

We are up here with the Romans, for few tourists come along since the bus drivers don't care to push their motorized beasts up the hairpin turns of the approaches to the Janiculum. However it is always a panic for us whenever a busload of tourists manages to make it to the summit upon a summer night. For so taken are they by the twinkling city below them that they snap away furiously with their cameras and flash cubes. Now these flashes which have a range of eight feet are fully expected to illuminate the entire Eternal City for a priceless addition to the album at trip's end.

Since we're up on the Janiculum we might as well see some other esoteric places like the lovely *Fontana Paolina* along the Passeggiata del Gianicolo. And around the corner, the American Academy, the school where classical scholars from the states can live intimately with the crumbled glories of Rome while they research them for their books or future classroom lectures.

If the gatekeeper is in a good mood let's try to glimpse the academy's pretty courtyard and witness its truly intellectual atmosphere.

What's that looming at the top of Via Angelo Masina? Why the Porta San Pancrazio, formerly the gate to the Via Aurelia. There's a family living in the tiny flat upstairs in the massive gate.

Across the street is one of the most splendid villas of all Rome — the Villa Aurelia which goes along with the job of Director of the American Academy. Quite a fringe benefit!

If the exigencies of a visit to the Janiculum have increased our appetites there are countless inexpensive, yet good, trattorie in this immediate area. We are in Monteverde, surrounded by shops of all kinds, in the midst of parks and apartment houses, among the warmest of the warm Romans. This is where we live.

Grazie della visita

XVII

The Steps

There has always been something innately beautiful and appealing about a long, graceful flight of stairs. In Rome they are ubiquitous and, fashioned of marble, they climb up and down the lazy seven hills.

Often to get from one street to a parallel road, or even to continue on the same street, requires the ascent or descent of marble steps (numbering sometimes more than a hundred) for a pedestrian, an alternate route for the motorist.

If we are walking home to Monteverde from Trastevere, which we often do in the exuberance and vigor that can come only from being in Rome, we grow weary in mere anticipation of the 93 steps we must traverse to get from the lower portion of Viale Glorioso to the upper. However, the sweeping panorama that awaits us — the rooftops, the cupolas, the campanili, the Castelli in the distant purple hills — amply motivates us on the way up and richly rewards us upon arrival. This too is surely one of the best places from which to view our adopted home town.

With our antiquated Fiat we swing left at the bottom of the steps on to Via Casini, right on Via Dandola, and left to pick up once again Viale Glorioso.

From Via Cavour up to Piazza San Pietro in Vincoli an arcaded stairwell awaits you and a most romantic counterpart will take you from the Via Cavour down to the parallel Via Urbana. From Via del Piramide to Via Faustina you will find another flight, from the bottom of Via Quattro Novembre to the Piazza Venezia still another.

And one may not drive on the Via Ferrara from Via del Quirinale down to the Via Nazionale unless one is unconcerned about such things as the car's shocks and the carabinieri's summons.

Thus it goes, from wall to wall in the Eternal City. But of course the most glamorous ornamented staircases are to be found not joining parallel streets. Rather seek them at churches, museums, monuments, and such.

Undisputed queen of the stairways is of course the *Scalinata della Trinita dei Monti* which the world knows as the Spanish Steps. This major Roman landmark, one of the most photographed Roman sights, an irresistible watercolor subject for artists, consists of 137 steps designed and built by Alessandro Specchi and Francesco De Sanctis in 1721-25 as a gift to the people of Rome from the French government. This rococo splendor covers the once muddy slopes of the Pincian Hill and provides a fairy tale ascent to the twin-steepled church and the French Academy adjacent. Recently the church, erected in 1492, was painted pink and the effect of the whole scene is now even more incredible than ever before.

The double flight converges on a landing, forks, and reconverges at the top. Gift of the French, the work of Italians, the steps were named "Spanish" because of the Spanish Embassy in the piazza below, which gained the same designation. From the balustrade at the top there is a thrilling view of what is probably the gayest square in Rome. By 9 A.M. one can watch the tourist buses approaching by the Via Tritone on the Via Condotti, spilling the garrulous "grand tourists" into the square and all over

On the Spanish Steps

the steps. One also is granted an incomparable view of the rooftops of the lower part of the city.

Loyal patrons by the score — hippies, flower vendors, costume jewelry merchants, artists, con-artists, students — are always there to welcome wide-eyed guests. Johnny looks forward to the Romeo with the Italian-speaking parrot perched on his shoulder. *Ciao!* it squawks, and *Buon Giorno* with a well-trilled *"r"* and *Prrrego* among other things. In spring and autumn we like an occasional brown bag lunch, complete with Frascati, in the midst of this lovely mayhem. One week last summer the Italian Junior Olympiad was held in Rome. A coach of a track squad from Milano would put his teen-age charges through their conditioning paces early each morning with several vigorous runs up and down the steps. A playground, trysting place, open-air market, outdoor library, the steps are also a favorite of Roman brides who, after their nuptials, whether in Trinita dei Monti or not, find them a great backdrop for their album shots.

Movie directors are forever setting up shop here for a scene or two. I was engrossed in girl-watching one autumn day here (my later account to Camille though was that I was sitting on the steps reading) when this guy, accompanied by a cameraman, started barking orders at a couple enacting a romantic scene. Along with everyone else I got up to get out of the way when the man with the little megaphone asked us to stay put and add to the naturalness of the scene.

So I was an unpaid extra in a TV travelogue on Rome, for the B.B.C., as I understood it. I've never seen the show or its reviews. So I don't know whether I'm celebrated in Britain or not.

In bygone days attractive girls would come fully arrayed hoping to be hired as artists' models. April and May provide a special visual treat when the steps are covered with potted plants of red and white azaleas. The twin-towered church, the obelisk at the top center, and the buildings on either side of the staircase provide an almost perfect balance to the whole place in a city that's bugs on symmetry. The ochre-colored building on the right as you look up, is the room where the English poet John Keats lived and died, now a Keats-Shelley memorial with a library of their works and Byron's. The poets' graves may be visited beneath the mourning cypresses in the Protestant Cemetery by St. Paul's Gate. In the building at the left you'll find Babington's Tea Rooms — a great place when you get a hankering for feathery light waffles or pancakes drenched in maple syrup with a tall glass of cold milk or a hot cup of English tea.

Less glamorous, but to the Romans more venerable, is the almost perpendicular flight of steps to the Church of Ara Coeli on the Capitoline, a site once occupied by the temple of Juno Moneta. It has thirteen fewer steps than di Spagna but presents a more formidable challenge with its steepness. As a result many visitors pass up a visit to this, the City Church of Rome and truly the Altar of Heaven. They do so needlessly, for there is a gentler access from the adjacent Piazza Campidoglio.

This superb square has its own unique staircase, more a ramp with grades, designed by Michelangelo, guarded below by twin fountain lions and above by another set of twins, the horse tamers, Castor and Pollux, in magnificent ancient statuary. Michelangelo's twin staircases to the Palazzo Senatorio in the Campidoglio ought to be mentioned here too.

A third staircase which climbs the Capitoline is that of the *Vittoriano* or Victor Emmanuel Monument.

Rising together to the first landing and to Italy's tomb of the Unknown Soldier, the stairs separate and converge at the base of the immense equestrian statue of the first king of Italy, and separate again to climb to the tremendous loggia above the Mussolini-famed Piazza Venezia.

Some lesser known, but in our view no less attractive, flights of marble stairs are to be found at the Church of San Gregorio on the Coelian Hill overlooking Via di San Gregorio between the Arch of Constantine and the Circus Maximus; at the Church of San Lorenzo in Panisperna on the summit of the Viminal, and an indescribably charming, though scarcely even noticed one at the Church of SS. Domenico e Sisto, at the beginning of Via Panisperna one block right of the beginning of the Via Nazionale.

Of course on any lineup of Rome's staircases, high on the list for its history, significance, and sanctity, must be the *Scala Santa* or Holy Stairway. These are the 28 steps that Christ climbed, on the first Good Friday, en route to his trial at the palace of Pontius Pilate, governor of the Province of Judea. They were dismantled from the palace and shipped by order of St. Helena, mother of the Emperor Constantine, to Rome where they are now housed in a chapel built especially for that purpose, across the street from San Giovanni in Laterano.

To get from our apartment on Via Fratelli Bandiera down to the next street, Via Aurelio Saffi, we use a splendid, unnamed flight of marble steps right on our property which I will therefore and hereby name the *Scalinata di Tamagnini* in honor of my Roman Mamma.

This is the site of daytime games and midnight (and later) neighborhood gab-sessions. Ron and Frank huffed and puffed up the stairs one night to announce that a movie company had just rolled up with all its crew, cast, and equipment and were about to fire away. Daniela and Paola were summoned along with Chico and the boys. I footed the gelato bill at Bar Faustini as we killed this hot night watching real live *telly* (as the British call it).

Old Rome had her stairways too and they must have been exquisite. Unlike the Greeks whose temples were ordinarily at street level, the Romans paid additional homage to their deities with houses of worship soaring high above staircases which ranged from 30 to 40 feet in height. The accesses to them, naturally, were decorated with sculptures, with an altar halfway up the flight, where religious sacrifices were conducted. Exemplary of this were the temples to Saturn and to Antoninus and Faustina. It may surprise you to learn that the Pantheon, now at street level because of the shifting sands of time, once had a superb staircase.

So cascading marble steps are another of Rome's specialties and are nothing new to the Romans; thanks in part to the fascinating topography of their city and in part too, to the Romans' long love affair with cascading marble steps.

Faremo una scalinata alle stelle

Via Veneto

XVIII

The Via Veneto

Via del Tritone descends to Piazza Barberini with its Bernini fountains. Swing around the plaza to the street at 11 o'clock. You are at the base of the sloping, twisting Via Vittorio Veneto, once a smart tree-lined boulevard sweeping through the old Ludovisi quarter, an aristocratic neighborhood of *fin de siecle* Rome, now a garish, neon strip.

Climbing to the twin-turreted Porta Pinciana in the rosy-bricked Aurelian Wall, the Via Veneto is the city's concession to Americans who go to Rome looking for American-type night clubs, with their astronomical prices. The Eternal City offers no night life of any consequence with the possible exception of this two-block stretch.

The inspiration for the film and the phrase, *La Dolce Vita*, the street was once the habitat of the chic and the elegant, the literati and intelligentsia, and the theatrical set of Rome. When it was discovered and invaded in post bellum Rome by hordes of tourists eager to gape at and rub elbows with celebrities, the latter soon abandoned the Via Veneto and sought sanctuary elsewhere. Most of the former patrons can be found these days over in Piazza Del Popolo at Rosati's.

Where stood stunning villas with lofty garden walls

now stand tourist agencies, and airline offices with their nauseating blinking signs, hotels with luxury prices and mediocre accommodations, and cafés of similar description.

It is a must stop for the most gauche among American visitors who converge on the place in the useless hope of seeing some stars of stage and screen. Romans, except for high-priced ladies of the evening and their business agents, gigolos, and con men, would scarcely be caught dead here and wryly refer to the strip as the American Ghetto of Rome. (We get a charge out of the pseudo world travelers who mispronounce it the *Via Va Netto* with the accent on the second part.)

Despite our little obloquy here, we would still recommend just one visit to the place to sit at Doney's or the Café de Paris and watch the nocturnal promenade. Before the tourists scared off all the names the street's population consisted of the watchers and the watched. Now it's down to just the watchers for gone too are the gossip columnists and even the scandal-mongering photographers known in exposé magazines as *paparazzi*.

Yet the Via Veneto is not all as bad as we've been portraying it thus far. There are, to be sure, some redeeming features to the area. Hotel Excelsior for example and its competitor Ambasciatori down the way still have enough of the old surface elegance to conjure up pictures of the Via Veneto's past glamor.

Another worthwhile stop would be the USIS library with up-to-date publications from back home.

Villa Margherita, once the sumptuous residence of Queen Margherita, is today the American Embassy to Italy.

But the passing parade, almost to a man, passes right by the one significant site on the street, the 17th century church of Santa Maria della Concezione. Built by the Capuchin Cardinal, Anton Francesco Barberini, twin brother of Pope Urban VIII, the church is still served by the Capuchin monks. In a city of extremes this is the greatest paradox of all — a monastery amidst night clubs and expensive hotels. A double staircase leads to the rather austere church. In the third chapel on the right lies the preserved body of Brother Crispino of Viterbo, whose canonization the order is vigorously supporting.

However, the high point of interest is the cemetery beneath the church. It consists of six crypts ornamented with the mortal remains of some 4,000 of the religious who died here between 1528 and 1870. Frankie and Ronnie and Johnny find it all so fascinating but their friends and neighbors, Daniela and Paola, shudder at the recollection of their one visit.

The crypts each have hundreds of skulls arranged to form alcoves in which lie the mummified remains of brown-robed friars. The soil of each chamber, brought to Rome from Jerusalem by Urban, has crosses marking the graves of other monks. Ceilings are decorated with symmetrical formations of knuckles and vertebrae and chandeliers of pelvic bones. Suspended from the ceiling of the last crypt is the skeleton of a princess of the Barberini family, holding in one hand a scythe and in the other, scales, traditional symbols of the inexorable march of time. What is the purpose, one asks, of this macabre display? It is not ghoulish the friars insist, but a visual sermon on the drama of life which must always conclude in death and a wordless exhortation to spend one's terrestrial years in virtue and in preparation for the endless life beyond.

Per omnia saecula saeculorum

On the busy and elegant Via del Corso

XIX

The Street Names

When this family goes to Rome for one fourth of each year it does so, to be sure, on a shoestring budget. No traipsing all over the Continent for this crew, nor even all over Italy. "We are in Rome," I keep saying, "and that alone ought to suffice for anyone regardless of his taste." I go on pontificating: "Samuel Johnson once observed that if a man is tired of London he is tired of life for there is in London all that life has to offer. Surely Rome has a thousand times more to offer than London so to be tired of Rome is to be simply mad!"

Mercilessly limited funds have taught us to embrace and practice the theme that the "best things in life are free." All of us have found many ways to have a good time in the Eternal City without parting with a ten lire piece.

One pastime I developed is reading and interpreting the street signs wherever I go in Rome. It is like a walking quiz in Italian, Latin, Roman History, Church History, the history of medieval and modern Italy. And I'm always smugly delighted in all those I can interpret or identify.

Street names in the Eternal City are like everything else here, so full of color, so poetic and so rich in history, unlike our *14th Streets* and *Avenue B's*.

Take a vicarious walk with me to see what I mean. But don't look for street signs on poles as we have back home. Here the name of the street is engraved on a slab of marble which is set into the second story of the facade of a corner building.

First question. Here we are on Via Alba Longa. What can you say about it? Don't you recall the hill town of that name whose shepherds moved to the region of the Tiber to establish on the Palatine a city which they called Rome?

Let's go on, equipped with imaginary winged sandals, gifts of Mercury, to fly back and forth across Rome in this chaotic tour — to Via Appia Antica.

Incidentally, it is altogether appropriate that this chapter be without much rhyme or reason for that is exactly the situation with Rome's streets. There are more than 8,000 street names in a city not too large geographically. Twisting, gnarled streets, not much wider than many of our driveways back home (some not as wide but with parking on both sides) are a way of life to the Romans. Chariot-width streets, irrevocably left over from antiquity, is what they are.

Ask a cabbie, born and raised in the city, to take you anywhere but to the very celebrated thoroughfares and the first thing he does is fetch his street directory and map his strategy. In an always fruitless attempt to ease the congestion, Rome's Commissioner of Traffic is forever creating one-way streets or reversing the direction of other one-way streets. If it weren't so harrowing it could be hilariously funny to watch the ant-like Fiats darting down streets which, as of this morning, are one way coming at them. Driving in Rome's streets is always a dangerous version of that bumper car ride in our amusement parks.

Evidently the city's streets have always been a hopeless jumble. I remember sympathizing with Vinicius in the novel *Quo Vadis* as, during the fire of 64 A.D., he frantically tried to find the tiny side street where his beloved Lygia lived. Speaking of fires you won't believe this but I'll run the risk of telling the story anyway.

My wife and I — the boys were at the sea with their grandparents — were down in the maze of Campo Marzio one afternoon when along comes this fire engine, siren wailing. Well don't you know, the thing screeches to a halt and the driver leans out to ask directions.

Where were we? Ah, yes, the Via Appia Antica. Whoever fails to identify this road picks up the tab at the trattoria tonight. It's only the *Regina Viarum* (Queen of Highways) that's all; the venerable Appian Way opened in 312 B.C. and after which is named everything from mineral water to frozen pizza.

Via Aurelia Antica is next. Care to guess? This was the consular road to the north as Appia was to the south.

Now we are at the corner of Via Romolo e Remo. No problem with that one. But what about Via Numa Pompilio? He was Romulus' successor, the second King of Rome.

On the next threesome we'll all win something: Viale Giulio Cesare, Via Pompeo Magno, Via Imperatore Augusto. *Viale* by the way usually indicates a wider thoroughfare, somewhat like our word avenue or boulevard.

If anyone's getting a complex at this point we'll throw him Via Giorgio Washington. Now no one can get completely shut out.

What famous sight can we expect to find if we follow to the end the Via Colosseo? The Via Circo Massimo?

If you are of Italian ancestry you might be pleased by one or more of the following: Via Napoli, Via Sicilia, Via Calabria, Via Abruzzi, Via Firenze, Via Milano.

Some names I find highly musical. Via della Conciliazione for example just rolls delightfully off the tongue. Johnny used to say it with such a splendid accent when he was five. This is the graceful boulevard which leads to St. Peter's. It is quite young (1929) and takes its name from the Conciliation, the accord reached by the Fascist government of Italy with the Vatican State. We enjoy the street names in Vatican City too, like a survey of Church history or a papal roster.

Rome's Christian heritage is also illustrated by street names such as Via della Porta Santo Spirito (Street of the Gate of the Holy Ghost) Via del Nazareno (of the Nazarene), Via del Cirene (for Simon of Cyrene who helped Jesus to carry the cross).

Ripa is Latin for bank of a river and Frankie's translation of Via di San Francesco a Ripa is St. Frank's Upon the Banks, his answer to the poetic, St. Paul's Outside the Walls.

Do you speak Italian? Well then you will know enough to look humble when you walk along Via dell'Umiltà. You will also expect to find a big bread store on Via della Panetteria, four fountains on Via Quattro Fontane, seven churches on Via delle Sette Chiese, and some dimly lit shops down Via delle Botteghe Oscure. There's also Via dei Giubbonari (jacketmakers) and Via dei Catinari (basinmakers).

Don't expect to buy pasta on Via Lasagna, however, for that street honors Luigi Lasagna, whoever he was.

Then there's the Street of the Vinegary Water (Lungotevere Acqua Acetosa) which is offset by the Street of the Holy Water (Via dell'Acqua Santa).

In his First Oration Cicero accuses Cataline of holding clandestine meetings on Via Falcarios (Street of the Scythemakers). In old Rome, men who plied the same trade would set up shops on the same street to make it easier for customers and deliverymen to find them (there being no Yellow Pages). *Staderarius* is the Latin for scalemaker or weighing machine maker and their neighborhood is still known as Via dei Staderari.

The practice remains, so that in looking for custom made chairs we go today to the Street of the Chairmakers,

Via dei Sediari, for tanned leather to the Street of the Tanners, *Via dei Conciatori,* for rosaries to Rosarymakers' Street, *Via dei Coronari,* and in anticipation of a rainy season to *Via degli Ombrellari.* And there's more of the same: the hatmakers are all on *Via dei Cappelari,* combmakers on *Via dei Pettinari* and basketmakers on *Via dei Canestrari.* (The Italian word for basket is *Canestra,* for ball it's *Palla,* ergo Basketball is *Pallacanestro*).

Out near the Olympic grounds is Via della Pallacanestro where basketball (growing in popularity) is played.

You might do well with Viale Guglielmo Marconi, Via Cristoforo Colombo, and Lungotevere (along the Tiber) Michelangelo. But could you cope with Via Machiavelli, Via Cola di Rienzo, Via Petrarca, and Via Resphigi?

Your knowledge of history will be put to a grueling test by the streets with dates for names.

Via Ventuno Aprile (21st of April), any high school Latin student could tell you is for the founding of Rome in 753 B.C.

Via Venti Settembre? On the 20th of September in 1870 Victor Emmanuel's troops entered Rome and made it part of the New Kingdom of Italy — the Capital in fact.

May 24th (Via Ventiquattro Maggio) 1915, saw Italy enter into the first World War.

And Via Quattro Novembre (November 4) commemorates the day the Austro-Hungarian Empire surrendered to Italy as the cost of World War I.

Via del Corso gets its name from the fact that it served as a course or track from Piazza Venezia to Piazza del Popolo for horseracing in the eighteenth and nineteenth centuries. Thus it was a great thing to have an apartment along the Corso whose balcony became a free box seat on racing days. Napoleon's mother so loved the races that he gave her the palazzo overlooking the track at the northwest corner of Piazza Venezia.

From here you are on your own in the street name quiz. If your feet have had it by now why not clip clop around Rome in a horsedrawn carriage which will go slowly enough for you to read the street signs in addition to gaping at all the sights. At the moment my sons are all badly in need of good haircuts and we must get over to *Via dei Barbieri* before they close.

Ciao!

XX

The Museums and Galleries

Rainy days in Rome have no adverse effect on the family mood because the boys and their mother know that when the *Pater Familias* gets home from the academy or from a guided tour he will haul them off in his horseless carriage to one or more of the city's endless museums or art galleries. Usually it will be to one of each, for the lads enjoy old Roman weaponry, mummified Egyptians, and that sort of thing, while my better-half can spot a Domenichino or a Caravaggio or a Titian quicker than the rest of us put together. And I? Why I just love anything that the old imperialists or early Christians left behind. You see then, don't you, why we have been known to pray for rain on occasion. With our clan, museum-hopping is a way of life.

"All Rome is a museum," many have said. To be sure, that is just how the government classifies the likes of the Forum and the Colosseum. And who would dispute the suggestion that each of Rome's splendid churches is in itself an art gallery? But we are about to discuss here the general type of museum, of which the city has an infinite number.

At the outset of the Renaissance the popes emerged as

zealous patrons, and collectors, of art. From this zeal many outstanding museums were born, the most illustrious of which is the Vatican Museum. A marvelous collection of artifacts from the Church's infancy can be studied in the Lateran Museum, behind San Giovanni. And the two incomparable museums in the Campidoglio were inaugurated by the popes. Renaissance Rome's nobility — the Borghese, Barberini, Colonna, Farnese, and Corsini families — were responsible for many more.

Before our litany of museums and galleries begins however, I would like to advise everyone interested in a scholarly approach to Rome of two English language libraries in the heart of the city. At 62B Via Veneto you will come upon the *Biblioteca Americana,* open from ten to one and again from four to seven-thirty daily excepting Saturdays. Nearby at Via Quattro Fontane 20 is the *Biblioteca Britannica,* with similar hours.

The tour that follows will be at best perfunctory but will serve at least to alert you, we trust, to the vast and innumerable collections of art available for public viewing in this fabulous town.

First stop will be the Michelangelo-designed palaces that flank the Piazza Campidoglio. On the right as you gaze at the Palazzo Senatorio is the Palazzo dei Conservatori. We pass through the impressive courtyard with the fragmented colossus of Constantine and by a sweeping marble staircase we reach a sign reading: *Primo Piano.* One tourist upon seeing this sign was heard to remark: "Wow . . . the first piano ever made! How do we get to it?" To which a fellow from the same group drily replied: "You're standing on it. *Primo Piano* is Italian for First Floor, Mac." The party of the first part soon recovered from his awkward moment when he laid eyes on such venerable masterpieces as the Etruscan bronze *She-Wolf,* the Greek sculpture of *Boy with a Thorn,* and the voluptuous *Esquiline Venus.* Greek and Etruscan vases are here by the

Frank at Constantine's foot in the courtyard of the Capito-
line Museum

score to delight the lover of antiquities along with marble sculpture from old Rome, and other objects from classical times, for one a sleek Roman chariot, for another a wooden (must have been rather uncomfortable) litter. Juvenal tells us that the wealthy Roman, while chauffeured to and from the office in one of these latter devices, was accustomed to catching up on his reading or his correspondence. We shan't leave the Conservatori without a study of Caravaggio's *John the Baptist* and some works by Rubens. That might be unpardonable.

Across the majestic square the Museo Capitolino awaits with its Capitoline Venus, a *Satyr* by Praxiteles and the ever renowned, *Dying Gaul.* Portrait busts of some of the emperors including the two mad men, Nero and Caligula, and other historic Imperial figures and a fine collection of Egyptian artifacts are among the other treasures on this fabled hill.

Descending into Piazza Venezia, turning right, and twisting with the road will bring us to Via Venti Settembre on the Quirinale to the Numismatic Museum offering a collection of all papal medallions from the early 1400's, some of Benvenuto Cellini's creations, and coins from every epoch of the city's long career.

A museum sure to be missed by most but worthy of a visit by all is the tiny Museo della Via Ostiense within St. Paul's Gate. The exhibit relates the role in the Empire's history of this highway to the sea.

For an amazing multiplicity of classical sculpture, including two discus throwers and an old prizefighter, we would take you to the Museo Nazionale Romano housed in Diocletian's devastated bathing establishment in front of the main railroad terminal.

A little journey is required for the Museo della Civiltà Romana (Museum of Roman Civilization) in the district called E.U.R. (Ay-yoorrr the Romans pronounce it.) The letters represent *Esposizione Universale Romana* the name

Mussolini drafted for his World's Fair which was finished, before it started, by World War II.

This is quite a place, symmetrical beyond description, full of buildings in the neo-classical fashion. After its service as fairgrounds this was to be the awesome Forum of the new Caesar. That dream along with all his others ended for the Duce when he fulfilled the Latin prophecy:

Intrabit ut vulpis; regnabit ut leo; morietur ut canis.

(He will enter like a fox; he will rule like a lion; he will die like a dog.)

Gradually the incompleted E.U.R. became a government and business center and a new locale for social life too. Out here a few miles beyond the walls of Aurelian along Viale Christoforo Colombo are pretty public gardens, a huge artificial lake for pedal boating, gracious cafés and restaurants, the Palazzo dello Sport (a Roman Madison Square Garden) by the famous modern architect Nervi. Looking down at this thriving district is Rome's one skyscraper (*grattocielo*, literally: skygrater), Al Italia's office complex.

As for the museum, on the left in Piazza Agnelli just before the traffic circle, it is a must for the classical scholar. A sprawling plaster model of the Imperial City with its stadia, circuses, temples, aqueducts helps to envision how Rome looked, more than anything I know. There is an elevated walkway all around it for your convenience. Throughout the vast halls of the museum are scale models of the Colosseum, the Circus Maximus, the Pantheon, and other landmarks. Miniatures of weapons, vehicles, fortifications may also be examined. And then there are the plaster casts of the bas reliefs on Trajan's Column.

Cross town in the Villa Borghese is a superb gallery-museum complex set in dreamily beautiful gardens. The Borghese Museum has a fine statue of David by Bernini. They say that Maffeo Cardinal Barberini, the young sculptor's benefactor, held a mirror behind the statue while his

204 ROME THE ENCHANTED CITY

protégé carved his own face into the marble. So we have then a great self portrait of the genius Bernini. Another work here by the same man, *Apollo* and *Daphne,* ranks high with all of us. As the pretty nymph is metamorphosing into a laurel tree I am brought back to my high school freshman year when we translated the Latin version of the story.

If you are not upset by nudity in sculpture ask to see the reclining statue by Canova of Paolina, naked from the waist up. You will be astonished at how Canova was able to work marble to convey the softness of human flesh. The apple she holds represents the one of gold given to Venus for being the most beautiful goddess on Olympus. This work has a reputation for controversy. At its completion the jealous husband locked it away in a closet. All Rome was scandalized that one of its nobility had posed in such a state of undress for a young artist. A century or so later, while on public display, it had to be discreetly draped so as not to offend a visiting head of state who was also an incurable prude, Adolf Whatchamacallit. The Vatican has never been too happy over this suggestive work.

Galleria Borghese, established by Scipio Cardinal Borghese, is considered the queen of all private art collections of Europe. The collection ought to be even richer than it is. But in the early part of the nineteenth century, Camillo Borghese wed the sister of Napoleon I, Paolina Bonaparte. Upon the Emperor's persuading, Camillo foolishly sold to the guy with the sideways hat, two hundred wonderful works of art. These can now be found in Paris' Louvre. The bill for fifteen million francs is still unpaid.

In the ceiling fresco by Lanfranco, Jupiter presides at a cabinet meeting, i.e., his Olympic council. This is a type of three-dimensional painting known as chiaroscuro, where figures seem to jut out from the surface like bas reliefs. You will see several corridors of this technique over in the Vatican.

On Viale delle Belle Arti there is Villa Giulia, Mecca for all Etruscan lovers. If it were bereft of its pre-Roman antiquities from Latium, Umbria, and lower Etruria the Villa would still attract us for we are fond of the building itself, built in part by Michelangelo. Its facade, atrium of Corinthian columns, semicircular portico walled-in courtyard, circular stairways, fountains and loggia delight us.

Galleria Colonna, located in Piazza Santi Apostoli, was established in the late seventeenth century by Girolamo Cardinal Colonna, for the purpose of exhibiting the family's collection of fifteenth century art. Those interested in the Venetian School come here for the works by some of the Flemish masters. As in Borghese, the art is displayed in superbly decorated rooms.

Rome's National Gallery of Ancient Art, housed in the regal Barberini Palace at the top of Via Rasella on Via Quattro Fontane, contains paintings from the twelfth through the sixteenth centuries, an outstanding coin collection, and a favorite Flemish oil of mine, that of the Dutch scholar, Erasmus.

For works by Titian and Rubens we go to the Galleria Spada in Piazza Capo di Ferro. If you like drawings, prints, and engravings from as far back as the fifteenth century you must go to the Gabinetto Nazionale delle Stampe at Via della Lungara 230 in the Farnesina.

And should you sometime be on a shopping spree along Via del Corso take time out, by all means, to savor the Raphaels, Titians, and Caravaggios in the Galleria Doria Pamphili, for surely. . . .
the *Ars* is very *Longa* and the *Vita* much too *Brevis*
to see it all as it is

Author and wife at Bar Settimio in the Trastevere District

XXI

The Cafés and Restaurants

Whenever the wife suggests: "Let's eat out tonight," depending upon where we are I quickly respond either, A) "Are you all right?" or, B) "Why not?" Sitting in our Jersey cottage I generally use response A, but in our Roman apartment it's always B. And so Camille, and the boys, come up with the suggestion much more readily and frequently in the apartment.

Back home it has become almost a trauma for me when the bill arrives in even the humblest of restaurants. In Rome I have, on many occasions, financed an evening's dining pleasure for all of us with 6,000 lire (a ten dollar bill). Just as Rome is a wonderful place to shop it is just as great for dining. The city's streets bulge with places to eat, a number of them somewhat expensive but here you'll see mostly tourists, rarely the locals. If you manage to avoid the glittering places on Via Veneto and the other glamor streets and patronize those we favor instead, you will go away better fed and far better off financially.

Before we get into the restaurant business however let us have an *espresso* or two at a sidewalk café. You would miss one of Rome's special charms if, in your understandable rush to see everything, you did not cultivate a fondness for the pleasures of café life and the sweet rewards of doing nothing (for a half hour or so a few times a day) but sipping strong coffee, or a cooling cocktail while watching Rome swirl about you.

And there are as many outdoor cafés as there are bars, of which there are hundreds within the walls. For every bar owner sets as many tiny round tables with their chairs as possible *al fresco*, i.e., out in the fresh air, knowing of his fellow citizens' love for this institution. In these places all the Romans' problems, from sex to taxes, from religion to the decadence of youth, are tackled over a relaxing drink. Open from early one morning into the beginning hours of the next, the cafés are ideal spots for a quickie breakfast of a sugar bun and a cup of java, resting stations throughout the rigorous day, evening watering places where one can say *Buona Notte* to Rome over a nightcap with traveling chums. A good deal of this book has been written at a table in the café garden of Signor Sabatini in Piazza Santa Maria in Trastevere, while the author's wife was reading all of Morris West's novels and Johnny was logging countless miles on his bike's odometer in the lovely cobblestoned square (off limits to motor vehicles). While we have a few favorite haunts, whenever we're struck with fatigue, or thirst, or spring fever, our favorite café always becomes that one just ahead. Believe us, they are all great, these sidewalk cafés, for the sidewalks of Rome are, one and all, great places to be any time, where history and romance and poetry surround you.

Rome has no counterpart to the American diners where a truck-driver or a businessman can drop in at six or seven in the morning and order a small banquet of ham or bacon with eggs, chipped beef with gravy on toast, cereal with fruit, juice, coffee, or a glass of milk. There is no need for a counterpart since breakfast in Rome is the same as you will find on the Continent — a continental breakfast, that is, a roll and butter with *caffé e latte* (a blend of half coffee, half milk). Ronnie says the rolls are pumped up every morning and Frankie swears he knows the gas station where they do it. The rolls really are quite big and hollow, but they've grown on us. We like them. You will sometimes hear lunch referred to as *seconda colazione* if its to be a light snack of bread and cheese and wine. The chief meal (*pranzo* or *cena*) will then be taken late that evening. But many Romans prefer midday for a complete dinner. Consequently the restaurants have two sessions, or sittings, to accommodate both preferences.

There are several types of eateries in the city with which you ought to be acquainted. Some signs will advertise a *Tavola Calda* or *Rosticceria*. These are very inexpensive places with all the food displayed in hot trays under glass. You will find good home cooking in these where you can pick and choose and assemble your own feast. Pizza garlic bread, fried potatoes, and cold chicken hit the spot with our group.

A *trattoria* (please accent the letter i) is simply an unpretentious *ristorante*, in furnishings and in price but not in the quality of food, likely to be found a block or two from major tourist attractions and patronized religiously by the neighborhood connoisseurs. Before we give a scouting report on some of the places we have come to enjoy we're going to conduct a crash course in Italian foods and beverages.

When you are seated you will likely find a plate of *pane* (bread) or a basket of *grassini* (breadsticks) already on the table. And always a cloth napkin. Paper would make a *brutta figura* (bad impression). Butter is served only upon request — and do request some because it is delicious - so you will have to say: "*Burro, per favore.*"

Pasto means meal. Therefore the concoction of *prosciutto* (ham) *salame, salsicce* (sausage) *olive, uova* (eggs) that is served first is known as the *antipasto*. Often this preliminary course is varied enough and abundant enough to constitute a pretty good meal in itself. But soup is on the way. *Zuppa di verdura*, as the name hints, is soup of greens, i.e., vegetables. This with bread, a glass of wine, climaxed in a cappuccino, often suit me fine. In a couple of places in the Monteverde quarter this dish is so good and so filling that I'll often drop in for nothing more. No resentment, no "how cheap can you get" scowls. The fact is the management is proud that I think so highly of the soup, and they extend the same genuine hospitality as if I had just brought a busload of well-heeled, heavy-tipping tourists for a six-course dinner.

A not so thick vegetable soup, *minestrone,* is also usually available, along with *zuppa di pesce* (fish soup) and *brodo* (clear broth). *Insalata* (salad, always so fresh here, perhaps picked and cleaned since you walked in) we never pass up.

The foundation of all Roman meals is the food called *pasta* made in tubes or rolls of varying shapes and sizes from wheat, flour, and water. Most common of the seemingly endless varieties are *ravioli* (meat stuffed squares); *spaghetti al pomodoro* (in tomato sauce) or *al vongola* (with clams); *pastasciutta* is served dry; *fettucine*, green or white strands with a smidgeon of sauce. (The Romans accuse our boys of drowning the defenseless noodles in a smoldering red sea.) One of the ways to my heart though is through *cannelloni* to which I was introduced by our chums Aldo and Cadia Miralli one day on a visit to Bagnaia, the little Tuscan town where they were childhood sweethearts. This slender, light roll of pasta stuffed with meat, and mushrooms, veiled with cheese, moistened with sauce would have induced the Olympians to forsake their *ambrosia*. Leaving Rome without sampling it is nearly as tragic as missing the sunset from the Pincio.

What is your pleasure in *carne* (meat)? Well there's *bistecca ai ferri* (steak on the grill), dependably good in Rome; *pollo arrosto* (roast chicken); *cotoletto di vitello* (veal cutlet); *fegato* (liver); *vitello scalopine* (prepared in marsala wine); *prosciutto cotto e carciofini* (cooked ham and baby artichokes); and our nominee — *saltimbocca Romana* (veal steak with strips of prosciutto fused to it).

Provolone, groviera, gorgonzola are the leading varieties of *formaggio* (cheese). Fruit in Rome is plentiful and tasty and we often climax the meal with a bowl of *frutta assortita*. If the warm-up course before the meal is the antipasto then what is dessert called? Why the *finepasto*, logically. *Dolci* (sweets), *pasticceria* (baked goods), *gelato* (ice cream), or a variation on any of these themes are sure to please. Linger over an *espresso* while waiting for the check which, especially if there's no wait for tables, might be some time in arriving, but don't be alarmed for that is the Roman way — *piano, piano* (slowly, slowly). But get alarmed if when you ask again for *il conto* (the check) the *cameriere* (waiter) replies *Subito!* (right away). For *subito* has a way in Rome of meaning in reality one hour, two, three.

Throughout the meal the national beverage, *vino*, has been freely flowing. Usually it will be brought to the table in a decanter instead of a bottle. For the five of us — yes even the kids here take it with their meals — (a cold glass of milk? What's that?) we order *un litro* (little over one quart). When just the wife and I slip away, a *mezzo litro* (one pint) might do. When dining alone and not too thirsty I might request *un quartino* (a half pint). *Frascati* is the popular dry white table wine from the hill town of the same name, consumed in great quantities in the Eternal City. Other good whites, *vino bianco*, are the dry and light *Soave*, the slightly sparkling *Verdicchio*, and the *Orvieto* from Etruscan country. In *vino rosso* there's the excellent *Chianti* from Tuscany, *Valpolicello*, *Bardolino*, and *Lambrusco* also from the northern regions. And all the whites and reds from the Castelli get our endorsement.

For something quite different in white we'll ask for a

bottle of *Lacrima Christi del Vesuvio*. But it's the red *vino liquoroso* of the same name that is out of this world. One day arriving home from the academy I find a note tacked to my apartment door. It is from Mario, our Roman brother in the apartment above, and written in plagiarized Latin: "*Tibi, non ante verso lene merum cado iam dudum apud me est. Eripe te morae!*" I recognize Horace's invitation to his patron Maecenas to come visit him at his villa in Tibur (modern Tivoli): "An unturned vat of ancient wine awaits within my house. Come quickly. Lose no time!" That was my introduction to the almost syrupy red wine from Naples. May I tell you the fascinating legend behind its name?

The name translates literally to Tears of Christ from Vesuvius. Neapolitan lore relates that when Lucifer was expelled from Heaven he fell into the beautiful Bay of Naples. In fact the region has been called at various points in history as "*un paradiso abitato dai demoni*" or, a paradise inhabited by demons. When our Savior visited the area one day He climbed the volcano for a better look and then wept bitterly at the decadence of man amidst such natural beauty. Where His tears fell on the slopes of Vesuvius, grapes grew, and these vineyards today produce *Lacrima Christi*.

If at times our thirst is just beyond the ability of wine to quench I'll have a nice, feathery light Peroni beer, my mate a *gassosa* (sugar-water) and my lads an *aranciata* (orangeade) or *coca-cola* (Coca-Cola).

On to Trastevere, over Ponte Garibaldi, where our particular favorite places to eat are found. Back in the sublimely chaotic streets of this crowded quarter we watch itinerant musicians parading proudly in their home-made uniforms from restaurant to restaurant, causing some consternation to the already harried waiters gingerly picking their way amidst a panoply of tables. In the immediate area are to be found Gino on Via Lungaretta, Alfredo and

Galeassi both in the popular Piazza Santa Maria, Taverna Trilussa on Via del Politeama. These we can recommend unequivocally to your stomach and to your budget. Unlike New York where you'd have to gag on the prices at some cafés, in order to star-gaze, it is quite possible to hobnob with luminaries of stage, screen, society, politics and the Church in a place where the food amounts to *summa cum laude* but the tab for a complete meal to three or four dollars. There might be at the very next tables an elderly conservative cardinal complaining audibly to a young monsignore about the wild liturgical reforms of Vatican II; a bejeweled, out-of-work contessa (not much call for them lately) lecturing her chihuahua on table manners; a film actor with the day's makeup still on (he's probably going back to work on a night scene) scanning the gossip columns in Il Tempo. The moderate priced Taverna Flavia near the Porta Pia, is a good bet if you are a celebrity fancier. Veal steak smothered in mushrooms is baked and served under cellophane at the Flavia.

Meanwhile back in Trastevere, there's La Cisterna on the street of the same name, Trattoria dal Facochio e Ottavio with a charming wine shop next door. But the liveliest spot of all is Rome's most successful restaurant, Da Meo Patacca, owned and run by an all-American football man from UCLA, Remington Olmstead. Rem came to Rome for a visit after the war, saw the wonders of the city, and was conquered beyond recall. Rome has been home for Rem ever since.

Situated just one block in from the Tiber in the petite, medieval Piazza dei Mercanti across from vine-covered, torch-lit walls of Renaissance dwellings, Da Meo comes alive each evening both on the inside with its rustic handsomeness and outside in its garden aglow with lanterns. Anchored at one end of the square is a large wagon stacked with wine barrels. The gaiety really begins when the troupe of excellent singers arrives and fosters a community sing of the old Neapolitan standbys like *Funiculi, Funicula; Luna Rossa;* and *O Marie.* When the horsedrawn carriages pull up and deposit their fares, the old world scene is complete. Caution! The place is expensive as places in Rome go (nine dollars or perhaps ten for a full meal with intermittent tipping of the musicians), so we've managed but one meal there and that was due to the largesse of our friend Harry Carr on his 1972 trip to Italy. But it costs nothing to watch and we've often killed part of a hot summer eve walking through Merchants' Square. What the boys remember most vividly about Olmstead's place is that they ate their roast chicken with plastic gloves, compliments of the house.

Now there are countless more good stops in Trastevere but this is not the time nor place to list any more. I'd be remiss however in not citing IVO at 158 San Francesco a Ripa for their pizza, and pizza garlic bread. Incidentally, do you know your pizza? *Pizza Margherita* is the normal species — tomato sauce and mozzarella cheese. *Pizza Napoletana* is adorned with fish, *pizza con funghi* with mushrooms, and *pizza capricciosa* with almost all things edible, or so it seems.

Down in the central part of the city we sometimes go to Quattro Fiume and Mastrostefano both at Piazza Navona and both moderate in cost. In fact the whole area is full of cheap, but good places to dine. At Pierluigi in Piazza Ricci we like the serve-yourself arrangement and the great choice of antipasto items. The Romans love to eat outdoors if weather permits but we've experienced many cozy winter eves huddled indoors at, say for example, Hostaria Farnese on Via Baullari or at La Villetta. In good weather it's always nice to dine beneath the thatched roof of the latter's garden. And the hospitality of the management and especially of the waiter Liborio Martino is without equal. We've been to, and enjoyed, the tiny *Torquato* on Via della Purificazione, one of the streets that spin off

Piazza Barberini. Ristorante Pancrazio, off Campo dei Fiori is an experience. Built over the ruins of the Theater of Pompey it affords a visit to the now subterranean hall where Caesar's assassination is alleged to have transpired. Sitting in Ristorante Ulpia one can gaze out at the adjoining Markets of Trajan. Our dear friend Father Hennessey likes Scoglio di Frisio at Via Merulana No. 256, the street which runs between the two basilicas, San Giovanni and Santa Maria. It claims to be Rome's true Neapolitan restaurant and supports the claims with sea food specialties and decorations representative of life on the bay.

One day long ago I played in a high school basketball tournament in Boston and to celebrate our victory the coach took us for a terrific meal at a genuine German restaurant. The one time we ate at Wiener Biechaus in Rome, with its German cuisine and strong beer, my thoughts drifted back over the centuries to that happy night in Boston. Camille discovered this one on the Via della Croce, which departs from the tomb of Augustus and arrives at Piazza di Spagna.

Tipping is not based on a percentage of the bill. Our friends taught us to leave a hundred lire per person to the waiter and for unusual service, a couple hundred more. And talking of service, another thing we run into in the restaurants is the eagerness to help with selection. We are not taken aback anymore whenever the waiter tsk-tsks our choices and pleads with us to let him pick out the meal. Now we just go along, and we have found that the odds are heavily in our favor that the meal turns out to be great.

So we recommend heartily that you Romanize your eating habits during your travels in Italy. Don't get talked into a package deal that includes meals back at the hotel. For the same money — or at most, pennies more — get out into the neighborhood trattorie and into the mainstream of Roman life. You can, wherever you go, count on a sincere,

Ben Venuto!

John with pony and cart at the outdoor market in Trastevere

XXII

The Shops and Markets

"Let's get out of here," Camille and Frankie both gasped, running from a small shop in Trastevere to Ron, and John, and me waiting in our doubleparked Fiat. "They're ready to kill each other!" On this, the second day of the family's first mission to Rome we were headed for the sea. My *Bella Donna* had asked to stop at a wool shop to get just the right colors for a cape she would knit on afternoons we chose to loll on some beach. My little legion was not yet acquainted with one of the key national pastimes, negotiating. With considerable effort I coaxed the wife back inside and proceeded to translate for her. Though the dialogue between the owner, a little guy on the shady side of seventy, and the young housewife, somewhat of a peppery, slender Lollobrigida with two pilot lights dancing in her eyes, was indeed animated and audible a block away, the innocuous exchange went round in circles thus:

"Hey, I'm a Roman, I live in the next street. Did you suddenly lose your memory. I'm not a tourist with an obese wallet!"

"Fine, Signora. I'll just give the stuff away! My family doesn't like to eat anyway."

No one considers all this a breach of the famous Roman courtliness, for bargaining is one of the genuine joys of life in the Eternal City. The discount is truly secondary. Primary is the competition, the battle of wits and durability, all of which provide still another outlet for the innate Roman gregariousness. At times I suspect the shop-keeper would think you didn't like him if you didn't carry on so. Half the spice would go out of his business life. After a short time in Rome you get a certain feel for when you may bargain, just how far you ought to go, when you are simply wasting your time. Since that frantic exodus from the wool place years ago Camille has come a long way both with her bargaining finesse and her command of the language. A couple of the merchants in our neigh-borhood complain (but with wry grins, which betray the fact that they always get the price they're after anyhow), that she now out-Romans the Romans. Even the kids have won their varsity B's in actual competition.

Rome is simply a splendid place for shopping, with a wide range of commodities at all price levels. So many items may be purchased here at as low as a third of the price back in the U.S.A., especially in the matter of leather goods and clothing.

Dickering is not possible in the big department or chain stores where, like Woolworth's, the sales clerks un-derstandably could never be authorized to alter prices. Still, for anyone visiting Rome with sufficient time to spare, these places deserve a stop. There is CIM near the main railroad station and Rinascente in the vicinity of Trevi Fountain. UPIM has a store across from Santa Maria Maggiore and another in the quarter behind the Vatican. Behind the apse end of the Marian Basilica there is a flower market, a feast of colors. But of all such places we like STANDA where the merchandise is dependably good, the prices likewise, and in my judgment, the sales girls exceptionally young and pretty. The tourist would do well to do some of his souvenir hunting right in STANDA. Things from the houseware department downstairs, like a set of canisters, or salt and pepper shakers, or a shopping reminder board, all marked with Italian words, make unusual and inexpensive gifts or personal mementoes of those glorious Roman days. Two suits that I got here a few years ago — for twenty-five dollars each — still draw raves from my American colleagues.

Some of the smaller shops have lately taken to putting up little signs announcing "*Prezzi Fissi*," fixed prices. In other words, "save your breath if you're here to get a discount." Nevertheless, we go ahead and start maneuvering for we have found that few of the proprietors mean it.

On the eve of our departure in early September we drive down to Santa Maria Maggiore where just across the street is Casa del Rosario. Here the prices are truly inflexible but so good that we still find them hard to believe. Catholic friends always cherish something blessed by the Pope and there is here a grand assortment of rosaries, medals, scapulars, etc. And there are plenty of non-religious objects too; plates for hanging, flags of the different provinces, pens and pencils with scenes of the city, silk kerchiefs with more scenes, guidebooks, and the largest selection of picture postcards at less than a penny apiece. Incidentally may we recommend to you the hobby that our boys improvised over here, i.e., collecting postcards of all the great sights of Rome. The photography on them is gorgeous and they are an inexpensive way of guaranteeing a good collection of pictures of Rome's beauties in case something goes awry with your films. Our kids mount them in scrapbooks and write a little commentary under each. A most educational endeavor it is too. Francesco, the proprietor's son, is a terrific fellow and if you get here tell him we sent you. Bring this book and show him the gang's picture on the back of the book. He'll get a bang out of it.

While we don't have the means to go on frequent buying sprees, we have gained considerable experience nonetheless from occasional buying, from constant browsing, and from daily conversation with our Roman comrades. Perhaps our readers will benefit in some small measure from the following observations.

For shoes, and this is something in which we have a little more expertise since the prices over here are too irresistible to resist (author's note: redundance deliberate), we favor Cesare down by the station (early in the morning), i.e., Stazione Termini. Fellow booklovers, leave the wife and kids here and come with me to the nearby cluster of bookstalls just off the Piazza Esedra. Of course all the works are written in the language of Dante but you do want to work on your Italian when you get back don't you?

Bufarini, a short distance away on the Via Nazionale, number 88, is a good bet for men's shoes, and for the whole family there's also Soree, across from Trevi fountain. And while you're there you might as well stop in at Perrone's across the piazza for gloves and scarves. They even sell golf gloves, genuine pigskin, for two dollars (six and seven back in the pro shops at home). Two doors down is a bar where you'd better get a large bottle of Galliano (thirteen dollars in New York, less than four here), perhaps some Strega, Sambuca Romana, even Johnny Walker, all at fantastic savings.

Before you leave Caesar Land you will have developed an appreciation of sculpture. So advance to the fountain, if you pass *Vai* collect your two hundred, and see the attractive woman at the top step about some fine marble statuary, small enough to cart back, at a low price. The vendor and his pretty wife alongside will sell you some costume jewelry. Give them all our regards and point out this allusion to them too if you have the book with you.

Sweaters and knit shirts are best bought at Lella on

Via Amendola, also in the Stazione neighborhood, where you will be served by the salesgirl, Paola, a fiery Latin beauty. As a matter of fact this whole quarter overflows with moderate price shops. Stay in the area a spell someday, wandering up and down the busy streets discovering your own treasure troves.

Brini at Via Barberini 79 will let you have men's suits for a decent sum. Art, and particularly oils? Walk along Via del Babuino from the Spanish Steps and turn right one block to the parallel Via Margutta.

Trastevere is best for antiques. Inch your way down the back alleys grandiosely called streets, past loafing cats, under flapping pennants of laundry strung between the buildings, through impromptu soccer games, glancing left and right as you go so as not to miss the charming vignettes down every side alley of this picturesque quarter, stopping whenever something in the window of a musty shop catches your eye. If you see something you really like, and the cost is not going to break you, by all means get it. We live but once! I'll always regret debating with myself whether or not to buy a framed (five by seven or so), yellowed photograph of a boy, perhaps ten or eleven, inscribed with touching Italian sentiments to his teacher, dated 1903. Four bucks was a little more than I wanted to spring for at the time. A few days later I resolved to get it. Gone!

Cameos come at a good price at APA in Piazza Navona, leather goods, including Gucci handbags, at Ceresa and Rampone in Via Tritone, glassware throughout the city. When I wish to buy my signora a jacket of leather or suede I drop in on my friend Vito Arbib at his factory showroom called *Pappagallo,* on Via Francesco Crispi No. 115A, just off the elegant Via Sistina. His prices, you will find, are about one third of those in the states for the same articles.

Moderate shops specializing in clothing can be found

on Via Sistina, between Piazza Barberini and Trinita dei
Monti as well as on Via Nazionale.

If you have money to burn, or if you enjoy eating your
heart out just window-shopping or celebrity-watching, you
might stroll the Via Veneto and the Via Condotti, where
you'll no doubt see Fellini's *dolce vita* stereotypes.

When in Rome do as the Romans do and what the
Romans do is go to market every day. There is an open air
market in Piazza Borghese where in addition to food there
are available old prints, books, antiques, and whatever
merchandise any of the vendors have been recently able to
lay their hands on.

Campo dei Fiori, the field of the flowers, just in a few
blocks from the Corso of Victor Emmanuel is Rome's
best-known outdoor market. The stalls shaded by enormous white umbrellas are garlanded with cheeses, salamis,
pepperonis, dried nuts, unplucked chickens. The rich mix-
ture of the canting voices of the vendors makes for an
amusing aria. This beautiful square of Renaissance harmony, with tired old grey buildings holding each other up
on the southern end of it, was the scene of Giordano
Bruno's burning at the stake in 1600 by order of the inexorable Inquisition. The brooding statue of the monk is an
intriguing centerpiece for the bustling square.

Every quarter has its market. There's the one on the
Via Sannio in the Lateran district. For Trastevere it's the
San Cosimato market near Piazza Santa Maria. Our neighbors and we go to the one on Via Cavallotti. At any of
these you will find, in addition to the fruits and vegetables
you are accustomed to at home, heads of cows, eyes of
pigs, skinned rabbits, tongues of other creatures and such.

All of Rome waits with bated breath for Sunday
morning however, for the fabled flea market at Porta Portese along the river side of Trastevere. I've never seen soup
or nuts sold here but surely everything in between: switch-
blades (American youths are always drawn to this display),

antiques, used bikes (John's cost three dollars, Frank's and Ron's five each; my motorbike $30; at summer's end we give them to some poor kids), hippie jewelry (elaborate concoctions of tin and wire and leather spread out on black velvet cloths), scrap metal, clothing. I was here last February and bought a cashmere overcoat for twenty-seven bucks, which I promptly draped over my shoulders, looking marvelously continental as I walked the cobbles. Mamma Tamagnini buys all her furniture here and may I tell you that her place is elegantly appointed. Picking up an ancient hopechest or rolltop desk might not be too clever for one soon returning to the states though, however low the price tag. For the shipping tab would be prohibitive.

There's a gentle old lady crocheting hats for sale, a guy selling unattached telephones, another with wind-up toys. You might like, for about a dollar and a quarter, an old twenty-lire piece made into a key chain with the effigy of Mussolini and the Duce's motto:

"*Meglio vivere un giorno da leone che cento anni da pecora.*"

("Better to live one day like a lion than a hundred years like a lamb.")

Watch the watch you buy here. It may have only some, or none, of the intestines it's supposed to have. These items have been known to run for a few hours after purchase and then strangely enter into eternal rest.

In any event, whether it be an open market, a little shop, an exclusive boutique, whatever you're buying, let your response to the first asking price always be those immortal words:

È troppo caro!

*Camille (center) with Daniela and Paola Guarnaccia in the
Park of the Orange Trees on the Aventine*

XXIII

The Villas and Parks

Civis Romanus has no lawn. He lives eternally engulfed by ancient marble, orange brick, and greying stucco. Consequently those oases of green throughout the city, the public parks, hold a tremendous attraction for the Roman, when he seeks umbrage from the relentless bedlam of the city, from walking ever vigilant along chariot-width streets with no sidewalks, from the sun-soaked piazzas.

In these verdant sanctuaries, most of which are closed to vehicles, the harried descendant of the Caesars can walk beside the still waters, lie down in green pastures and restoreth his soul enough to return to the riotous status quo of the Eternal City.

The visitor to Rome suffering from jet lag, or tour-bus drag, would also do well to take a camera, a lunch, a book, and a *simpatico* companion and retreat to any one of the city's parks for an unforgettable afternoon. Especially for the history buff can we enthusiastically recommend such an interlude. For even more than the majestic debris of the Forum or the gutted remains of the Colosseum, these shaded places, with their handsome palaces set like jewels amidst gleaming lakes and lush gardens and taciturn statuary embraced by lofty walls, take us back to the grandeur and spirit of late Republican and early Imperial Rome. They are in the best tradition of the patrician villa of both eras.

Frankie and Ronnie and Johnny are accustomed to the pleasures of a backyard. In Rome we have none but the boys have no complaints. Within eight minutes on foot they have their choice of three great parks whenever they feel the need to work off excess nervous energy.

Closest is the Villa Sciarra which hides behind the towering Janiculum wall. Offering plenty of grassy plains for ball playing, bowered paths for jogging, tiny ponds for sailing toy yachts, a mini zoo, and a few playground rides, Sciarra is a dream of a backyard for three young Americans. Situated between our apartment and the American Academy it was my delightful shortcut to school. On my way back at about one in the afternoon on brutally hot days Camille would often surprise me there with a cold Peroni beer and some chunks of cheese. Then, reinvigorated, I would sometimes get my studying done on the spot and have clear sailing the remainder of the day.

George Washington with his great right arm would have been able to throw a hundred lire piece from here to the Gianicolo, another of our "backyards."

The third of our neighborhood's parks is the Villa Doria Pamphili, once the estate of Prince Camillo Pamphili nephew of Pope Innocent X. At the beginning of the old Aurelian Way is the soaring triumphal arch to Garibaldi who once headquartered here. It also marks the spot of the bombed *Casino dei Quattro Venti* (House of the Four Winds) a fitting name for this airy place where Roman families come each summer evening to take the *bel aria*.

Down in the center of Rome there are the parks that the visitor is more likely to have heard about. Should you find yourself of a lazy Wednesday or Saturday afternoon in or around Piazza di Spagna, climb the fabled steps and at the top turn left down Viale della Trinita dei Monti. Slake your thirst in the out-of-this-world outdoor Café Giardino just a little way down on your left, and then head, refreshed, for the Villa Medici across the street. In the 1600's the estate of Cardinal Alessandro de Medici, the place, claimed by Napoleon in 1801, is now part of the French Academy. Outstanding French students who win the coveted *Prix de Rome* get to spend three years studying in this terrestrial paradise. Open to the general public only on the two afternoons mentioned above, the Villa Medici is a complex of rolling gardens adorned here and there with fragments of Augustus' Altar of Peace and with a monument to the brothers Cairoli who died in a battle against the papal forces in 1867. Their touching simple last words are engraved on the pedestal: *"Arrivederci Roma."*

A pretty staircase will take you to the upper terrace, *Il Boschetto,* from which you may view the adjacent grounds of the Villa Borghese.

We come to Villa Borghese often to enjoy the pine forests and fountains and sculpture. The boys love it for the rowboating on the lake. In the center of the lake is a tiny island with a miniature temple to Aesculapius, its entablature displaying beautiful Greek lettering. The brothers Korn also enjoy the large zoo here where you can be photographed sitting with a tame (but ferocious-looking) lion. With the boys occupied at boating or zooing, Camille often steals away to the Borghese Gallery and its works by Canova, Bernini, Raphael, et al, and I to the museum of the Villa Giulia overflowing with Etruscan art and sculpture.

There are several approaches to these sprawling grounds which were put together in the 1600's by Cardinal Scipio Borghese. The most impressive, I think, is just outside Piazza del Popolo in the Piazzale Flaminio. From here you pass through the 6th century towered gate by Belisarius, the Porta Pinciana. This most picturesque of all the parks has a flowered promontory called the Pincio. These famous gardens, executed by Valadier in the early 1800's, hang high over Piazza del Popolo, the great round square which you'll recall boasts identical twin baroque churches, a massive gate, a great obelisk of Rameses II in the center guarded at its base by four lions spouting water, flanked by fancy cafés alive with the *In-Crowd,* the *Beautiful People, of Bella Roma.*

Pompey the Great lived in a lavish estate on this cliff and so did his contemporary, the Epicurean General Lucullus. The latter was known for his smashing dinner parties whose guest lists read like a *Who's Who in Roman Politics.* And through the ages the Pincio has remained a beautiful pleasure ground.

Romans gather here late in the day, every day, to watch the great ball of Apollo drop behind the Vatican while the lights begin to twinkle across the city's dusky streets which stretch out below in all directions. Remember what the Romans say about experiencing this at least once.

So come here some day to savor the rosy glow of Rome's evening and wait a bit till the moon bathes the city in a mellow light. Then turn, walk among the palms, and take the lovely winding descent down to del Popolo to join the crowd.

Pretend now that it is another day and we are making our weary, dusty, way back from a pilgrimage to the catacombs beyond the walls on the Appian Way. We choose not to enter the old city through mighty Porta San Sebastiano but instead turn right and walk along the wall of Aurelian to the Porta Latina. Just inside the gate to the left is a walled-in park.

We had stopped there on a few occasions our first year in Rome and it was never more than a lovely park to us. One day Frankie, who loves to work on his Italian, gets into a conversation with the caretaker and mentions my studies in archaeology at the academy. Whereupon the gentleman hustles over to our bench all excited and asks: "*Signore, vuole vedere qualcosa interessante?*" (Sir, how would you like to see something interesting?) My broadest smile speaks for itself and in a wink we are all taken behind the man's house, which is the result of a marriage of a medieval dwelling to the foundations of an old Roman building, where we descend to a small catacomb.

Buried down here too are some tombs of the legendary Scipio family, including one of Scipio Africanus who took Carthage in the Second Punic War. Frankie's been encouraged to strike up conversations ever since.

In the same quarter of the city you will find the Parco di Porta Capena which encompasses the massive ruins of the Baths of Caracalla. Here you relax where the bathers strolled and gossiped and where their little ones frolicked. For the little ones today there is the ride in the cart pulled by Shetland ponies.

Head toward the Colosseum from this point and high on your left along Via San Gregorio you see the terraced gardens of the Farnese clan in and around the ruins of Tiberius' palace on the Palatine. The profoundly romantic and historical air of this place is desecrated only by the metal sign exhorting: "*Bevete Coca Cola*" on the facade of the little café.

Ascend the Aventine across the valley through narrow streets contained by high garden walls with overhanging wisteria and you will soon arrive at Parco Savello (also known as the Park of the Orange Trees) with its flawless symmetry and belvedere of the Tiber and the Trastevere.

Almost all of the seven hills can boast of a public garden or two. On the Caelian there is the Villa Celimontana where one can enjoy the marble antiquities including an altar and a small obelisk.

One of the Esquiline's summits, the Oppian Hill, offers the Parco Oppio adjacent to the extensive ruins of Nero's golden palace.

Everyone is familiar with the Capitoline's glories but few know of the secluded, generally deserted little park reached by bearing right at the Palazzo Senatorio and up a steep flight of stairs through a glass door. We love the vistas out over Rome in the Parco del Tempio di Giovi.

If you are driving, take a ride outside the walls along the aged Via Nomentana to the Villa Torlonia. This mansion with its marvelous gardens was the private residence of Benito Mussolini in his heyday. Second century Jewish catacombs tunnel their way beneath the house. A second Villa Torlonia (this one called Villa Torlonia Ex Albani, having been owned formerly by Cardinal Alessandro Albani) awaits nearby on Viale Regina Margherita.

The Cardinal had put together an enviable collection of classical sculpture, 300 pieces of which Napoleon confiscated and sent to Paris. This was the inspiration for one of Rome's countless maxims which states: *"I Francesi son tutti ladri"* (The French are all robbers); to which the response is: *"Non tutti, ma buona parte"* (Not all, but a good part). If you remember Napoleon's last name you'll appreciate the double entendre.

Happily however, the collection has been replenished. This park is only quasi-public for, in order to visit, one must apply in writing to the Ammistrazione Torlonia at 30 Via della Conciliazione.

Out farther along the Tiber hard by the Olympic grounds sits the Parco della Rimembranza. Perambulate here among the variety of trees and the monuments and enjoy the views of the river and distant Rome.

There is no end to the sights of Rome and you will no doubt see many. But on your last full day here borrow a few hours from the ruins and churches and fountains and give them to a park or two, there to contemplate in bucolic tranquillity the wonderful time you've had in the Eternal City.

Pax

XXIV

The Climate

It has been said that Rome enjoys but two seasons, winter and summer. The implication is that it is always either uncomfortably cold or unbearably hot. But from my point of view the observation misses the mark considerably. That Roman summers can be sultry there can be no denying, but even the longest excessive heat waves break after a week or a week and a half and give way to a stretch of more reasonable conditions.

Some insist too that the heat is aggravated by severe humidity but such has not been our experience. Vis-à-vis the sticky summer days of the New York area, Rome's clime comes off quite nicely. For example, one does not fry in muggy heat in the aftermath of a summer shower in Rome. Rather the rains invariably freshen the air, and result in comfortable temperature and moisture.

Everything that is done in Rome — building, eating, drinking, politicking, loving — is done with a concentrated passion. Even raining. It comes down literally in nearly horizontal sheets. And it even thunders with a Roman accent. On our first encounter with Roman thunder we feared the end of the world had come, it being like no sound we had heard anywhere before.

The climate of Rome, the more I think of it, is in perfect harmony with Rome itself. That is, it is beautifully chaotic, lusty and enigmatic. May I submit that Rome has four distinct seasons. Her winter, December and January, is often rainy but with frequent stretches of premature spring. Even in these, the coldest months, the average temperature is still a mild 51 degrees, only 5 degrees less than that of Los Angeles. Snow is a rare occurrence, sometimes as little as once in five years — and when it does come it is hailed as an event by the Romans who rush out to see their basilicas and ruins adorned in white. For they know that the blanket will vanish within hours. It always merits a front page photo or two in *Il Tempo* and the other *giornali*. By the way, palm trees are part of the Rome scenery so how bad can winter be?

Spring arrives to stay some years as early as the first week of February. This winter the boys played in short sleeves on many February afternoons. However when the sun gets low it's time to bundle up again. By the end of the month though, the sidewalk cafés are in full bloom and will stay that way until well into December, for the Romans love to eat and drink outdoors even if the weather is not always exactly ideal for it. The spirit of Springtime in Rome is best captured I think in the Sunday promenades in the Villa Borghese, the sunset watch on the Pincian hill, the carriage ride past the azalea-bedecked Spanish steps.

Autumn in Rome, our choice, is as beautiful as the song so titled whose last line declares: *Let winter come, all my Decembers — are spent just dreaming of — the way we fell in love — one lovely autumn in Rome.* Indeed Camille and I spend all our Decembers this way — dreaming of how we fell eternally in love — with Rome and her people and her places — particularly in the Autumn of A.D. 1969. The sky in this season is such a limpid blue with the lines of the apricot-colored buildings and the baroque churches with their breezy white statues on high so sharply defined

Scene just north of Rome . . . a visual aid for sensing the climate

against it, that Rome, lovely throughout the year, must be regarded as at her very loveliest now.

But the summer has the reputation of a villain. When July and August arrive the Romans (those who can afford to) depart, either to the countless Tyrrhenian beaches or to the cool uplands of the Castelli Romani. This is in keeping with a tradition that can be traced back to the Republic.

We know from his own correspondence for example, that Cicero kept a summer villa in Pompeii on the Bay of Naples; and Horace writes longingly of his rustic retreat in the Sabines. The popes of the last five centuries have eluded the discomforts of the summer by abandoning the Vatican for the Papal Villa high over Lake Albano in Castel Gandolfo.

About the Castelli we speak at some length in the following chapter. But some of our favorite beaches we can commend to your attention here.

If lively crowds appeal to you, try the number of beaches that all come under the heading of *Ostia Nuova.* For 1,500 lire (little more than two dollars) we get our family of five into the life-guarded beaches, a cabana for dressing, and two beach chairs. For another 300 lire we get an umbrella for the day. There are impromptu volleyball games at which all are welcome, soft drink and ice cream stands, pinball machines and such for the bambini.

First time out to Ostia take the inexpensive train at the station across the piazza from the Pyramid. You'll feel so European peering out the window as the train (a poor man's Orient Express) wheezes, rumbles and creaks its way for a half hour across the countryside. On the right side you'll see, amidst the pines, the ruins of Ostia Antica.

While the boys prefer the hubbub of the Ostian sands, Camille and I, and our checkbook are enamored of several free beaches up along the consular highway, Via Aurelia.

Their appeal is more than economic however. They are wonderfully romantic and irenic to boot.

We frequently pack a lunch and hie off to Fregene; or to Santa Severa where we drape our robes and towels on the stones of a perfectly preserved medieval castle; or to San Nicola where we stroll up the beach to see the Etruscan sea wall or some World War II pillboxes and barbed wire; or to Santa Marinella with some pretty garden restaurants in town.

If the wallet doesn't squawk we like to, once a week or so, stop on our return trip at Cere, in off the highway about eight kilometers. The narrow winding road up to the hilltop town is always good for a thrill, the town itself a real charmer and the *pièce de résistance* — the turret of an Etruscan fort where we take our dinner. A bill for us five and for a couple of guests — the grandparents, or my sister Anne and my niece Faith, or Harry and Sharon Carr or whoever's passing through — might approach the mind boggling sum of 8,000 lire.

We started out on this chapter talking about the climate of Rome and here we are dining on a cliff in Cere. *Mi scusi.*

For my part there's no pressing need to go scurrying off to the hills or beaches however hot the city gets. For Rome's abundant charms — there's always so much to see and do — serve as very effective mental air conditioners for me and I scarcely feel any discomfort even on the most scorching days. These same charms are heaters in winter and umbrellas in the rain.

Now if I had my druthers, I druther come to Rome in autumn. By then the Romans have reclaimed their city from the tourists, the Holy Father is back in his window at Sunday noon, and the temperature is perfect for whatever you've scheduled.

Il tempo fa bellissimo!

Castel Sant' Angelo

XXV

The Castelli Romani

It is another blistering July morn here in *Urbs Aeterna.* My signora and I have just breakfasted in the cool of our terrace on the peak of the Janiculum. My Three Sons (remember that program with Fred MacMurray?) have already gone off with the Pannetta boys, Roberto and Maurizio, to the Villa Pamphili for a day of baseball and soccer. While my wife is watering the copious plants of our solarium, and screeching each time she spots a lizard, she continues to insist that today I speak to you of the Castelli Romani. *Va bene!* (O.K.!) Today I discuss the rolling velvety hills, smothered in olive trees and picturesque villages, that one finds when he heads south from Rome along the new Appian Way. I will quickly agree with Camille, in that even the most hurried visitor to Rome should find a day or two to give to these volcanic hills that rise lazily from the Roman Campagna. They are their loveliest in spring and fall, but sleepily beautiful in this season too. Just a short run from the Capital is required for this grand glimpse of typical small town life in sunny Italy.

These distant mountains, from thirteen to twenty or so miles from the city, are clearly visible from all of Rome's promontories.

Called *Castelli* because of the medieval castles that arose on the many summits of the Alban hills, these towns are actually built on the sites of hilltop hamlets that predate Rome.

Castel Gandolfo, for example, is the Alba Longa founded by Ascanius, son of Aeneas, a thousand years before Christ. The Gandolfo family from Genoa settled here and the dwellings of its clients which clustered round the family castle increased in time to a rather sizable town. More about this place shortly.

When they grow weary of the sea our boys lobby with me for a "day in the Castelli." I'm easily persuaded for I have a very warm spot in my heart for these towns and their natives, and their renowned wines. So after Camille gets back from the marketplace with a supply of *provolone,* salami, *prosciutto,* rolls, pizza bread, fruit, we become for a day at least, the Beverly Hillbillies in reverse (I guess that makes me, Jed; and Camille, Granny) fleeing the big city for life in the hills.

Usually our neighbors Daniela and Paola Guarnaccia are along, or the little Miralli boys, Corrado and Dario, sons of our good and great friends Aldo and Cadia Miralli, as we chug out the New Appian Way in our green Mini-Morris. Mario and Paola Tamagnini always give us one of their cars when we are staying in Rome. This little toy has served us well and faithfully thus far this summer.

When you come to Rome hire a car, if you have the courage, not from Avis, Hertz, or Maggiore (you'll go to the poor house with all of them), but from the little independent guys who have three or four in fairly good shape to rent. Try my old friend Di Laurenzio at his garage on Via San Francesco a Ripa. For a few dollars a day rental, plus gasoline, you'll have wheels under you, and your coverage of Rome will increase a hundred-fold. If he's fresh out of cars get the telephone directory, look under *Auto-Nolleggio,* and keep calling until you hit pay dirt. These

guys never speak English but you'll communicate some-how. *Vouloir c'est pouvoir!*
Buses galore go out to the Alban country but a car ex-cursion to the Castelli beats that way by far. *Quanto tempo ci mette per andarci, Signore?* ("How long does it take to get there, Sir?") *Mezz'ora, Lui responde.* ("A half hour," he replies.) No matter where you're heading from Rome, be it to the Castelli or to Ostia Antica, or to Anzio, or to Etruscan country, the Roman always has that stock answer, *"mezz'ora,"* to the question "How long?" With all these places it happens to be a fair estimate but he'll as likely tell you *"mezz'ora"* for Viterbo, Venice, or even Vienna. We often drive up to Bagnaia (just beyond Viterbo on the consular Via Cassia) with the Mirallis, and Aldo makes a gallant effort to reduce the normally two-hour trip to that inevitable *"mezz'ora."* Mario gives it the same college try when he chauffeurs us to Siena each August for that summer madness *Il Palio.* On these occasions our rosary beads get a vigorous work-out in the back seat throughout the course of the flight, er . . . ride.

Meanwhile back on Appia Nuova we've been passing such incongruities as a soccer field and a golf course amidst the ruins of the Claudian aqueduct, *Cinecittà* (Ita-ly's Hollywood) and a Trappist monastery, shepherds tending their flocks in the wheatfield near the airfield of Ciampino.

We are coming upon a fork in the road with a sign of-fering these choices: 1. Via dei Laghi; 2. Albano. Electing *numero uno* we dilly-dally our way to the lofty, cozy town of Castel Gandolfo (Pop. 4,000) with its Papal Villa, sum-mer retreat of the pontiffs of the Church for the past five centuries. The Villa, designed by Carlo Maderna, who worked on St. Peter's, with its matchless terraces, gardens, and vineyards, hangs five hundred feet above the serene Lake Albano. In prehistoric times this was a volcanic crater which in the course of time spent itself as a fiery furnace and filled up with rain water to become the gorgeous soupbowl of blue water it is today. From a clifftop restaurant on the edge of town a *seggiovia* (ski-lift) affords our boys and their friends a thrilling ride down to the lake while Camille and I steal away for quiet conversation over a cappuccino. Rejuvenated, we join the lads for a delightful interlude of swimming and boating. Albano is about 600 feet deep in the center so do be careful. The hours fly by and then we drive — they ski-lift — back to Gandolfo to mingle with the *animali locali,* as the natives call themselves.

On summer Wednesdays, if I'm not working, we arrive here early in the morning to join the throngs of excited pilgrims come to see the Holy Father in his weekly public audience. Precisely at ten, Paul arrives to the delirious cries of *"Viva Il Papa!"* borne aloft on the *Sedia Gestatoria* (portable throne) so that all may get a better view of their Holy Shepherd. That first summer when we would come to the audiences Johnny, then only six, would be borne aloft on the *umeris patris* (shoulders of his daddy) so that when Pope Paul passed by us they would look straight into each other's eyes and exchange loving smiles. Johnny's cherubic face with its button nose, topped by a mop of blond curls is an easy one to remember and once, when I was introduced to His Holiness because I was writing a series of articles on him, the Pope wished me luck and then asked how my *bambino biondo* was.

You must try to get to one of these audiences. We never fail to be thrilled at the sight of the Holy Father. Whether it is the Holy Office that he holds, or because of his personal charisma, he electrifies the multitude from the time he is carried into and out of view. No one is immune to a great surge of emotion. Some smile almost as if in ecstasy, others shout in hysterical joy, many experience a lump in the throat. My sister Anne who accompanied us to

six audiences one summer, wept uncontrollably each time.
One July Sunday in 1972 my boss, Dr. George Gordon, and his pretty granddaughter, Madelyn Miller, visited with us. This was their last day in Rome and they wanted to see the Synagogue, Solemn High Mass in St. Peter's, and the Pope. The first two requests were easy to fill but we were standing on the steps of St. Peter's at 11:40 with the Pope scheduled to make a brief appearance at Castel Gandolfo in twenty minutes. With Camille, her mother, and our two guests safely aboard, I raced the heartless clock, set the Via Appia Antica all-time speed record, and screeched into the town center with a minute to spare! We were the last ones admitted before the Swiss Guards closed the gates to the courtyard. Mission accomplished.

After such excitement we unwind with a walk through the main piazza which features a Bernini church and fountain. Then when the last bus of pilgrims has pulled out for Rome we drive with our picnic basket up the road a piece, passing the outdoor mosaic Stations of the Cross of the Seminary of Propaganda Fide, to the little bar of our good friend, Giancarlo.

He sells only drinks here but he has tables on a pretty vine-covered terrace over the lake so the locals, and we, always bring our own chow. Lunch here must be something like lunch in Paradise. The tranquillity is unequaled, the beauty of the place indescribable.

A two-mile ride brings us to Albano where Pompey, and later Domitian, had villas. In fact the reservoir that Domitian commissioned is still in service. There are some catacombs here too, and lovely churches and villas.

Camille often requests a stop at Marino for her favorite Castelli red wine. Roman wines are poor travelers we are told, and they are at their best taste in the areas where they are made. Thus the best place to drink Marino red is in Marino, Frascati white in Frascati *e così via* (and so on).

Following the road high above the lake we come into

view of that picture postcard town of Rocca di Papa with its medieval dwellings clinging for dear life to the mountainside. At the white stucco, Spanish-looking church of Madonna del Tufo, about a kilometer short of the town, there is a promontory just perfect for photographing Rocca di Papa as a whole. Arriving in the town we gasp at the steep streets and marvel at the inhabitants' indifference to the ridiculous topography. Children rush to welcome us, two tattered waifs clean the windshield and extend their palms, an ancient mariner-looking character asks if we need directions and proceeds to tell us, unsolicited, all about the town.

The family recalls with amusement the first trip to Rocca di Papa and the time we decided to stop at "that wine store down the hill there." With our eye on the distant sign, *Vini,* we eased the car down the almost perpendicular slope and, applying brakes, hand brakes, turning off the engine, and leaving it in gear we could not pull to a stop. Continuing to barrel down hill we landed in the square of the lower part of the town and had to circle up and around again to make a second pass, this one successful. Stop in at these wine cellars for a few minutes. Enjoy the local grape while you watch the oldtimers playing cards, swatting flies, and exchanging racy stories.

As we leave the town we look up to majestic Monte Cavo. When time and energy allow, we make the 1,000-foot tortuous but scenic ascent to the popular restaurant there, not for a meal, but for an unforgettable view. This is the highest point of the Alban Hills and the panorama is without end.

It is not far now to Frascati, a town of much significance for me. During the academic year I make my living teaching the life and times and works of Marcus Tullius Cicero, the preeminent orator of all history. Here was the ancient town of Tusculum where Cicero had an idyllic villa, which he called *Tuscolana,* with a well-stocked wine cellar and library, with its garden walls, and a farm and vineyard beyond. Here he entertained a few close friends during his illustrious political career, here he would walk for hours in happy and profound conversation with his beloved daughter Tullia, and here he spent his tragic twilight writing his philosophical treatises.

At Frascati we sit at one of the endless cafés and sip the same wine that Tully so enjoyed twenty-one centuries ago. Sightseeing here includes the cathedral, the Villa Aldobrandini and the Capuchin monastery.

South over these hills that watch Lake Albano is the charming town of Nemi, which is perched over Lago Nemi another ex-volcano which lost the fire of its youth. "Stop the car!" Ron insists each time through here. Ron is a great strawberry fan and in the woods that encircle the lake they come fist-size. Son number two leads us on a strawberry pick. On the road into the town we pass the children who have set up strawberry stands, the way our kids have lemonade stands back home, and we make a purchase or two.

"Look at that woman with the laundry basket on her head en route to the town trough!" There she will join the other *signoras* in spicy gossip while they beat the daylight out of their dirty linens. The goddess Diana was once the town patroness and a beautiful temple to her stood here.

Velletri is the lowest of the hill towns, and is well worth a visit with its basilica and with its Shrine of *Divino Amore* in honor of Our Lady of Divine Love. In any hour of peril, Romans come here in great numbers to invoke the protection of the Virgin Mother. It was thus in World Wars I and II.

On the feast of Corpus Christi, Genzano completely carpets the street leading down to the church of Santa Trinità with flowers. Two Roman ships were salvaged on this shore of Lake Nemi by teams of archaeologists.

Grottaferratta with its elegant villas, Palestrina with

its ruins of a huge temple to Fortuna, and tiny Rocca Priora are other members of the Alban Hills that we can warmly recommend.

But twenty-six kilometers from Rome in another part of the Castelli is situated the hill town most visited by tourists, Tivoli. Standing on the site of ancient Tibur, reached by the highway still called Via Tiburtina, its great claim to fame is of course the Villa d'Este built for Cardinal d'Este, son of the infamous Lucrezia Borgia from that medieval cloak-and-dagger family.

In Tivoli we find cool relief from the Roman summer and outstanding and reasonable places to eat, especially *Ristorante La Lanterna*. The saltimbocca Romana, fettucini, and the local table wine add up to an almost royal feast. From some of the town's terraces, on a clear late afternoon, the white dome of St. Peter's Basilica can be seen outlined against the distant purple.

Villa d'Este is something else! It is a wild baroque fantasy perched above the medieval town, consisting of a sumptuous palace and more than four hundred roaring fountains amidst a wealth of strikingly colorful gardens. There is the street of the 100 Fountains, the great Fountain of the Organ, the deafening waterfalls under which you may walk, the *Rometta* (or little Rome), a fountain symbolizing the Imperial City on the Tiber.

Seen by day the Villa d'Este, often mistakenly referred to as Tivoli Gardens, is a dazzling delight. Seen illuminated by night, it is a never-to-be-forgotten extravaganza. P.S. The real Tivoli Gardens are in Copenhagen.

From Tivoli a short distance up the road to Avezzano is Vicovaro, noted for its extraordinarily beautiful women and for the villa of the Augustan poet, Horace. A most welcome refuge from the hurly burly of the capital, it provided inspiration for most of the poet's entertaining odes. Yet Horace apparently could take being away from the excitement of Roman society life only so long for he often

confessed: *Romae Tibur amem, ventosus Tibure Roman.*
(When I'm in Rome I long for my villa in Tibur, then at
Tibur I can't wait to get back to Rome.)

On the road back to Rome we watch for signs to *Villa
Adriana* (Hadrian's Villa). Turning left and continuing for
three kilometers we come to a fancy portal with a guard
house. A small fee admits us to Hadrian's Camp David,
now a vast expanse of gently crumbling ruins. He was vi-
tally interested in architecture and while on tour of his
sprawling empire he sketched the temples and monuments
that impressed him most and resolved to erect replicas of
them on the grounds of his country estate. The estate was
intended to provide Hadrian with a vacation retreat from
the rigors of Capital politics and a terrestrial paradise for
his retirement. It had libraries, theaters, baths, banquet
halls, lodging accommodations for hundreds of guests,
cypress-lined promenades, groves of olive trees, vineyards,
three huge pools — a world in itself fortified by a wall five
miles in circumference. Sadly, it is recorded, the Emperor
enjoyed the facility but twice before he was stricken with
dropsy. Taken to the Imperial Villa on the Bay of Naples
in the vain hope that the sunny clime would bring about
his recovery, he breathed his last there and his funeral cortege wended its melancholy way back to Rome across the
Tiber to the still incomplete mausoleum on the Vatican
bank of the river.

Nevertheless we are welcomed today by the Italian
government to take the archaeological adventure of walking the grounds of Hadrian's villa and enjoy this unusual
glimpse of Imperial opulence. Inexpensive M I P. (Min
istry of Public Instruction) guide booklets on all three sites,
Villa d'Este, Horace's Farm, and Villa Adriana are readily
available.

Let us get back to Via Tiburtina for I assume you are
by now weary of hill towns. Let us head for Rome.
Arriverderci Castelli!

*Romans pausing at Porta Portese where they may enjoy a
cup of soup then shop for boots or bolts*

XXVI

The Romans

So you're coming to Rome! Well then you ought to know something in advance about the people who will be your hosts for one week, one month, *ma che fortunato!* one year?

These Romans — how they will captivate you with their marvelous Mediterranean manner. How they will exasperate you with their maddening idiosyncracies.

But if you ever get annoyed, consider this: You are in Rome! Rome! Where one street leads to St. Peter's, another descends to the Forum, another rumbles to the catacombs. What grand compensations for occasional tiny annoyances!

At the very top on our list of things to see in Rome are the natives. For we never weary of watching these adorable, good-looking, and enigmatic people. In fact I've come to suspect strongly that it is their boundless hospitality, infectious gaiety, and unbelievable gregariousness and cordiality — far more than the city's marble wonders — that draw us irresistibly back, again and again, to the banks of the Tiber.

You will too, upon arrival, be impressed with that cordiality. Whether you put up at a ritzy hotel or the most

modest pensione, the management will leave no stone unturned to make you feel that you belong. If you have no
plans consider the convenient Pensione Villa Franca four
blocks up from the railroad station. My dear chum Gianni
Schifano, the owner, along with his staff Franco and Angelo, will ensure your comfort and truly provide for you a
home away from home.

From living in their midst we, the Mrs. and I, our
sons, and our dog Princess, have come to love the Romans
and cherish our friendships with them. I recently asked
Camille and the boys to submit lists of their observations
on them while I did likewise.

The following pages will provide, in no special order,
the results of the survey and in turn, I hope, provide some
small insight at least into the nature and character of today's Civis Romanus.

For openers, the men of this city are perennial world
champions in the sport of girl-watching. Perhaps this is so
because the girls of Rome are so worth watching. Byron's
memorable comment on the Italian woman went like this:

> *Heart on her lips,*
> *And soul within her eyes,*
> *Soft as her clime*
> *And sunny as her skies.*

Standing in clusters at every corner or sitting at those little
round sidewalk tables, the men roll over all other con-
tenders for the championship by vigorously voicing their
approval of the passing feminine parade.

The objects of their affections take no offense whatever and in their thoughts laud the watchers for their obvious
good taste. I have learned to enjoy watching these Latins
watching Camille.

The closeness of the Roman family is something to
behold. This covers not only the immediate family but ex-
tends even to the uncle who's been in the city for the last
three months trying to find work, the recently widowed

aunt, the grandparents upstairs or even in the same apartment. No one in the clan is ever turned away for that
would be inhuman, even barbaric. Watch them sit down to
the main meal of the day. They do not segregate themselves by age or gender or any other classification. They
are a unit taking profound joy and sincere interest in each
other. See how affectionate they are especially toward the
children whose very physical and spiritual health call for
an abundance of love and warmth!

Such softies! Camille smiles in admiration when she
recalls our landlady's thirty-two-year-old son Mario, who
loves to put on an air of Maurice Chevalier insouciance,
weeping inconsolably when he had to give his frisky Dal-
matian, Dobro, to friends in the country because city life
was not safe for it.

Health nuts! Their daily commitments, however
heavy, in this hectic capital must never be allowed to interfere with their beloved *siesta* and *passeggiata* (after dinner
stroll). If at all possible the Roman will return home at one
in the afternoon for dinner, followed by a nap. Then it's
back to work at four. Finding this impractical he will dine
leisurely at a nearby trattoria proceeding thence to the
nearest park for a snooze upon a bench. Even the dogs observe the tradition and screech to a halt at midday to plop
down anywhere.

Generally the midday meal is the big one. The evening
repast is taken quite late — at eight-thirty or nine or even
later. The staples of the Roman diet are bread and wine.
Silone points out in his classic novel, *Pane E Vino,* that the
Italians have always seen great symbolism in the two.
Bread is made from many ears of grain signifying unity,
wine from many grapes. The bread and wine of communion, the Body and the Blood. And bread and wine take
nine months to make, Silone notes. The same length of
time it takes to make a man. The grain is sown in November and harvested in July. It takes from March to Novem-

ber for the grapes to mature. Mario's little boy Lorenzo, born in October was surely conceived in February, the proud father insists.

A bottle of *acqua minerale* good for the digestion, must be on every table. Only fresh meat, and eggs, and vegetables, and fruit — purchased that morning at the open air market — will do. Frozen, canned, carbonated foods are *anathema*. They constantly warn each other against using too much salt; no good for *il fegato* (the liver).

The mother will walk blocks to a particular fountain to draw its water if she believes it superior for boiling the pasta.

On all our lists of observations a common denominator was the great Roman skin. Perhaps their wonderful complexions are attributable to their finicky dietary habits. We think at once of the families we are close to: the Tamagninis, the Guarnaccias, the Mirallis, the Faustinis, and the Ferronis. Never a blemish among them, nor among those familiar faces of every day — the busdrivers, the nuns, the streetcleaners, the teenagers.

It can be said that the Romans live to eat but it must also be pointed out that they certainly eat to live. Each meal is almost a religious service starting with the ceremonial: *"Buon appetito!"*

In the states we won't let the kids go in swimming for almost an hour after eating. Here the rule is three or four — better make it four and a half hours. Frankie and his two kid brothers go nearly bats whenever we lunch at the Tamagninis' summer place, the Villa Lidia, near Ostia. Here is this fantastic, in-the-ground pool just begging to be swum in. (Is that grammatically correct? To be swum in? *chi sa?*) Anyway, as they sweat their brains out, the kids are watched over by Mamma to be sure they observe the long moratorium on all swimming activity.

Nothing real hot or ice cold goes down into the Roman stomach. Watch the natives in the place exchange knowing glances whenever an American asks for ice in his soft drink at a restaurant or bar.

On their walk through a park after the meal and the nap, they will buy for ten lire each some of those twigs they like to suck and chew on, which they credit with properties that also wonderfully aid *il digestivo.*

Romans love to eat out. Go over to Trastevere any night in the week and you will see what I mean. But as much as restauranting, they enjoy having guests for dinner at their places. We often recall a November Sunday afternoon when Camille's sister and brother-in-law, Ann and Jack Stasi, her aunt and uncle, Mary and John Gatto, and my sister Anne Korn and niece Faith Christensen visited us in Rome for the first time. They had all come over on one of those package tours. After showing them our flat, we took them upstairs to meet our Roman family. Paola took care of the initial amenities. Mario became instant bartender. Mamma, after embracing our kin as though they were hers, insisted we spend the day, evening, and night right there. She faded gracefully from view and with young, pretty Rosanna Warren, daughter of author Robert Penn Warren ("All the King's Men") who was living with the Tamagninis while studying at the Academy of Fine Arts, prepared a royal feast.

Mellowed by hours of flowing Frascati and Verdicchio, the fifteen of us, our four hosts, our six visitors, and our family of five, watched from the windows and terrace of Mamma's elegant penthouse as the autumn fires in Rome's skies went out and the twinkling lights of the Castelli came on. There are no superlatives yet coined to do justice to the following banquet, though Mario insisted it was nothing much.

He related Rome's long history of dinner parties and told of how Agostino Chigi once impressed that old patron of Renaissance art, Pope Leo X, at a dinner in his pergola over the Tiber. After each course all the gold and silver dinnerware were tossed over the wall into the river by the servants. His Holiness swooned at such opulence. After Leo departed for the Vatican however, Chigi had his staff haul up the nets in which the plates had been caught.

This then was how our relatives were introduced to traditional Roman hospitality on their very first day in the Eternal City. We had started up the stairs to Mamma's at two in the afternoon for a ten-minute visit. The church bells on the Janiculum had a half hour ago heralded the arrival of Monday.

Time had flown, for the Romans are zestful conversationalists. Well educated and quite literary, abstract and esthetic, they'll talk about the economic crisis, what the Vatican said today, the Via Veneto's latest scandal.

They'll discuss the didactic poetry of Lucretius, the liberalism of Seneca, the works of Dante, Petrarch, Pirandello, Silone and Mario Puzo. (*The Godfather* was a smash here.)

But a favorite topic is "Life in America." They love to hear about the New World.

Since they are such inveterate political animals, lively campaigns, rallies, protests (occasionally quite violent) are practically daily occurrences. They take an active interest in politics, one citizen told me, because they are all hoping to meet that *pezzo grosso* (a big shot) who can get them or their sons employment in a bank, a museum, or any of the government agencies in the Italian capital. It is a challenge to find just *a* job here. To find a good one requires that *pezzo grosso*.

Pomp, pageantry, parades, festivals, uniforms, all have special places in the Roman's heart too. This no doubt comes down through the centuries from the dazzling triumphal shows on the Via Sacra in Imperial Rome.

They have not yet become blasé about holidays or holy days here. Christmas Eve is the most stirring. The lovely hymn *Tu Scendi dalle Stelle* is to be heard everywhere; traffic cops perform their impossible tasks as gifts (from grateful pedestrians) of wine, cheese, and other foodstuffs pile up around their pedestals; Piazza Navona overflows with Romans who come with their bambini to see the colorful displays. On Good Friday night the Pope, in solemn procession, reenacts the tragic events of the Via Dolorosa by carrying a huge wooden cross to the Colosseum. For this, all Rome turns out. Two days later it's a different story, when the joy of the Resurrection is manifest in the happy faces of Romans of all ages promenading in their Easter finery through the streets and squares and gardens.

They are enamored of music. Church bells, Gregorian chant wafting from the monasteries, the watery music of the great fountains, popular ballads, and even hard rock, each have their devotees. Romans will tell you to listen to the music of the rustling pines, of the lilting Italian of the children, of the *uccellini* of the parks. They hear music everywhere. Even the thunder sounds Wagnerian. You will have your choice of outdoor concerts in the summer months. We favor those in the splendid remains of the Basilica Maxentius.

But it's at the opera — indoors at *Teatro dell'opera* or outside at *Terme di Caracalla* — that they really demonstrate their love for song with a throaty: *Bravo!* or *Bravissimo!* as the dying hero or heroine of Puccini, or Verdi, or Donizetti completes another lusty aria. And they really *do* sing themselves. School kids on the way home, window washers doing their thing, delivery men unloading wine barrels, salesgirls in STANDA, fruit vendors, the whole lovable lot of them.

Romans can be both provincial and cosmopolitan, mundane and urbane. Long ago a Roman by the name of Marcus Aurelius wrote: "My city is Rome, so far as I am Aurelius, but so far as I am a man, it is the world."

Capable of irreverence in the midst of piety, but never

to the extremes of the movie, *Fellini's Roma,* they enjoy an occasional ribald anecdote or a satire on the hierarchy. While they tend to be somewhat frugal they nevertheless are fashionable dressers, male and female. The man will often have but one suit but it's one of quality. With a few fine shirts and ties, and always polished, genuine leather shoes — whether he drives a bus, waits on tables, cleans fountains during the week, on Sunday he will manage to appear to have stepped off a magazine cover.

Since he wants always *fare bella figura* (to make a good impression) he takes his suits without pockets to avoid unsightly bulges. The little purse he totes then is for his wallet, keys, comb, cigarettes etc. A long-sleeved shirt, however hot the weather, is a must; Bermuda shorts a travesty.

One unbearable summer midnight in the middle of the annual *sirocco,* that sultry wind from Africa which saps one's vitality, I could not sleep. Standing in my shorts behind the potted plants on our balcony I heard a young male voice softly rendering *Una Furtiva Lagrima.* Leaning over, I saw this Latin lover — suit, long shirt, and tie — pass beneath the street light, arm around his *inamorata,* cool as you please. Vergil wrote that love conquers all *(omnia vincit amor)* and these people, born lovers all, apparently espouse the theory.

My friend Joe Mase spent more time on his visit gaping at the sartorially sharp Roman males than at the monuments and palaces, and began to worry about himself.

As for the signorine, Camille will tell you that they are always elegant and tasteful in their attire. You will never see one in public in jeans, bobby sox, hairpins. They've too much *amour-propre* for that.

All those jokes about Italians speaking with their hands are accurate, at least in the case of the Romans. Everything is done with a dramatic flourish here, even talking. Expressive eyes, lips, foreheads, shoulders — all are expected to pitch in and help the hands get the message across.

Surrounded by churches, they are nonetheless not the best church-goers on earth. But their devotion to the Virgin Mary is genuine and demonstrated in the ubiquitous corner shrine, usually in the form of a mosaic medallion borne aloft by solemn angels in the facade of a building.

Courtliness, perhaps residual from the period when Italians were the stars of diplomacy and their language the diplomatic tongue of the continent, is also among their hallmarks. They are great letter writers. Never would they think to embarrass a visitor to their city however much he might deserve it on occasion. A nun friend of mine, Sister Mary Daniel, had asked me to chauffeur her about the city one day so that she might increase her slide collection. From dawn to dusk — she in full habit with cameras in the ready, and I alongside in tee shirt and blue jeans carrying her pocketbook, we pounded the eternal pavement. Everywhere the natives were gracious enough not to bat an eye at *The Odd Couple,* but the tourists, not so restrained, poked each other silly when we passed.

Use whatever Italian you have when you are here. You will be lauded to the heavens for it and you will find everyone a ready and willing teacher.

Let me cite another incidence of this courtliness. Joe Mase and I were returning from Naples one afternoon. Just before the toll booth for the *Autostrada* we noticed a handsome chap hawking bottles of whiskey. Since we were to be dinner guests at the Mirallis that evening Joe wanted to bring a gift. We negotiated the guy down to about five dollars for two bottles, one Johnny Walker (popular here) the other Chivas Regal. I joshed that it was probably water and the three of us howled.

That evening we gave the Johnny Walker to Aldo, warning him that it might be water — *ha, ha.* He opened it, poured a shot glass, sampled it, and broadly grinned: *"È l'acqua!"* But he quickly recovered his composure and his diplomacy enough to insist that it was good water. *(Ma è buon acqua!)*

All this gentility, strangely enough, still won't deter them from sneaking ahead of you in any line — at the bank or at the butcher's or at the train station. With an inexplicable abhorrence for straight lines they will cluster around the teller's window or the cash register clamoring for attention. Having left you somewhat miffed they'll smile their disarming smiles, leaving you feeling quite sheepish for the murderous thoughts you were just harboring.

Tourists sometimes get abusive with the street vendors if the latter get too pushy. Not the Romans. "They have to live too," they'll remark; "one must admire their enterprising natures." Enterprising indeed. They will set up shop anywhere offering merchandise (often somewhat warm) from belts to sunglasses to nude statuettes to rosary beads, having mastered just enough French, German, and English to conduct negotiations. ("Hay Buddee, wonna bye a niza wotch?")

Others will sell services — guide, taxi, escort. Some, men and women, will buy black, cop-looking hats, slap a toy badge over the peek, stake a claim to a busy block and hustle change by parking cars. Tourists courageous enough to drive are almost always fooled into thinking they are municipal personnel and pay several hundred lire automatically. The Romans know better of course but still tip them for the genuine services they provide — helping you to back in, helping you to pull out, and watching over your car in the time between. Some are in the entertainment business. You have the sidewalk magicians, singers who stride right up to your outdoor table and start crooning, flutists who slither up and down the street — all depending on tossed coins for their revenue. The family's favorite is the wrinkled Latin leprechaun who haunts Piazza

Navona playing the old Neapolitan standbys with a leaf in his mouth. In this city of art you'll find even the sidewalks frescoed in chalk, the artist squatting next to his work — hat upside down as a receptacle for your donation.

Beggars, some legitimate, make up a huge part of Rome's work force. The City of the Seven Hills, of Fountains, of Churches, is also the City of Palms. The gypsy likes to hold a baby, soiled and destitute-looking as herself, the better to evoke pity and a bigger take. *Rent-a-baby* agencies have sprung up as a result. Urchins will come up and shine your shoes or clean your windshields with a dirty rag before you realize what's happening. Prosperous Romans are patient with and considerate of all these types and like to think they can distinguish between the needy and the faker.

Oh, how the Romans love to give advice. Whether it's accurate or not is not so important. It is the giving of it that counts.

"Peaceful" describes them well too. Unpleasantries they have learned to block from their minds. Days after World War II they preferred not to discuss it any more. *"La guerra è passata già,"* they would note. (The war is a thing of the past already.)

On foot they have two speeds here a) slow and b) dead stop. Behind the wheel, look out! Roman drivers enjoy the dubious tag of *Pazzo* (crazy). Cars are still a novelty here and early each morning the *Demolition Derby* begins, lasting until the Colosseum is drenched in moonlight. Johnny Gatto, no Sunday driver back in America, bailed out ashen white after a five-minute scrimmage with those Kamikazi Fiat pilots. Soon after the war there was much government speculation about a subway to cure the unsnarlable traffic in the ancient streets. The citizens had their doubts: "Men will walk on the moon before we ever get a subway here." In July of 1969 Neil Armstrong left this planet to walk upon another. In July of 1975 the construction of Rome's subway crawls toward completion. Traffic violations are committed with impunity because for example if you were to, say, go through a red light in Largo Argentina, the cop would not dare pull you over simply because there is nowhere to pull you over to. He'd have to catch up with you on the Appian Way somewhere. A terrible parking problem exists in Rome but the drivers solve it every day by hanging their little bugs anywhere and everywhere — up on the sidewalk, two deep if need be.

Though the older generation frets about the erosion of the old values and what the kids are coming to, time has still pretty much — happily — stood still in the schools insofar as discipline and no-nonsense instruction go. University-bound kids still must master the likes of classical Latin and Greek and Philosophy and Elocution in addition to at least one modern language. My teacher at the Institute of Dante, ran a tight ship regarding homework, attention and attendance in class, though all of us were doing postgraduate work. Consequently I fell in love with her just as I did with all my wonderful teachers throughout grade school.

Visit the Romans in the different charming quarters of the city and you will note some differences; a sort of neighborhood chauvinism, the district's own patron saint or two, local festivals such as the colorful *Noi Antri* over in Trastevere each July. Trasteverini swear they even have their own dialect which, of all others, is closest to the ancient Latin. They are the true descendants of Caesar's Rome they'll have you know. Try to meet the sophisticates of Parioli, the longanimous Roman Jews in their Ghetto on the Tiber, the phlegmatic craftsmen down in the Campus Martius, and all of us up here in Monteverde Vecchio.

Gambling fascinates the male — whether it be casual at cards or Bocce, or organized and legalized such as *Totocalcio* (based on the National Soccer League). In Trastevere stoopsitting is the favorite outdoor sport for women.

From what I can see, the Romans, much more so than any other prominent society in the world, have kept the ways of their forebears in antiquity. The citizens of Augustan Rome loved their public gardens, and architectural fountains. Back then the really affluent resided in richly furnished villas, the rest in apartment houses with little balconies. They were big on statuary and all kinds of art. They prayed in the great temples to the gods, frequented the baths, took after dinner walks, drove out into the campagna to take the air, "complained," Juvenal wrote, "about the weather, the taxes, the noises of Rome." Dinner parties, rooftop-sitting, political hurly burly were also popular.

Change the temples to magnificent Catholic churches. Instead of frequenting the baths, make it the beaches at Ostia and you have today's Romans.

So perhaps now when you come you will be ready for the Roman temperament. Take the old counsel and do as they do while you are among them. Your trip will be an even greater success if you do. Study their ways and learn.

They love their city, their past, their traditions, their life style.

The Roman's genuine affection for his city is I think best illustrated and typified by the Sgambati anecdote.

In the 1890's Signor Sgambati was the rage of the music world. Vienna, Paris, all the European capitals were vying for his services. An offer arrived one day from London which proved irresistible. The music lovers and critics there awaited the composer's arrival with wild anticipation and open arms.

On the day of his departure Sgambati went to the railroad station, purchased a ticket, checked his luggage, and walked to the appropriate platform. As he boarded the train the stark reality of what he was about to do hit him full force. This was more than he had bargained for! Going to London to begin a new and more glamorous and more lucrative adventure was one thing. Leaving Rome was quite another! He retrieved his belongings, destroyed his ticket, and quickly returned to his house on the Via della Croce, there to spend, in sublime contentment, the rest of his life.

They are in love with life and live to the fullest every marvelous minute of it, heeding the sobering words of the proverb:

Tempus fugit

XXVII

The Signora

The most unforgettable character I've ever met is my *Roman Mamma*. Indeed she is so terribly interesting and fascinating that her life story sounds more like fiction than fact. May I assure you that the following account is non-fiction.

Signora Irma Tamagnini (*"Mamma"* to me and my wife and *"Nonna"* to our three sons) owns a grand palazzo in an old but lovely quarter of Rome. Each summer we rent an apartment from her for three months. She has so completely captivated us that we do, in fact, regard her as another mother and grandmother.

She has led an extraordinary life and I shall attempt to provide here at least a perfunctory look at it.

The Signora, a striking Italian beauty even today in her mid-sixties, was born in the enchanting, immured, medieval town of Siena, famous for its *Palio* festival each August. The *Palio* (Italian for pennant or banner) is a bareback horse race held in the great town square on August 16th, in honor of the Blessed Virgin.

It has roots in the 13th century. Siena is divided into 17 wards and each ward enters a horse and rider to vie for the coveted standard. The race, which requires but three minutes to run, is preceded by a tradition-steeped pageant, complete with medieval costumes and centuries-old ritual, which lasts more than three hours.

It was in this fairy-tale setting that the Signora as a little girl, whose beauty and charm were even then the talk of the town, grew up and went to school. And to this day she never tires of reminiscing about the vibrant life of this most picturesque of the Tuscan Hill towns.

A product of the district of *La Lupa* ("The Wolf"), it is here too that she still returns each summer to wave the *lupa* colors and cheer lustily for her old neighborhood's representatives in the parade and in the race. And after the annual madness, it's a grand tour of old comrades' homes and the town's ginmills to renew friendships, lift a decanter of domestic chianti, rejoice in victory or commiserate in defeat, into the next morn.

Irma was but a child when her strength was tested. She lost her *"angel"* mother whom she adored, and was raised then by her father and a stepmother.

One day, long ago, the 19-year-old *"Belle of Siena"* decided to make her life in the capital of the world, the Eternal City of Rome.

So, with great expectations, she boarded a rickety train at the city gate and headed south for what would prove to be a wonderful rendezvous with destiny. It was spring and throughout the scenic but grueling odyssey the young woman's fancy had been turned to thoughts of love and romance on the banks of the Tiber.

Up ahead in the car was, among others, a handsome, distinguished gentleman, totally oblivious to the glances of a girl almost a third of a century his junior. He was one of Italy's most celebrated sculptors and was to become the preeminent sculptor during the Mussolini era. Engrossed in his reading, he patiently awaited the train's arrival at his destination, short of Rome.

Signor Tamagnini, upon the conductor's bark, gath-

Mamma Tamagnini with Camille and author

ered his papers, donned his coat and quickly disembarked. Walking along the motionless train through the bustling station, he sensed someone staring at him. Looking up he saw this vision of loveliness gazing somewhat forlornly through the window. At once enraptured by what he saw, and with the train slowly pulling out, he leaped aboard again.

Walking down the aisle with what little composure he could muster he chose the seat next to the vision. The artist, a 48-year-old, highly eligible bachelor, wasted no words. He introduced himself rather thoroughly, told the signorina that she was the greatest work of art he had ever seen and asked her to marry him. She consented, pending her father's endorsement. Upon arriving in Rome, the pair purchased tickets for a return trip to Tuscany.

That very night Signor Tamagnini was back in Siena asking the girl's father (who, *mirabile dictu,* turns out to be an old comrade) for her hand. Thus was launched a marriage that was to be unbelievably fruitful, exciting and idyllic. The middle-aged groom took his young bride back to the capital to resume his hectic life there. From the union were quickly to come two sons: Giancarlo, now a civil engineer living in Frankfurt with his German wife and their two children; and Mario, still of Rome, an artist of stature himself, and the husband of a college professor of philosophy, who are the proud parents of Lorenzo, born in October, 1972.

The newlyweds were soon part of Rome's social whirl, what with the Signore moving in some rather fast artistic circles. He was even commissioned by Benito Mussolini to carve Il Duce's likeness for coins, busts, and to work on other art projects of state.

All this while his wife was becoming very active in women's church organizations, through which she was to become the lifelong friend of one, Monsignor Angelo Roncalli, whom the world will recall as Pope John XXIII.

Life was to be full of surprises for Irma. She soon discovered that among her husband's abundant charms was a great impetuosity, a wild unpredictability.

For example there was the night she had prepared the usual regal feast for the man in her life. He arrived slightly late, as was his custom, exchanged amenities with the object of his affection, feasted, and then expressed a desire for a cup of cappuccino. The devoted wife hastened to ready the coffee pot but the man had other ideas.

With no explanation other than, "I know a place that serves a great cappuccino," he took the signora by the hand to the car, thence to Fiumicino Airport, where they boarded a plane for Sicily.

Two hours later the Signora found herself sitting and sipping at a sidewalk café in Palermo. After paying the check the couple caught the next plane out for Rome. While *Britannica* and *Guinness Book of World Records* don't record it, it is my suspicion that this was the costliest cup of cappuccino in the history of man.

Every day was Valentine's Day in the artist's view and his gifts would range from a long-stemmed rose to a long winter coat.

The Signore, whose works grace the piazzas of many Italian towns, died seven years ago having provided his dream girl however with abundant and joyful memories. Has she since sat around and brooded? No, our Roman Mamma has a simple philosophy about life's hardships — *"tutto finisce"* (all things come to an end). And so she philosophically viewed her great loss as the completion of another phase of her life and the beginning of the next.

An intellectual, she is too absorbed in too many things to live in the past. Her interests are numerous and varied. She loves the opera and is partial to the works of Puccini. Poetry of all ages, but especially Dante's and the prose of contemporary Italian writers also receive her time and attention. She enjoys turning out verse of her own as well.

She loves to paint and work with ceramics. We have some of her creations in honored places in our Jersey home.

The Signora is a remarkable seamstress and has always created her own clothes. She has in her wardrobe, for example, a stunning grey, pinstripe suit which she fashioned from an old suit of her husband's.

Mamma is also the nurse of the block. Though she has no medical training whatever, she ministers tirelessly to the sick, giving orders, injections, and comfort as she goes, all still perfectly legal in Italy. She has an insatiable thirst for knowledge and is, in truth, the very embodiment of Michelangelo's personal motto: *"Ancora Imparo."* (I'm still learning.)

This year she has been taking lessons in clay sculpture and is already producing masterpieces.

She rehabilitates old furniture. She designs and then creates new pieces of furniture such as beds, desks, end tables.

When not engaged in one or another of her endless projects, she enjoys vigorous walking tours of her beloved Rome. While still loyal to Siena, she is totally Roman. Ask her what her favorite season is and the reply is *"questa stagione"* (the current one), for she really feels that Rome is exquisitely lovely in all months, all weather, all seasons.

She is a zealous student of Roman history from the Republic through the Renaissance through the Vatican. I have been the intellectual beneficiary of many of her walks, for as we stroll arm-in-arm through the streets, past the ruins, in and out of the churches, she disseminates information with insight, profundity, and eloquence in a way no guide, textbook, or professor could ever hope to do.

Nostra Mamma Romana has the vigor of those a fraction of her age. She thinks nothing of a 24-hour train ride to Germany to visit Giancarlo's bambini or an auto trip to Yugoslavia, jaunts that would stagger many of us.

On one trip to Germany not many years ago, she gave a young British chap a graphic lesson in etiquette. Arriving last in the cuchette, she, with all due feminine politeness, asked the youth who was occupying the upper berth if she might have that choice spot in view of her age, her gender, and the length of her trip.

He claimed not to speak a word of Italian (though as it later came out he had just spent a year studying it in Perugia) and pretended not to understand her. The Signora importuned some more. He was intransigent. She asked again. He grew brusque. She grabbed one leg and yanked and it was London Bridge all over.

Then chattering angrily in Italian the way Ricky Riccardo used to in Spanish on "I Love Lucy," she lamented the young man's deficiencies in basic courtesy and, picking her way around his supine form, scampered to the upper perch. Before the ride was over, however, she had won the victim's respect and friendship, and still corresponds with the lad, now an attorney in London.

Mamma also belongs in the culinary hall of fame and one invitation to dinner in her Janiculum Hill penthouse with its breathtaking panorama of Rome convinces the visitor of this.

Signora Tamagnini has a deep concern for all her fellow men. During the war she was active in a crusade to alleviate the plight of the Jewish community in Italy and remains active today in the battle against discrimination.

She has all the tenderness of St. Francis of Assisi for all of God's creatures. I have seen her tend to wounded birds and she even loves the *pipistrello* (a little bat). The thought of killing any living thing is to her abhorrent. Even an insect who finds its way into her kitchen will merely be picked up, given a brief lecture on where it belongs, and set back outside the window.

Her own apartment is a festival of colors from the countless plants which enjoy her tender, loving care.

The Signora is a brilliant conversationalist and the hours spent in her company have the wings of minutes.

She has a *joie-de-vivre* which is infectious and our lives will always be the richer and fuller because of our relationship with her. My *"Bella Mamma"* is for us at least — Cicero, Caesar, Augustus, notwithstanding — the greatest Roman of them all.

Grazie tanto, Mamma

XXVIII

The Petrine City

In His last days Jesus had exhorted the Apostles to "go teach ye all nations." Taking Him literally, Andrew set out for Egypt, Matthew for Ethiopia, Mark to Egypt and so on.

The primitive Church was on the move. A spreading missionary program was shaping up. From all this there gradually developed a hierarchy. The top echelon consisted of the Apostles whose leader was Peter.

Wherever the Apostles took the Church they established advisory councils called by two names: *episkopos* (Greek for overseer) and *presbyteros* (Greek for old man) from which have derived, in order, the words "bishop" and "priest."

Peter began to receive reports from different regions that the Christian poor were being neglected. Surely if the Jews helped their destitute with alms the Christians could do no less. For the message of the Lord was not only to ensure the spiritual salvation of man but also to ease his worldly suffering. The head of the Church thereupon commissioned a new clerical order called diaconi (Latin for servants) to minister especially to the needs of the impoverished.

These clerical ranks have remained to our own day in the deacons, priests, bishops, cardinals, and Pope of the Roman Church.

Christ died on the cross and rose from the tomb in the year 33, in the reign of Tiberius Caesar. For the rest of that decade Peter oversaw the spread of the Church from Jerusalem. In the forties he too journeyed forth into distant lands.

It is a fairly undisputed theory that Simon Peter, by now over 60 years of age, arrived in Rome in 55 A.D., in the reign of the deranged Nero Caesar. The leather-skinned, bearded, broad-shouldered Galilean had walked for many days from southern Italy to reach the capital.

In the spring of 59 the man who would forever be viewed in history as the partner of Peter in the propagation of Christ's gospel in the seat of the Empire, entered Rome. That man, Saul of Tarsus, formerly a bitter foe and persecutor of the faithful and later called by the name Paul, had been converted to the cause of our Lord in the most extraordinary fashion. A devout Jew though a Roman citizen, Saul had recently been assigned by the high priest to go to Damascus to lead new attacks there against the Christians. Approaching the city he was struck down by a brilliant light and lost his sight. He heard clearly a voice inquiring "Saul, Saul, why dost thou persecute me?" He was helped into the city by passers-by. A Christian called Ananias baptized him and his sight was restored. After this he discussed religion with Christians in their homes and a great change took place in him. Saul astonished Jews and Christians alike when he began to preach Christ in the synagogues. In the next three decades he became the most traveled Apostolic missionary bringing the Word to many nations, converting thousands, building churches. Now Paul had reached Rome, the fortress of paganism.

If the Holy Land was the birthplace of the Church promised to the world by the Savior then surely Rome was

John and shepherd pose for a sort of biblical scene on the Appian Way

its incubator. For it was in that metropolis that the Church, after a most difficult birth, teetered on the brink of death for the first three centuries of its existence. It was at Rome that the Church made its first real efforts to talk and walk. It was at Rome too, that the Church developed into the robust, dominant, powerful institution it has remained to this day, and shall so remain with the guidance of the Holy Spirit, to Judgment Day.

Peter's task in the world capital is herculean. Paul's presence in the city must be a source of comfort and strength to the first Supreme Pontiff of Holy Mother Church. Upon the fisherman's muscular shoulders rests the conversion of decadent, pagan Rome.

His work daily finds him teaching, preaching, ministering to the city's poor, the sick, the lame, the troubled, the oppressed. Burying the dead is another of his duties. Burying the dead? Here the Christians owe a debt of gratitude to Rome's Jews. The Jews could not in conscience cremate their deceased, which was the Roman practice. The children of the Jewish political prisoners in the administration of the consul Pompey, in order to circumvent the law of cremation, went subterranean. They dug an elaborate network of tunnels and passages later called *catacombs* whose walls were carved into niches to receive and entomb mortal remains. Now the Christians began to follow this example. They created even more sophisticated *necropoli* below the soil. Part of Peter's pastoral work includes accompanying the bereaved to the coolness of the catacombs for interment ceremonies.

Among his commitments too are the appointing of more bishops to aid in the administration of the growing Church, the ordination of more priests, the resolving of great ecclesiastical and theological questions, and the combating of heresy which seems to be rearing its ugly head everywhere.

Days, weeks, and months fly swiftly by for the Pontiff

in the imperial city for he truly thrives on his work. The reputation of his sanctity and goodness grows to legend dimensions.

The first Bishop of Rome and Head of the Church of Christ manages to find time, however, in his crowded daily regimen for meditation and solitude. His appeal is broad based for he is held in esteem by those in luxury as well as those in squalor.

Most of the time Peter can be found in the turbulent *subura* on the Esquiline Hill, yet at other times in the verdant surroundings of a garden of a well-to-do friend on the fashionable Aventine. While he truly loves the poor, he despises not the affluent and seeks their conversion as zealously.

Perhaps it is while strolling and praying on the Aventine that he sometimes pauses at the eminence to gaze at the Vatican Hill across the Tiber. There in the cooling, setting sun of a Roman afternoon he can discern a lone charioteer in vigorous workouts in the stadium situated on the slopes of the distant hill. The charioteer? His Imperial Majesty, the cherubic-faced but satanic-hearted young emperor.

We might suppose that in such moments Peter's ardor sweeps his imagination away to visions of converting the demonic Nero himself to the gentle ways of Jesus Christ and of convincing the ruler to use his vast temporal power to the greater honor and glory of the Messiah.

A call to dinner by the servants of his host quickly brings the alien fisherman back down to earth as his thoughts leave Nero and turn to the amenities of mealtime. Over a lucullan Roman supper, not altogether agreeable to the ascetic Peter whose customary repast consists of lentil soup and dried peas, the conversation ranges from politics to philosophy to theology and inevitably to the growing membership of the Holy Church. The task of presiding over a universal Church is fast becoming a colossal one.

While tradition has little to say about the collaboration of Peter with Paul in ecclesiastical matters it stretches one's credulity not at all to suppose that the two most prominent leaders in the Christian movement were a great source of strength to each other in this period. Though Paul was brought to Rome to stand trial for disturbing the peace in the province of Judea he had been placed under house arrest. He had mobility and was free to preach and teach the Kingdom of God.

Can't we assume then that whenever their busy schedules would allow, Peter and Paul would seek each other's companionship, solace, and counsel? Their paths must occasionally cross too as they celebrate the Holy Sacrifice in the homes of various faithful, distribute food and clothing from the prosperous to the deprived, minister to the sick, bring solace to the dying, or preside over conferences of the spiritual leaders of the Christian community.

Reminders of their partnership abound in the Eternal City today. Astride the great piazza of the Basilica of St. Peter's stand their splendid statues, again flanking the beautiful main altar of the Basilica of St. Paul's Outside the Walls, and again throughout many of Rome's churches and even down in the catacombs.

Peter's followers are zealously devoted to spreading the word and goodness of the Carpenter from Nazareth and people from all walks of life are being drawn to the faith. Even hardened atheistic, or at least agnostic, Roman legionaries are among those streaming into the fold. A few Roman senators have also embraced the new religion.

What is the disposition of the civil authorities and the general public toward the practitioners of this worship? A general attitude of bemusement, fascination, and tolerance pervades the citizenry and the government regarding those who, as Pliny later wrote, "meet very early in the morning to take bread and wine and chant prayers to a mere mortal but render harm to no one."

Indeed those who have embraced the new way along with their bishop are being viewed as so many harmless, fanatical, eccentric cultists who are so foolish as to eschew the pleasures of the flesh and pursue the joys of the spirit. "This cult," the Romans are gossiping, "will pass away just as surely as all the countless others which have visited us for a time from alien cultures and have vanished."

This state of affairs continues. The infant Church grows while pagan Romans snicker. Until July 19, 64. Then disaster strikes. As that typically sultry Roman summer afternoon draws to a close and the glowing hues of twilight play on the marble wonders of the Forum, a shout is heard on the Aventine. "The Circus Maximus is ablaze!" Flames gut the Jewish Ghetto around the corner and tenement districts on the Esquiline as a summer breeze gives wings to the internecine embers. The fire spreads with lightning suddenness. By midnight the center of the city is a fiery furnace. Panic reigns. People, particularly children, the aged, the lame, are trampled to death. Everywhere the din of screaming is deafening as Romans are being burned alive. The city's firefighters stand by hapless and helpless. Hundreds, maybe thousands, make their way to the Tiber, leap into the turgid stream and are drowned. Others climb precipices only to be confronted with another wall of flame. Wooden *insulae* (apartment buildings) are veritable tinderboxes. Hoodlums loot and slay. The conflagration rages for nine days and nine nights. Tens of thousands perish, hundreds of thousands are left homeless.

Following the disaster, frustration and despair are rampant in the charred streets, squares, and back alleys of Rome. The community's spirit has been crushed. In their anguish the victims are searching now for someone on whom to hang the albatross. The Emperor of course! Why it is he, with his vile ways, who has incurred the wrath of Olympus; he who has turned Rome into another Sodom or Gomorrah. "Storm the palace," is the cry of the frenzied mob. "Let us sacrifice Nero and perhaps the gods will be placated."

Upon receiving word of the awful unrest in the city and of the terrible animosity his subjects now harbor for him, Nero swings into action his propaganda machine which grinds out the allegation, "The Christians, those mad, little cultists are to blame." A vicious lie campaign is launched against the Christians. Human sacrifices, cannibalism, drinking the blood of children are some of the charges. To lend veracity to the indictment the words of Christ are quoted, "Unless you eat My Body and drink My Blood you shall not have life in you."

To increase the credibility of all this, members of the Christian sect are rounded up and hauled to a kangaroo court where the machinery of Roman justice moves with fierce swiftness.

The public's emotions are only warming up. For Nero's actions have triggered a wave of pathological hatred for the disciples of Christ. All Christians are now proscribed. This marks the beginning of a nightmare that shall not end until the reign of Constantine nearly three centuries hence.

Nero has snatched victory from the jaws of defeat. He now gives the howling mob its pleasure. Christian men, women, boys and girls are dragged from their homes, beaten senseless, incarcerated, thrown to wild beasts in the arenas of the city.

One night during this pogrom the Emperor gives a lavish party in his fabulous gardens. He dispenses with the usual form of lighting and lets hundreds of Christians, doused in flammable liquids, tied to stakes, and set aflame, illuminate the grounds, their screams providing the musical background for the festivities.

Still not satisfied, his Imperial Majesty declares Peter and Paul as public enemies numbers one and two respectively.

Peter's heart is breaking as the genocide rages on. He can hide no longer. The Bishop of Rome has decided to surrender with the hope of making a deal with the government to end the bloodshed. "A fair deal can never be made with a tyrant," his friends, with great difficulty, convince Peter. "You must flee, not so much for yourself as for the Church," he is told by all.

On a torrid Roman night Peter is smuggled to the south gate of the city and under the cloak of darkness he makes his way down the Via Appia. As he nears the second milestone on the highway he is stunned to his knees by a clap of thunder. Coming out of his daze he sees, in all His glory, our Lord. *"Quo Vadis, Domine?"* (Whither goest thou, Lord) he inquires emotionally. *"Venio Roman iterum crucifigi,"* (I come to Rome to be crucified again) is the reply. Peter, the lovable, bumbling, pathetic hulk of a fisherman weeps and apologizes profusely for abandoning his mission. He returns to the city to resume his work for as long as God might grant him the life to do so.

At this time the Church goes, literally, underground in droves. Down in dark, dank, foreboding cemeteries they sleep, eat, continue to dig, and take in more refugees. By the dancing light of candles Peter celebrates the Eucharist daily. Peter and his bishops and priests lead the weary, frightened, but ever fervent faithful in hymns and litanies. The simple yet eloquent sermons of the Pontiff console the crowds sitting and kneeling in the eerie corridors.

Peter continues to go above ground in his work though he is the target of an incessant vigorous, city-wide search. In the arenas where daily more of the faithful are being torn limb from limb and devoured by ravenous beasts, Peter, incognito, mingles with the throngs, silently blessing the condemned from high up in the stadium. The sadistic Roman spectators are confounded by the unwavering courage and perfect willingness of the Christians to be martyred.

As their bodies are being mangled and consumed some are actually smiling peacefully, others chant the popular hymn "Christus Vincit! Christus Regnat! Christus Imperat!" (Christ is conquering! Christ is reigning! Christ is ruling!)

Word of Paul's arrest and imprisonment saddens the Christian community. The police are closing in. On a June morning in 67 Peter is detected, chained, and hauled off to the Mamertine Prison near the Forum. The sentencing is quick. He is cast into that foul, vermin-infested hole beneath the jail known as the Tullianum Dungeon. Paul has been there some days now. The two weary, blinking old men embrace and talk of the joy of seeing their Lord soon. Here the two Apostles await their execution.

Paul, a Roman citizen, is afforded a less humiliating death than his beloved bishop. A detachment of troops escorts the chained missionary outside the city to a spot on the Via Ostiense, where he is beheaded.

Peter, an alien, is scheduled for the degrading death of crucifixion. Before a capacity, hysterical, delighted crowd of Romans in the Circus of Nero on the Vatican, he is dragged behind his cross, being too sick now to carry it, into the center of the arena. The crowd roars its approval. The din can be heard in the Trastevere and even down in the Campus Martius.

His only request is that he be crucified head down deeming himself unworthy of the same death as his Lord. The Galilean's request is surprisingly granted. His remains are buried outside the circus on the gentle, marshy slope, where they lie even today, beneath the main altar of St. Peter's Basilica.

Thus ends the reign of the Prince of the Apostles, the first Supreme Pontiff of Holy Mother Church, our first Pope. And thus begins Rome's story as the glorious Seat of Christianity.

Tu es Petrus

XXIX

The Catacombs

In contrast to the unexampled splendor of *Urbs Aeterna,* as the Rome of Nero was already being called, there was growing just outside the walls a mole-like, subterranean *Urbs Mortuorum.*

This vast city of the dead, now known to the world as the catacombs, burrowed its way for hundreds of miles through the accommodating volcanic soil of extramural Rome.

It is to this incredible land that we go in this chapter. While catacombs can be found along virtually all the ancient highways leading from the city the most interesting and historic among them are situated to the south.

To reach the Catacombs of San Callisto, San Sebastiano and Santa Domitilla one, if he is ambitious, scholarly, and religious, will go on foot, commencing at the Mamertine Prison (as historic a starting point for such a pilgrimage as can be found) where Peter and Paul were incarcerated, down the Via Fori Imperiali passing the superb ruins of the marketplace whence emanated the edicts of persecution against the early Christians, bearing right around the massive Colosseum whose arena floor was so often drenched with Christian blood, through the arch of

Constantine whose edict at last arrested the bloodshed, down the Via San Gregorio with the gutted palaces of the emperors high up on the Palatine to the right. Upon reaching the remains of the Circus Maximus he will turn left down the tree-canopied Via delle Terme di Caracalla to the Porta San Sebastiano, through the mighty gate, out on to the super highway of the old empire, the Via Appia Antica.

Now our friend is but twenty minutes away from the beginning of the catacomb region. Proceeding along the historic road, immured at this stretch by the walls of private villas and farms, he passes on the right a restaurant of sidewalk tables with the rather auspicious name of *Ristorante Quo Vadis* and soon after on the left, the chapel of the same name marking the spot where in 64 Peter made this inquiry of Christ.

He is now in catacomb country, for twenty-five yards straight ahead rises the iron gate of the Cemetery of San Callisto.

The less energetic may take the No. 118 bus from the Colosseum to this point.

Catacombs — intriguing and mysterious in their name alone.

But the devout who dug these endless galleries in that long ago twilight of the Empire did not use this term. *Coemeteria,* they called them, resting places for the departed.

The first time the term catacomb is used according to De Rossi, the 19th century pioneer in sacred archaeology, is in a ninth century document discovered in Naples referring to the particular cemetery of San Sebastiano. The Greek words *Kata* and *Kymbas* mean "by the hollows" and this cemetery was situated in the naturally depressed area near the tomb of Cecilia Metella and the Circus of Romulus along the Appian Way.

The term gradually came to be used comprehensively for all such burial sites. But while *coemeterium ad catacum-*

The Basilica of St. Domitilla at the Catacombs

bas was the term for St. Sebastian's, other grave sites had their own names, e.g., *ad duas lauros* (at the two laurels).

What then were the catacombs? Of what interest ought they be now for us? Among Imperial Rome's plethora of laws was one prohibiting burial within the Capital's walls. As a consequence of this statute all the grand roads stretching in every direction from Rome became oblong cemeteries along which the pagans raised impressive mausolea to contain their funerary urns.

Their epitaphs still speak to us from the ravaged remains of these sepulchers. Judging by some of the messages of the first and second centuries before our era, the Roman citizenry was ripe for Christianity with its promise of life hereafter. One citizen issues in stone from his grave on the Via Appia this heart-rending and blood-chilling plea: "I was nothing. I am nothing once again. You who still live, eat, drink, and rejoice, then come with me."

The pagan custom was cremation. But the Jewish community of Rome entombed their dead. Being out of the mainstream of economic life in the city the Jews could not afford above-ground tombs. Therefore, they went underground. They found to their pleased amazement that the subsoil of Rome and its environs consisted of layers of soft tufa, easy to hollow out yet strong enough to support the terrain above. Many centuries before this, we should add, the Etruscans in the north had dug subterranean cemeteries, and to the south the ancient Sicilians and others. This was so wherever was to be found the soft tufa.

This chocolate-looking, porous substance yielded to the digging efforts of even the women and children. The Jews tunneled their way beneath the pagans' area and cut out niches in the corridors to receive the mortal remains of their loved ones. The niches were then sealed with terra cotta and mortar. One such Jewish cemetery, now open for visitation by the public, is at No. 119 Via Appia Antica. This site is especially interesting for its Greek epitaphs and

Hebraic adornments of menorahs, cornucopias, and other representations of ancient Judaism.

It was then, from the people of the Old Testament, that the embracers of the New learned the technique of "catacombing."

The Christians, following the example of their Divine Master, and with their belief in the resurrection of the body, rejected cremation and would wrap their deceased in linens and lay the remains in tombs.

Since after the fire of 64, when they had become *personae non gratae* to the Roman populace, they could not, even their wallets permitting, afford further agitation by erecting tombs to compete with those of their pagan tormentors.

Thus they too went underground. Contrary, however, to the romanticized account that the Christians dug this vast network of galleries as hiding places, the original purpose of the flock of Peter was the same as that of the Jews, i.e. for burials. The passages were later, though, to serve as places of refuge during the more violent persecutions such as those of Nero, Valerian (257-258) and Diocletian (303-313).

The persecutions since the first under Nero had waxed and waned. In prosperous times the Christians were left alone and even participated in the mainstream of daily life in the city. However, let there be a famine, a bad stretch of weather, an epidemic, a national calamity of any kind and the cry, "The Christians to the lions!" would be raised. On these occasions the catacombs would then be used as much for worship and escape as for interment.

No one then as now would have hidden for very long down in the vaults, however, for rheumatism (or pneumonia) was as much a reality for the ancients as for us. Yet we do read of some accounts of rare incredible stretches passed by some of the persecuted in the subsoil of Rome's classic campagna.

Pope Liberius for example is reported to have evaded the Emperor's gestapo for more than a year in the galleries of Sant'Agnese on the Via Nomentana.

Now the question always raised by first-time visitors to these sites is: "How did they dig without detection?" The answer is simply: "They didn't have to, at first."

Despite the barbarism of the times toward the infant faith, the law that all cemeteries, regardless of religious affiliation, were inviolable was rigidly observed. *Violatio sepulcri* was an act abhorrent to all Romans. Besides, it would have been fairly impossible to conduct such extensive digging without giveaway mounds of excavated dirt gracing the countryside.

In fact the Christians, as the Jews, would purchase the property before digging. The deed to it was recorded with the town register in the Tabularium.

An extraordinary point about this though is how the workmen were able to dig so blindly and yet avoid going beyond the legal dimensions of the property above.

How then precisely were the catacombs dug. First a stairway would be cut down and through the surface. Then a corridor was holed out usually about a yard in width and seven to eight feet in height. From here there would be cut more corridors, leading off the initial one, which would join with others parallel to the first. This would continue until the whole complex resulted perhaps by plan, more likely by Divine Providence for protection in the dark decades ahead, in a labyrinth.

Into the walls were carved *loculi* (niches) of varying dimensions depending upon the physical size of the deceased. As observed earlier the *loculus* would after the entombment be sealed with terra cotta, or, if the bereaved family could afford better, perhaps with marble, and in the case of greater affluence, perhaps alabaster. An inscription would often be carved into the material — perhaps the family and Christian name of the poor soul along with a

Christian symbol or two such as the fish, the dove, the olive branch, the Greek letters (chi rho ☧ the first two letters of the name Christ) or *IPHNH* (in Greek, "Peace").

Greek was the liturgical language of the primitive Church. In Greek the letters of the word fish (*IXΘUΣ*) are also the initials of the five words which translate to: Jesus Christ Son of God, Savior. Hence the symbolism of the fish. In later times the Latin words *In Pace* were added. You will notice other Latin graffiti too, such as *Sursum Corda* (lift up your hearts) and *Vivas in Christo* (may you live in Christ).

There were, besides the *loculi,* other types of final resting places down in the catacombs. The *arcosolium* was a much larger niche — about 10 feet long, 6 feet deep, with an arched ceiling perhaps 6 feet at its highest point.

The *sarcophagus* was rather a marble casket often resplendent in sculptured reliefs.

Cubiculum was a little room, often purchased as a family crypt with a capacity in its walls for as many as twelve bodies.

These and the *arcosolia* would often be covered with a layer of stucco and the stucco covered with frescoes of a religious theme.

One other arrangement was the *forma,* a grave cut into the cubiculum floor.

There were other forms of decoration for the burial places besides inscriptions and carvings. Small flasks containing perfumes would sometimes be fixed in the mortar. This pagan custom survives in our practice of placing fresh flowers on the grave. More sumptuous tombs were graced by mosaics. The oldest paintings in the catacombs date to the end of the 1st century. Scenes such as Abraham's sacrifice, Jonah and the whale, Moses drawing water from the rock, Noah, Daniel in the lion's den, Lazarus, and the Good Shepherd are predominant. There are also some portrayals of the Blessed Virgin and Child.

When a network of galleries filled up over the years, the keepers of the cemetery would dig a second stairway through the floor and begin to tunnel out another level. Therefore the upper tombs are of an earlier era than all the lower.

Pope Fabian (236-250) had divided Rome into seven regions each with one or more cemeteries. Priests were placed in charge of the upkeep of the cemeteries. Funds would be solicited from the rich to finance the digging and materials needed for the graves of the poor.

Wealthier converts like Flavius Clemens, martyred cousin of the Emperor Domitian, Priscilla, Lucina, and Domitilla permitted fellow Christians to share the subterranean graves on their own property.

The rising number of converts to Christianity resulted in the filling up of the second level, creating a need for a third, then a fourth, and so on.

Some of the catacomb sites, for example San Callisto, have seven levels of galleries, the shallowest being about 25 feet below ground level and the deepest more than 80 feet.

Adjacent catacombs would sometimes be merged into a large network by breaking through walls of adjacent cemeteries. San Callisto consists of several lesser sites. The total length of turning, twisting galleries lined with loculi from floor to ceiling has been estimated as low as ninety miles to as high as one thousand miles, which would exceed the length of all Italy.

Farmers tilling the soil as far as the old part of Ostia have come upon light shafts leading to Christian catacombs. Estimates of the number of bodies entombed in *Roma Sotteranea* range from 500,000 to the several millions. The latter figure is considered exaggerated by modern scholars since the Christian community in Rome was thought to be rather small in number up to the days of Constantine. Some church census accounts put the figure at 10,000 in the year 200, at 100,000 in the early 300's.

So we may assume that the dreary status quo of the catacombs went uninterrupted for the first two centuries of their existence. Solemn Christian funeral processions would daily wend their way along the Via Appia past pines and cypresses, the open and closed umbrellas of Rome's tree society, through rows of lavish *columbaria* landscaped with ilex and poplar, brightened with wreaths of acanthus and myrtle, to the melodies of hummingbirds and wild fowl, over enormous paving stones and under the sweeping arches of colossal aqueducts to the tranquil countryside asleep under Rome's uniquely azure skies.

Rows of cypresses dotted the area of the Christian sites as well. For this symbol of death dates to old Eturia, and was adopted first by pagan Rome and then by the Rome of the Christians.

Sacred burial rites, perhaps with funeral Mass, were celebrated for the repose of the soul of the departed and for the consolation of the bereaved. The faithful, chanting hymns, would pick their way through the dark foreboding streets of this city of the souls by the gentle light of tiny oil lamps.

These lamps (*luminaria*), made of iron or clay, continue to be found by the thousands down in the galleries. In fact that is today the best way to tour the passages because your eyes will then see the same endless hallways of inspiring gloom in the same aspect which the eyes of Peter and Paul and the other first bishops of Holy Mother Church saw them.

This isn't so easy to do anymore however. For the general public has access but to a small portion of the galleries of any of the sites and this is usually illuminated however bleakly, by the electric light and the flashlight of the guide.

Archaeological students however are granted such privilege and as such I was one day accompanied with my wife and sons through the fourth level of galleries of San

Callisto by an old friend assigned as a guide there, Brother Joseph Mascarenhas. With a knowledge of six languages and an inspiringly eloquent style of explaining the history and sanctity of the catacombs, Brother Joe's guide services were in constant demand and he thus had the pleasure of escorting the mighty and the humble through this hallowed ground. Because of the danger to the lungs and limbs mentioned before, Brother Joe and his fellow monks have to be reassigned to some warm dry clime after a tenure of just a few years. Our friend, a living saint we think, now ministers to the poor in Bombay.

He used to descend to the depths, in midsummer, with long, thermal underwear beneath his black soutane. Johnny, Frankie and Ronnie still chillingly recall one anxious moment we had in the depths during my research there when Brother Joe's lamp went out just as he had temporarily lost his way. This we imagined was the just horror that befell so many of the imperial police when in the late third and early fourth centuries they abrogated the law of the cemeteries' inviolability and raided the catacombs.

The Emperor Valerian was the first to interfere with Christian burial societies and forbade religious services in the catacombs.

Since in the last two centuries persecutions of Christianity had become more frequent and more violent and churches above ground were being raided and confiscated and the faithful rounded up, the catacombs now again took on the additional function of an underground church where Christians would come to pray at the tombs of the martyrs, especially at those of Peter and Paul *ad catacumbas,* and worship under the fear of impending doom.

As a result the Christians became more secretive and set up dummy entrances to the catacombs to deceive the police. Many entrances had to be sealed off and new ones established via trap doors in farmhouses of some brethren or of some sympathetic, trustworthy non-Christians.

Two accesses were always provided to any site. Look-
outs would be stationed at each so that a warning could be
passed along if the Emperor's hatchet men approached
one. The worshippers would then make their heart-pounding escape through the other.

There are eyewitness reports extant of such raids. Cyprian, the famous bishop of Carthage, explained in a letter
to a friend: "Xystus was put to death in the cemetery on
the eighth day before the Ides of August (August 6, 258)
and with him four deacons."

We know too from other documents that Cyprian,
five weeks later, while celebrating Mass and preaching in
the cemetery of San Callisto was, "beheaded when soldiers
suddenly forced their way into the assembly. The worshippers had surrounded their bishop to defend him at their
own peril but in vain." Another account reveals how Pope
Zephyrinus and St. Tarcisius, the young deacon, were
stomped to death while carrying the Sacred Host through
the corridors on their way to a Eucharistic celebration.

So we see the catacombs in this dark hour as a mole-
like city where both the living and the dead comprised the
population in a mutual mission to spread the Church of
Christ in the face of Roman might. And the Church grew.
The blood of the martyrs became Her very elixir of life.

Thousands of inscriptions in the catacombs demonstrate clearly that Christianity was finding its way into
some of the most illustrious families of Rome.

The persecution of Diocletian, lasting ten years, was
fiercer than all earlier ones. So many of the catacombs at
this time suffered the profanation of berserk pagan gangs.
Hymns of the sacred liturgies would often fade in a flash as
the brown hallways echoed the impassioned screams of
women and boys and girls, as the men and especially the
clergy would be slaughtered before their very eyes.

This carnage was to continue till the ascent upon the
throne of Rome by Constantine, when in 313, with his

edict of Milan, the Christians were granted freedom of worship and the faithful no longer had to practice the sacred rites clandestinely. The Church emerged triumphantly from the awful darkness, and public churches above ground began to spring up like daisies across the length and breadth of Rome Eternal. Splendid basilicas, partially in the ground, were also raised directly over the tombs of certain of the martyrs, such as San Sebastiano in the Via Appia, Sant'Agnese in the Via Nomentana, and Santa Priscilla on the Via Salaria.

But the catacombs continued to be used as places of burial too by those who wanted to sleep eternally near the tombs of the martyrs and as sites of worship by those who wanted merely to visit them for the boundless inspiration they afforded.

St. Jerome wrote in A.D. 354: "When I was a boy going to school in Rome, my classmates and I would go on Sundays to the sepulchers of the Apostles and Martyrs. Many times did we go down into the tunnels. These are excavated deep in the earth and contain on either hand as you enter, the bodies of the dead buried in the wall. It is all so dark there that the language of the prophet seems to be fulfilled: 'Let them go down quick into hell.' Only rarely is light allowed in to soften the gloom and then only through a hole not a window. You take each step carefully as, immersed in deep night, you recall Vergil's words: *Horror ubique animos, simul ipsa silentia terrent* (Everywhere there is horror, at the same time the silence itself terrifies the minds)."

Now the barbaric invasions of Rome were starting. It was becoming impossible to bury outside the walls. The barbarians while encamped in the campagna had time to ravage the cemeteries. Christians were now using the grounds of the churches, and the churches themselves, for final resting places. With the remains of most of the Church's supreme pontiffs to that time and those of all the other martyrs in serious danger, Pope Paul I began to translate the catacombs' precious relics to the city's churches.

The devout continued however to make pilgrimages to the Roman countryside to descend to the "hollows."

Then in the mid-eighth century when the Lombards and others sacked Rome, again and again the Christian cemeteries were prime targets as the barbarians carried off bones and relics of the saints for their own churches.

Popes in the 800's, beginning with Paschal, launched a massive reburial program. One inscription in the Church of Santi Apostoli tells that Pope Stephen VI in 886 helped carry many bodies here on his shoulders. A familiar sight in those days was wagonloads of human remains crawling solemnly along the highways, through the gates, past the battered traces of the grandeur of Rome, and across the city where the churches would serve as warehouses for the dead while graves were hurriedly being dug on Vatican Hill. The largest warehouse was Hadrian's pagan Pantheon, now a Christian church. As a result the Church acquired the name it is still known by: *Santa Maria dei Martiri.* In Vatican soil today, then, lie tens of thousands of souls who made the supreme sacrifice for the faith. This explains why that terrain is held in such reverence by Catholics today.

The picturesque Roman Campagna was now deserted. The abandonment of the catacombs was complete. Entrances were sealed either purposefully or accidentally by the shifting sands of time. Their locations were forgotten, not to be uncovered again until the 16th century, when workers in the countryside would go down into lightshafts and bring up huge slabs of marble for many uses.

In June 1578 some workmen digging for *pozzuolana,* a volcanic deposit useful for making cement came upon a subterranean cemetery by the Porta Salaria with many levels of frescoed galleries.

Now all of Rome, recently having been rescued from the intellectual void of the Dark Ages by the sun of the Renaissance, was abuzz with excitement.

Systematic excavations were commissioned. St. Phillip Neri for one, at the time of the Reformation, loved the catacombs and used to spend much time down in them in meditation. He favored the galleries under San Sebastiano as do I. For it was to this site — we may pinpoint the very crypt — that the bodies of Peter and Paul were transferred for security during the more vehement persecutions. Peter had been exhumed from his grave on Vatican Hill and Paul from his on the Via Ostiense. More than 600 graffiti in San Sebastiano corroborate the tradition.

One reads: "I, Tomius Coelius, have this day partaken of the *refrigerium* (a ceremonial meal) here at the tomb of Peter and Paul."

But the famous inscription of Pope Damasus fixed on the walls of the same small room are the most positive literary proof: *"Hic habitasse prius sanctos cognoscere debes nomina quisque Petri pariter Paulique requiris."*

Which means . . . "Here you should know that the saints once dwelt, you who are seeking the names of both Peter and Paul."

This Petrine and Pauline tradition is widely accepted as accurate by today's archaeologists.

I'm hard put to choose for second place between the Cemeteries of San Callisto, Sant'Agnese, and Santa Domitilla.

Sant'Agnese, of them all, has the most unopened tombs where the remains of Christians tormented and executed seventeen and eighteen centuries ago have gone undisturbed. The others for the most part reveal only row on row of empty loculi.

For the visitor to Rome on a short trip it would be unrealistic to hope to see the dozen or so catacomb sites now open to the public. My counsel, drawn from the experience of many inspiring days spent in underground Rome, would be to choose one from these four.

Today those of us with a profound interest in the catacombs stand deeply in the debt of the most celebrated of all practitioners of sacred archaeology, Giovanni Battista de Rossi, whose tireless and lifelong efforts are responsible for most of what we see and know of the catacombs.

The definitive work on the cemeteries which I can recommend enthusiastically for your personal library is: "The Roman Catacombs" by L. Hertling and E. Kirschbaum.

I'd like to add one further note of interest in this account if I may. And that is that in our own lifetime the catacombs rendered again to Mother Church a service as a place of refuge and resistance against a modern tyranny, Fascism.

For it was down in these burial places in the 1930's that Pope Paul VI as the young Monsignor Montini, held clandestine meetings for the Catholic student organization, FUCI, in its crusade against this new foe of God's Church and indeed of mankind.

When in Rome, then, do not fail to go *ad catacumbas,* the places which, more than any mighty basilica or the splendor of the Vatican, testify in an eternal, silent eloquence to the unwavering faith of Imperial Rome's Christian community. Where side by side the rich and the poor, the great and the meek, the young and the old, entered into the eternal joy of the Lord. No more moving sermon on the love of Jesus Christ has ever been preached.

Dominus vobiscum

St. Paul's Outside-the-Walls

XXX

The Churches

I love churches, always have. When I was a little boy from a devoutly Catholic family, my home lay in the late afternoon shadows of a magnificent gothic cathedral. Following the example of my older brothers, Ray and George, I became an altar boy. In those days I thought there was nothing better in life than the smell of incense, the sight of a priest in cassock meditating at a kneeling bench after Mass, stained glass windows, saintly statuary, flickering candles, all in an incredibly beautiful architectural setting.

Holy days, and especially Holy Week, were exciting and inspirational times for me, with their solemn ceremonies. The atmosphere was celestial when the mighty organ signaled the start of the ritual, the procession began, and the great choir praised God with Latin hymns. . . . *Gloria in Excelsis Deo.* . . . "Surely," I thought, "this is the kind of music they listen to in Heaven."

Even when there were no services I would be at the cathedral to say a rosary, or to follow the Way of the Cross, or simply to gape at this wondrous work of art that man had raised as an act of devotion to the Lord. I was enchanted by the medieval aura of the whole place and even at such a tender age had come to seek it out again and again as a place of tranquil refuge from the turbulence of daily life.

Thus, early on, I became fond of stone, and marble and mosaics and flying buttresses, and forged irrevocably my image of what a House of God ought to be. And so I come back to Rome where I can have my choice of nearly five hundred splendid stone churches which bring me back to the St. Patrick's of my boyhood and rejuvenate my spirit. If Rome had no Colosseum to offer, no Fora, no cafés, no fountains, I would still come just to pray in her great Christian shrines.

Even the most ambitious guide books handle but thirty or forty of the churches so that such a number would surely be beyond the scope of a volume like this. However, being familiar with a couple of hundred, we, my family and I, are eager to acquaint you with a few that delight us most.

In the early 1800's Pope Pius VII permitted the establishment of non-Catholic churches within the Holy City. Now there are about a dozen. Among them, three Episcopal (including St. Paul's Inside the Walls, so called to distinguish it from the mighty Basilica of St. Paul's Outside the Walls), two Methodist, a Presbyterian; one Baptist church, and one Synagogue, the beautiful Tempio Maggiore on the banks of the Tiber. The different Catholic rites — Armenian, Greek, Maronite, Slavonic, Byzantine — can all be found in this city of Peter and Paul.

Much of the character of Imperial Roman building came into Christian expression as throughout the city altars to Christ soared in triumph over pagan temples. Through her churches too, Rome demonstrates a shining devotion to the Madonna with almost a hundred bearing her name. Even the mayor and council lay a wreath at the column of the Blessed Virgin in Piazza di Spagna each December 8th, Feast of the Immaculate Conception, whereas the town fathers of antiquity paid similar homage to Venus who was then worshipped as *Mater Romae.*

That Rome is so photogenic is due in large part to her churches as their baroque domes glisten against the sky, and their statues atop the facades peer out over umbrellas of pine. May we recommend that you visit as many as you can. We feel safe in believing that if you stop in at those we are about to discuss you shan't be disappointed. But do go with the right attitude and a good disposition. Visit them not only for their spiritual nature but for their roles in the city's history, and for their wealth of art as well. Don't be like the impatient lady I overheard one day as she reboarded a tour bus in front of Santa Maria Maggiore: "If I see one more church I'll flip!"

We will take you first to some of Rome's original parishes where Peter and his friend from Tarsus must surely have celebrated the Eucharist on many occasions. Thence on a swing of some churches from the Rome of the monks or the Middle Ages, followed by a few of the Baroque Age, concluding with a number that are special to us for a variety of reasons. Incidentally the face of contemporary Rome is mostly the result of the Baroque artists of the eighteenth and nineteenth centuries.

One of the most unusual places to see in Rome is the aged Church of San Clemente, on Via di San Giovanni halfway between the Colosseum and the Lateran. On this site lived Clement, the fourth Bishop of Rome (88-98) who had known Peter. He gave over part of his papal residence for use as a church. Such house churches were already numerous in Rome and even before the Constantinian era there would be more than three hundred.

Clement suffered under the persecution of Trajan and was exiled to the Crimea where he eventually was martyred, by drowning, in the Black Sea. His relics were later returned and are now enshrined in the altar of the upper basilica. I specify "upper" for there are three levels to San Clemente. After the Edict of Milan a large basilica was erected in and over the ruins of the martyr's home. This was destroyed in a fire by the invading Normans in 1084. Two decades later Pope Paschal II built the present structure upon the debris of the fourth-century church. It consists of three naves separated by columns. The marble enclosure which you will see is the *Schola Cantorum* (Latin for School of Singers, i.e., the choir) so characteristic of the city's ancient churches. Transferred from the lower basilica the schola is richly ornamented in bas reliefs commissioned by Pope John II in 532. On either side is an *ambone* (marble lectern or pulpit), one for the reading of the Epistle, the other for the Gospel. Resting alongside the remains of Clement are those of Saint Ignatius, Bishop of Antioch, who was martyred just up the street, in the great arena.

Behind the altar is a throne for the titular cardinal. Each member of the Sacred College has a church in Rome. (For example Cardinal Cooke's church is San Giovanni alla Porta Latina, while Cardinal McIntyre of Los Angeles has Sant' Anastasia. Cooke's predecessor, Francis Spellman, raised funds in the states for some badly needed restoration work on San Giovanni in the fifties.) May we direct your attention also to the Chapel of the Passion decorated by the eminent artist Masaccio with scenes representing the life of Saint Catherine of Alexandria. Out in front of the church of Clement is a most charming atrium or courtyard. Regrettably the present main entrance to the church is not through the quaint fourth-century porch but from the side street. Many visitors inadvertently miss the court.

Raphael would come here often just to study the colors and the natural lighting effects. Some of the sarcophagi that you will see about the church are pagan antiquities, some Christian. Would you like to impress your friends on how to distinguish? Those engraved D.M. are pagan, the letters standing for the words *Dii Manibus* or Gods of the Lower World. The Christians played on this symbolism by engraving D.O.M. on their marble caskets,

for *Deo Optimo Maximo,* i.e., To the Greatest and Most
Excellent God.

Now for what attracts most about San Clemente. For
some centuries it has been in the charge of Irish Dominican
priests. In 1857 a Father Mulooly was carrying on some
restoration when workmen accidentally discovered the
long forgotten lower basilica. The pastor ordered formal
excavations which continue to our day. The digging has
continued through the fourth-century church right on
down to the rooms of Clement's house. More probing has
recently unearthed masonry work from as far back as the
Rome of the Kings, five and six centuries before the coming of our Lord. As a result it's not a cliché to say that here
one may walk back through time, but a fact. For when one
enters San Clemente he has just left a twentieth century
street and sped back nine hundred years (when the upper
basilica was consecrated). Descending a steep flight of
marble stairs just off the sacristy he finds himself in the
main aisle of a fourth-century church and seven hundred
more years have rolled by. At the end of the left aisle a
stairwell awaits that will take him down to the first-century
papal household and he will be standing where Peter and
Paul stood.

While we are down here we will direct you through the
various rooms with their pavement tiles in the herringbone
pattern so endemic to that period of Rome. The rushing
waters you hear are on their way to the Tiber through the
Cloaca Maxima. In exploring the remains of Clement's
home the excavators decided to break through one of the
walls and to their ecstatic delight they came upon another
dwelling with a *mithraeum* or chapel to the god Mithras.
Mithraism was a popular cult at the time. It competed with
Christianity for converts. You will observe in the chapel an
altar with a relief of the god slaying a bull. Notice too the
ledges where the cultists, all males, would sit while con-
suming the bread and wine which was also part of their lit-

urgy. They would do this and pray and meditate while soaking their feet in the blood gushing from the sacrificial victim.

So you have a first-century situation where people came to worship in two faiths, in adjoining homes, perhaps unknown to each other. Fantastic, no? Here in San Clemente one gets, I believe, the most vivid impressions of what the primitive Church was like. My boys will always drop whatever they're doing if they hear that I'm heading for San Clemente. They never tire of roaming around in this most unique place where Roman history reveals itself in layers.

The chill in the subterranean regions gets to you before too long so let us make our way back up to the middle church and I will show you about. Standing in the narthex of this old place I'm always reminded for some reason of the death scene in the movie Romeo and Juliet. The frescoes in the nave, astonishingly well preserved, are from the sixth through the eighth century and relate events in the life of the fourth pope. Try to imagine the solemnities that took place here over the course of several centuries. Envision the priest elevating the Sacred Host up there on the altar set in that wonderful apse.

All good things must come to an end, even our visit to San Clemente but it is right that this be so for there is much to be seen. You will be leaving Rome, sadly, in a few days so we must hurry.

Turn left with us now outside the triple church and walk uphill a few blocks to Santi Quattro Coronati. This church honors the earliest known Christian artists. Having refused to paint murals and carve icons for the dying pagan religion they were put to death by order of the Emperor. Like San Clemente, one of the original parish churches of the city, Quattro Coronati was restored under Pope Leo IV in the ninth century. With its extraordinary paintings in the Chapel of St. Sylvester, it is a favorite among students of art history. Sylvester is the patron of Rome's sculptors. The chapel is usually closed but we'll get the key from the nuns in the adjacent convent. I hope you will have the time to see one of the great but little known beauties of Rome while we are here, the thirteenth century cloister just outside the door on the left. You may also be interested in knowing that a Temple to Minerva from the sixth century B.C., stood here, the rubble of which is incorporated in this church's foundations.

For many devout pilgrims to Rome our next stop, *Santa Croce in Gerusalemme,* is almost as much a focal point of devotion as St. Peter's and the catacombs. This is the repository of Christendom's most sacred relics. As the church's name would suggest, a piece of the Holy Cross is housed here along with part of the *INRI* plate, two thorns from Christ's crown, one of the nails that fastened Him to the cross, and the finger that the doubting Apostle Thomas inserted in the wound of the Savior.

These Christian treasures were brought to Rome from the Holy Land by Emperor Constantine's mother, Helena, later canonized. The Emperor established this church expressly for housing the great relics. Helena, having once embraced the new faith, became a zealous collector of sacred objects, going to Jerusalem herself to supervise the efforts to retrieve them.

It was known that the Cross and all other materials used for the execution of Christ were buried in a ravine alongside the sepulcher provided for the body of the Messiah by Joseph of Arimathea. Under Jewish law such objects had to be buried since they were considered defiled by their use. For the next century this ditch was a site of worship for the followers of Jesus, causing considerable pagan and Jewish resentment and unrest. Emperor Hadrian, annoyed by it all, ordered the ravine filled in and soon after had a pagan temple erected over it to discourage Christians from approaching the site. What he was unwittingly doing however was clearly marking the spot for posterity. This accounts perhaps for the preservation of the wood which might otherwise have rotted in the ground, for thanks to the marble of the temple above, it was not subject to the erosive effects of rainwater.

Not too far from Santa Croce, in the vicinity of Santa Maria Maggiore, are the ancient churches of Santa Prassede and Santa Pudenziana. The saints were the daughters of a Senator Pudens who risked his political career by hosting Peter and Paul, and by actively helping their crusade. Paul refers to this gentleman in one of his epistles. Parts of the Senator's home, where clandestine services were conducted by the two Apostles, have been uncovered beneath the church of Pudenziana. Noteworthy here too is the lovely facade with reliefs representing the holy sisters, as well as the apse with a fourth century mosaic.

Over in Santa Prassede we will see columns from pagan temples, more mosaics, sarcophagi with the sisters' relics, a sanctuary of rare red marble from Egypt, and a beautiful courtyard. One unusual mosaic shows Peter and Paul with avuncular arms around the shoulders of the Senator's daughters. Several of our Roman friends are devoted to the memory of Pope St. Pius X and often come here where his relics lie.

To reach the remaining ancient parishes on our tour we must cross the river to Trastevere. Santa Maria, situated in one of Rome's finest squares, rises on the site of the papal palace of San Callisto who had a chapel here in 222. The original church was built over the ruins of the palace in 340 but was severely damaged in the invasion of the Goths in 408. This was the first of Rome's churches to be dedicated to the Virgin. The present church dates from 1130 and we like it for its mosaic facade, Romanesque bell tower, all the columns gathered from Imperial buildings, the ornate ceiling. My interest in archaeology is rewarded here by the first century pagan mosaics in the sacristy and by the knowledge that material from the Baths of Caracalla was used rather extensively in the construction of Santa Maria in Trastevere.

Through the neighborhood open-air market a street takes us to San Cosimato, now closed to the general public. The little sixth century porch entrance reminds one of San Clemente. If I see one of the Benedictine monks I know here I'll try to get us into the church for a few moments and especially to the twelfth century cloister, lovely even in neglect, so perfectly medieval.

On the other side of Viale Trastevere and down some back alleys is Santa Cecilia. The church we see now is mostly the ninth century work of Pope Paschal I. After the Saint appeared to him in a dream and told him where her remains, long thought hopelessly lost, might be found in the catacombs, Paschal had the body exhumed and transferred here. Of special interest to us is the house of Saint Valerian, husband of Cecilia, beneath the church. My wife would recommend to your attention the courtyard with its large urn fountain and the adjoining convent offering a very pretty thirteenth century cloister.

Three churches of the early middle ages that we know you would enjoy are: Santa Maria in Cosmedin, San Giorgio in Velabro, and Santa Maria in Ara Coeli. The first two are situated in the ancient Forum Boarium, the third upon the precipice of the Capitoline Hill.

Some sixth century Greeks, ironically fleeing *religious persecution* in their homeland, had come to this city where the phrase got its infamous start. They established a parish, *Santa Maria in Schola Graeca,* between the Circus Maximus and the river. They built a fine church upon the rubble to the pagan Greek demi-god, Hercules. In the twelfth century the church was renovated. Now it was so richly ornamented with dazzling mosaics and frescoes, instead of with the customary austere Greek icons that the Greek word *kosmetikos* (decorations) was attached to the name, resulting finally in Santa Maria in Cosmedin, or the Cosmetic Saint Mary's. We love its Schola Cantorum, and the columns, no two alike, from all over the Imperial city, with their variety of capitals, some Ionic, others Corinthian. Arabic and Greek are the liturgical languages here and the Byzantine rite is observed. There is a gallery for women, consistent with the Greek custom of segregating the sexes at worship. Ye of Irish ancestry take note. A portion of the skull of St. Patrick is contained in a reliquary here. (Students of antiquity, do not miss the mini basilica below, reached by a short flight of steps to the right of the central altar.) The colors of the frescoes are so delicate that one guide book calls the church the most gentle and feminine in Rome. Perhaps this explains its popularity with brides. The priests of Santa Maria in Cosmedin are very hospitable and eager to show you the eighth century mosaic of the Blessed Mother in the sacristy. Before we leave why don't you buy a stack of their stationery to add a touch of elegance to your future invitations and thank you notes. In the form of a greeting card, it has a line drawing on the front showing the exterior of the church, its Romanesque bell tower, and the baroque fountain in the park across the street.

Also down here in the Greek quarter, just around the corner is San Giorgio, and well worth a stop. This historic old church sits back only a couple of hundred yards from the river and often suffered flood damage whenever "Father" Tiber got into one of his moods. In a city obsessed with symmetry, in architecture San Giorgio is asymmetrical — as the ceiling clearly shows. Like its neighbor it uses columns from Roma Antica.

It is a relatively short and pleasant walk to our third church of the middle ages. *Ara Coeli* or Altar of Heaven is appropriately named you will agree, after the arduous ascent we must make to reach it — 124 marble steps. They were dismantled in the 1300's from the Temple to the Sun

God. Saint Helena lies here in eternal rest. Late in the life of Augustus Caesar, on this site, an oracle prophesied to him the coming triumph of a Hebrew child recently born of a virgin to whom the whole Roman world would someday bow. By order of the Emperor a temple to the Unknown God was erected where now stands Santa Maria in Ara Coeli.

In late afternoon, the pock-marked, pink brick facade, which never did get the marble veneer originally intended for it, is particularly pleasing to the eye. Before we depart from Rome, Camille always makes a last stop here, a) to pray in this lofty House of God and, b) to visit the little shop in the sacristy for some very inexpensive prints and water colors excellent for framing, which will make for wonderful gifts.

At the rear steps of the church overlooking the Forum, Gibbon would often sit in the evening. He found the Gregorian Chant of the Franciscan Monks wonderful music by which to write "Decline and Fall of the Roman Empire." Left of the main altar we find a door leading to the chapel of the renowned *Santo Bambino*. This wooden statuette carved by a Franciscan in Jerusalem out of olive wood is considered to have great healing powers, especially for children. The more zealous will insist that it was carved by angels. During the Christmas season it is displayed outside at the top of the steps. Occasionally the monks will take it on a sick call. Generally it is displayed in a glass case. All of the watches and rings and other jewelry with which it is decorated are tokens of gratitude from people miraculously cured of some malady. Letters of both petition and thanksgiving, from around the globe, you will notice stacked around the Infant.

If the fantasies of the baroque style appeal to you, accompany us to Santa Maria della Pace in the neighborhood of Piazza Navona. We are always impressed with its delicate air, its octagonal shape, and with the painting of Our Lady with the Infant Jesus (which is said to have bled when struck by a madman's rock) over the altar. Bramante's cloister of 1504 enhances the charm of della Pace.

Baroque fans really delight in our next church, Sant' Andrea della Valle. Excluding St. Peter's and the Pantheon's cupolas, Sant' Andrea's dome is Rome's largest. Even with its facade blackened by the exhaust of the thousands of vehicles that pass it daily, this work by the indefatigable Carlo Maderno is most imposing. Popes Pius II and III repose here beneath extraordinary paintings by Domenichino on the life of Sant' Andrea. Opera lovers return often to view the Attavanti chapel, remembered as the scene of the first act of *Tosca.*

Il Gesù, Jesus' church, is exemplary of baroque design with a double-storied facade and is the main church of the Jesuit Society. Once inside, our attention will be arrested by the great dome, and then by the gold sarcophagus of the order's founder, Saint Ignatius, beneath the ornate high altar. Ignatius prayed in a cell to be found in the cloister of the Gesù. On New Year's Eve in this 1568 church one may see Romans of all classes and every walk of life worshipping at the special rites offered to welcome the coming twelve months.

Piazza del Popolo offers no less than three outstanding churches. If we enter through the Porta Flaminia, as we should, just inside the gate on the left we will come to Santa Maria del Popolo. Sitting at the foot of the Pincian Hill and in front of Nero's burial place, this Santa Maria is virtually a gallery of great art. Bramante, Raphael, and Bernini are represented here. But the church is often visited today by fans of that artist who is only just recently receiving the recognition long due him, Michelangelo da Caravaggio (1564-1610). Now considered the giant of western realism in painting, Caravaggio exhibits two of his works here, one his unforgettable portrayal of the conversion of

Paul. For more Caravaggios run, don't walk, to San Agostino thence to San Luigi dei Francesi where you will discover three. Continue your Caravaggio hunt someday in the art galleries of the Vatican and the Villa Borghese.

Across the huge square, witness the *gemini,* identical twin churches from the mid-1600's, flanking the Via del Corso. Santa Maria del Montesanto on the left is so called for the friars from the Sicilian town of Montesanto who keep the church. Over the main altar is a sixteenth century icon of Our Lady. At this altar on August 10, of 1904, young Angelo Roncalli, having completed his seminary studies in the Holy City, was ordained a priest. Angelo, still a farm boy at heart, probably laughed the most at the tired, old joking forecast at every ordination: "Someday you will be a pope." In reality he was taking the first step of a long holy journey — in geography but a couple of miles — to the throne of Peter. People of every religion, of every ideology, of every age in every nation around the world would forever love him and remember him as the good Pope John XXIII.

This church and her twin, Santa Maria dei Miracoli, were the creation of those late Renaissance greats, Carlo Fontana and Lorenzo Bernini.

Rome has another set of twin churches, Santa Maria di Loreto and Santissimo Nome di Maria, on the edge of the Trajan Forum just off Piazza Venezia. The former was built as the guild church of the Baker's Association and was opened in the Jubilee Year of 1550. Not all the churches are parish churches. Many others like Santa Maria di Loreto were erected as houses of worship for the various guilds. Santa Maria dell'Orto was commissioned by (so help me) the local spaghetti makers, while San Giuseppe Falegname served the carpenters, and so on.

Santissimo Nome is a twin only in design not in age, having been completed in 1738. Originally called Santa Maria di Vienna, it celebrated the liberation of Vienna from the Turks in 1683 by King Sobieski of Poland. Statues of saints line the tops of the facades, crowned by attractive octagonal domes, over which Peter, upon the column of Trajan, strains to look toward Vatican City.

We must leave the walled-in part of Rome by way of the Porta Pia and travel along the consular highway, Via Nomentana to Number 324 if we wish to see the church my wife insists is the loveliest of all, Santa Costanza. Upon arriving however we find first the seventh century Sant' Agnese with its beautiful wooden ceiling and decorations taken from the catacombs below where there are many still undisturbed early Christian graves.

Set in the cloistered gardens out back is the church of Santa Costanza, with the quality of a delicate jewel. This early Christian sanctuary, circular in shape like the mausolea of Hadrian and Augustus, was originally the sepulcher of Constantina, daughter of the benign Emperor. Never shall you forget the charm of this place. In the apse is an impressive sarcophagus of red porphyry, a copy of the original casket of the princess which is now in the Vatican collection. The Saint's remains have been transferred to a crypt beneath the altar. This enchanting church in-the-round has a cupola supported by twenty-four slender columns, and fourth century pagan mosaics with scenes of people dancing on grapes for the preparation of wine. Of all Rome's churches, we are now standing in the most popular one among brides. What girl would not love such a storybook wedding in an imperial mausoleum, now a Christian chapel, bedecked for the occasion in lush, green carpeting, with its altar graced by endless flowers, with elegant gold chairs of seats upholstered in green velvet for the bridal party, and kneeling benches draped in purple?

Returning to the Porta Pia let us proceed along the Via Venti Settembre until we reach the corner of the Four Fountains. On the far left corner is the delightful San Carlino alle Quattro Fontane, an amazing work by Borromini in 1638. Wanting to underscore the incomparable splendor and magnitude of St. Peter's, Borromini built this church within the exact dimensions of the floor plan of any one of the four supporting piers for the great basilica's cupola. So large is St. Peter's then, Borromini was saying, that one pilaster could contain a sizable church.

The sacristan appears grumpy but is really an adorable old guy so don't be afraid to ask him for a look at the sweet courtyard with its double-deck portico. Go ahead, ask him. Whenever I come to San Carlino and see the aged gentleman I think: "What a serene way to have passed one's years, tending to this little holy place, a haven of calm at one of Rome's busiest junctions." Buy a package of slides or some postcards of the church since it is very difficult to photograph both inside and out.

Sant' Eusebio always pleases us, especially on January 17 when the church becomes a menagerie. On this day the Romans bring their pets here for a special blessing. Some kind priests in recent years have been going out on the same day to Rome's ruins to bless all the alley cats who can't make it down to Sant' Eusebio on their own very well.

San Benedetto is special to us. This little medieval church in Trastevere has a painting of the Madonna beneath which Benedict prayed the daily office, and an exquisite brick campanile. Furthermore, it is on the site of Benedict's house and a nun will show us, upon request, the Saint's monastic cell with the stone he used for a pillow.

Our family's adopted patron saint is Anthony of Padua, for many reasons. For this reason, and for the urn of precious green Egyptian marble beneath a side altar, and for the church's art, we go often to Sant'Antonio dei Portoghesi.

This little tour of Catholic churches will terminate in the Jewish Ghetto of all places, where we come to little San Gregorio. It is known to the Romans as the Jewish Chris-

310 ROME THE ENCHANTED CITY

tian church for it is frequented by inhabitants of the Ghetto who converted to Catholicism. We favor it because we can go there on a Sunday now and then and worship with many of our friends from this quarter.

Ite, missa est

XXXI

The Basilicas

Pilgrims of the very early Middle Ages revered the many holy places of Rome and in particular those renowned shrines which came to be known as the Seven Pilgrimage Churches. Ever since the first Jubilee Year (or Holy Year) in 1300, one may gain a special indulgence by visiting all seven sites between Vespers of one day and sunset of the next. These seven houses of God are: San Sebastiano ad Catacumbas, Santa Croce in Gerusalemme, San Lorenzo Fuori Le Mura, and the four Patriarchal, or major, Basilicas — Santa Maria Maggiore, San Giovanni in Laterano, San Paolo Fuori Le Mura, and San Pietro in Vaticano. True to our good Catholic upbringing my wife and I, soon after our return to Rome each year, take our sons on this pilgrimage in order to gain the special spiritual benefits. But I must say we have a much easier go of it in our Fiat than did our forebears on foot.

The first of the seven we discussed in our coverage of the catacombs; the second, in the segment on Rome's churches; and the last will be taken up alone in the chapter that follows.

Therefore we shall begin this account with San Lorenzo which, as its full name indicates, lies beyond the old

Roman walls. On your way to Tivoli and its rich villas you will pass by this holy and historic place and you ought really to give it some of your time. In 330 Constantine had this basilica built over the tomb of poor Saint Lawrence, archdeacon of Rome, who was martyred in 258 under the demonic Valerian by being roasted alive on a gridiron. Later on, in the seventh century, another large church was built, orientated in the opposite direction, over the tomb of another martyr. The apses of these two churches abutted each other. Devastated by attacks of the Saracens in the 800's, both churches were restored and altered. Then under Pope Honorius III the two adjoining churches were made into one very long basilica by removal of the apses. This accounts for the unique edifice we visit today. It is really two churches in one. Ancient ionic columns line the endless center aisle, and beautiful frescoes of the last century brighten the old walls. Tenth century mosaics provide the pavement and four columns from antiquity support the canopy over the central altar, beneath which rest the earthly remains of Saints Lawrence and Stephen. Pius IX so loved this place he asked to be entombed in the lovely chapel in the vestibule.

This is the one Roman church which suffered physical harm in World War II when on July 19, 1943, allied bombers missed their mark, the nearby railroad yards, and caused extensive damage to the venerable basilica. One of my all-time favorite photographs is one of Pope Pius XII standing at the site minutes after the tragedy, his white soutane splattered with the blood of the casualties, arms outstretched in a marvelous and moving paternal gesture as he tries to comfort the frightened residents of the neighborhood who cluster desperately around him. Just behind the Holy Father in the picture can be seen a future pontiff, Monsignor Giovanni Montini, then Pius' top aide, now Pope Paul VI. All of Rome was heartsick at the damage to this sacred place and the Vatican was quick to undertake

Interior scene of the Basilica of St. John Lateran

its restoration which was complete and miraculous. Nearby is the large cemetery of Campo Verano. So San Lorenzo is the scene of many funeral Masses. Whenever we go we make an effort to visit the simple but charming Romanesque cloister of the eleventh century which is part of this shrine.

What would a visit to Rome be without a stop at very old Santa Maria Maggiore? According to tradition the original church on this site was built by divine inspiration in 352. Pope Saint Liberius, the tradition claims, had a vision, one summer night, of the Blessed Mother. She requested him to build a large church in her name at the place where he would find snow the next day. On the following morning the city buzzed with talk over the mysterious snow that fell during the night on the crest of the Esquiline Hill. Liberius hurried up from the Lateran and at once took a stick to trace in the snow the outline for the church he would build here. Funds were granted for the project by a wealthy man named John. One of Rome's loveliest customs takes place here on the 5th of August each year. The miraculous snowfall is recalled when at the consecration in the Mass thousands of white rose-petals are dropped from the dome.

Large parts of that original basilica are incorporated in the current structure whose majestic travertine facade is from 1741. Here you will see one of the most attractive *loggias* in Rome, and surely the highest bell tower, which commemorates the return of the Popes from Avignon in 1377.

Santa Maria, as do the other three patriarchal basilicas, has a papal altar upon which only the Bishop of Rome may celebrate Mass. We mount the flowing staircase and pass through the lofty vestibule to enter this beloved shrine of Mary. Athenian columns are the main aisle's guard of honor. The whole interior is a spectacle of beauty and elegance, the floor of cosmatesque marble, the ceiling gilded with the first gold from America, the rich mosaics from the fifth century some of the finest examples of early Christian art. Over the papal altar is an ornate bronze canopy which is held aloft by four columns from Hadrian's Villa. The altar itself is the covered sarcophagus of the patrician who financed the original basilica. Below the altar repose the remains of Matthew the Apostle. Down in the crypt called the Confession (not to be confused with the confessional) is the kneeling image of Pius IX. The Confession, along with the papal altar as we mentioned above, and the *Porta Santa* (the Holy Door which is opened only in Jubilee Years such as 1950, 1975, 2000, etc.) are common denominators to the four major basilicas. In Santa Maria it is the farthest left door that is the holy one.

Descending the Esquiline and using a great obelisk as our beacon we reach, after a fifteen-minute walk, or a half-hour ride (such is the state of Rome's vehicular traffic), the Basilica of St. John in the Lateran. Over the entrance engraved in the expressive facade is the Latin proclamation: *Omnium Ecclesiarum Urbis et Orbis Mater et Caput.* (Of all the Churches of the City and the World, the Mother and Head.) From an enormous piazza on the Caelian Hill we can study the awe-inspiring edifice, its front crowned by giant marble likenesses of Christ and His Apostles, with Judas conspicuous by his absence. Orientated, as are all the major basilicas, toward the east, San Giovanni is especially splendid when drenched in the first splashes of sunlight coming up over the Alban Hills.

This truly is the Mother and Head of all churches by virtue of it being the first commissioned by the Emperor Constantine after three long centuries of the darkness of the catacombs. Since that era it has remained the Cathedral of the Bishop of Rome, and as a result enjoys in many respects even a higher status than St. Peter's great church over on *Mons Vaticanus.*

We cross the square and enter through the large portico at the extreme right of which we find the *Porta Santa*. The two huge bronze doors, through which we shall soon pass, watched Caesar and Cicero and other statesmen come and go many times — not here but in their original habitat, the *Curia* or Senate Building, cross town in *Forum Romanum*. Now we step inside to be overwhelmed by the marble splendor and vastness of the basilica. Most impressive to my family and me is the immensity of the statues of the Apostles and Evangelists which seem to be gazing down on us from every angle. Of great interest to us too are the foundations of Roman military barracks, twenty-five feet below the pavement, which we were privileged to see through my status as a scholar in Roman Civilization at the Academy.

Here the main altar consists, in part, of the wooden table upon which Peter offered the Holy Sacrifice and below which, for seventeen centuries, have been enshrined the heads of Peter and Paul. Supporting the canopy are four bronze columns said to have been transferred to Rome from the Temple of Solomon in Jerusalem by Titus. Pilgrims have always been drawn to St. John's too because it is another repository of a great number of Christianity's most cherished relics. In the Confession kneels Pope Martin V (1417-1431). Extraordinary thirteenth century mosaics adorn the apse while all about are the tombs of popes and cardinals. Noteworthy too, I think, is that for an extensive restoration in the 1300's much marble was taken from the already ravaged pagan Temple of Antoninus and Faustina in the Forum. And it wouldn't be a bad idea to ask the sacristan to open one of the side chapels for a look at a dramatic *Pietà* by Montauto.

A side entrance to the basilica has a grandeur all its own, boasting twin bell towers and a wonderful loggia. When the Pope comes here for Good Friday services he uses this entrance. Adjacent is the celebrated rotunda called the Baptistry of St. John's, with a deep baptismal font of green marble of the type used in early times for baptism by total immersion. As so many of Rome's renowned churches do, San Giovanni also offers an eye-pleasing cloister, a haven of piety, laid out by Pietro Vassalletto seven centuries ago.

Upon exiting from the cathedral our attention is arrested first by the sweeping vista that includes the old wall and the Porta San Giovanni to our right, then by the baroque beauty of the Church of Santa Croce in the distance, and lastly by the monument of the mendicant St. Francis and his fellow friars across the square.

But to our left waits something very special, spiritually and historically, the Chapel of the *Scala Santa* or Holy Stairs. In 326 St. Helena went to the Holy Land and had the twenty-eight marble steps leading to the upper level of Pontius Pilate's gubernatorial mansion dismantled and sent to Rome. For on the first Good Friday, nineteen and a half centuries ago, Jesus ascended these steps to be arraigned and sentenced, and then descended them on the way to His crucifixion. They are held in great veneration by the faithful and the more devout can be seen daily climbing the staircase on their knees, while offering a prayer at each step. At the top of the stairs we will find an old chapel which was once the private oratory of the popes and is still referred to as *Sancta Sanctorum* (the Holy of Holies) for its treasury of precious relics. Inside is a painting that tradition attributes to St. Luke.

For the next to last stop in this pilgrimage we must leave the ancient part of the city and go beyond Aurelian's fortifications to reach the imposing, the mighty, Basilica of St. Paul's Outside the Walls, on the Via Ostiense. Never will we grow blasé about this great temple. My professors at the academy maintained that of all the Christian basilicas, it is St. Paul's which most retains the architectural character of the old structures in the Forum, the basilicas of Aemilia, of Julius Caesar, of Maxentius. The power of their suggestion enables me to envision, whenever I first enter St. Paul's great hall, toga-clad lawyers and judges, striding gracefully among the columns, lobbying here and there in little groups, senators being followed by their amanuenses and buttonholed by harried constituents. Soon the spell is shattered though, for as my eyes adjust to the lack of light I begin to see the dramatic Christian symbols that surround me.

To enter we had to pass through the largest atrium in Rome, a colossal colonnade of dazzlingly white marble. We had to pass left or right of the powerful effigy of Paul in the center of the court, with the fire of God in his eyes, and the burdens of his mission and his trials on his broad but sagging shoulders. Panels of colored Capadoccian marble highlight the lower portion of the facade while above there glistens the famous gigantic mosaic of the Divine Master, flanked by His faithful servants Peter and Paul. "Peter and Paul," "Peter and Paul." It's a recurring theme in Rome.

Constantine had, around 324, ordered a basilica erected over each of the tombs of the two Apostles. St. Peter's rose on the Vatican while out here, on the sea road, the basilica to Paul began to take form. And what a masterpiece of architecture it was. And yet it was not enough. Increasing throngs of pilgrims from abroad and a growing Christian community at home moved the Emperor Valentinian II in 386 to raze the old and build a much larger church. This wonderful and wondrous shrine was to survive the ravages of time, the buffeting of storms, the vicissitudes of history to the summer of 1823 when it was tragically and heartbreakingly destroyed by a fire. Rebuilding was begun at once thanks to generous funds provided by the Roman people themselves. We like to examine the prints of old St. Paul's in the sacristy. What a loss to Rome, to the world. Yet the new St. Paul's ranks as one of the most awesome religious edifices on earth.

Back inside the five-aisled basilica we take a crash program in papal history, via the large mosaic medallions, on the upper walls, of Peter and his two-hundred and sixty-two successors, with the image of the reigning pontiff illuminated. Another of Rome's endless legends tells us that when St. Paul's runs out of space for papal medallions the world will come to an end. Frankie has come up with a prognostication of two centuries while Johnny and Ron think the world has somewhat less time than that.

Flanking the steps that lead to the high altar are still two more tremendous statues of Paul and his aging bishop. Many of the columns here were salvaged from the old church and they, before that, had been rescued from the Basilica Aemilia on the Via Sacra.

The main altar, for use only by the Holy Father, covers the tomb of the martyr. (His body lies here, Peter's beneath his Vatican basilica. Don't turn back! It is only their heads that are kept in San Giovanni. Such dismemberment of the martyrs' remains was common practice in the early Church.) Ornamenting the apse is a gleaming mosaic of Christ and the Evangelists. When one descends into the Confession he may pray close by the tomb of the great Apostle. As always, a cloister of monastic serenity awaits. Here it is through the door to the right of the altar. Whenever I come out to St. Paul's, which is often, I have difficulty in leaving, for the atmosphere is so conducive to prayer and meditation that I feel as though I'm breaking up a warm conversation with God.

But we have miles to go before we sleep — about four. On to St. Peter's, to complete the pilgrimage. . . .

Orate pro nobis

St. Peter's in Rome

XXXII

The Basilica of St. Peter

Rome is the Queen of Cities and has a crown to prove it — the massive, sparkling white dome of St. Peter's Basilica. From the terrace in the Pincian gardens, from the pretty Park of the Orange Trees on the Aventine, from the enchanting Bridge of the Angels one sees this jewel by Michelangelo, the loftiest achievement of the Renaissance, floating in the blue, high above the monuments and palaces and other churches of the city. To appreciate though, just how much St. Peter's cupola dominates the skyline of Rome, one must view it from some distant hill town or while driving in on one of the consular roads.

It is Sunday morning and the church bells are singing their praises of the King of Kings. The bambini are arrayed in their finest, white shoes freshly polished, rosaries and prayerbooks in tow. The bigger girls in the family, their Mediterranean beauty enhanced by long delicate black or white mantillas, have the little ones in hand. While the really bigger girls are in the strong protective hands of their well-tailored courtiers. And all are under the proud and watchful eyes of Mamma and Papà who bring up the rear. They are on their way to the Vatican for Mass, their path guided by the soaring dome which serves as a lantern to the faithful to come worship at the greatest shrine in all Christendom.

From every direction the people converge on St. Peter's Square, welcomed by a hundred saintly figures in stone upon the colonnade of Bernini, and by Christ and His Apostles who watch from the top of Maderno's facade.

We will approach from the left bank of the Tiber along the modern Via della Conciliazione. After a short distance we pass on our right the impressive church of Santa Maria in Traspontina. The walk becomes ever so slightly more arduous now as the street slopes upward to Vatican Hill. Beneath all the obelisk-shaped lampposts which line this boulevard are stone benches where we may take the load off our feet for a spell. All along too there are cafés where we may do the same and have a cool drink at the same time. But if we are hoping to receive Communion at Mass we will give these and all the *gelati* and softdrink wagons a pass. It might be a good idea, time permitting (and it usually is since there's a Mass starting every few minutes at one of the many altars in St. Peter's), to browse in the souvenir and religious article shops on Conciliazione where you can gather some last-minute items; medals to be blessed by the Pope, a guide book of St. Peter's and Vatican City, a lace mantilla, or more film, of which you never have enough in this wonderfully photogenic place.

Having left the last of the shops behind us, we cross the busy traffic circle and enter into the warm maternal embrace of Holy Mother Church. Bernini represents that embrace with his two mighty colonnades which reach around the sprawling piazza, gently gathering all of the people in it to bring them inside the most glorious of all God's houses on earth.

Before we enter the Basilica let us contemplate first the many wonders of her spacious front yard, which stretches more than a thousand feet in length and in width nearly seven hundred, and which can hold about a third of a million people for such momentous events as an Easter Sunday Papal Mass, or a solemn procession preceding a canonization ceremony, or a papal coronation or funeral. That towering brown needle in the center of Piazza di San Pietro is a good starting point. This obelisk, perhaps forty centuries old, was removed to Rome from Heliopolis by order of the Emperor Caligula. Nero used it to decorate the dividing island of his race track which stood just to the left of where St. Peter's now stands. It was the mute witness to much spectacle and much savagery, including the crucifixion of Peter. Where Peter was buried, a short distance away, Constantine on November 18, 326 opened the first basilical church in honor of the Apostolic prince, with the main altar positioned directly above the martyr's tomb. This shrine was to survive a thousand years until that patron of the arts, Nicholas V, alarmed by the extent of the deterioration, ordered it razed, to be replaced by one of even greater splendor.

Though he died soon after the decision, Nicholas had set in motion the great machinery that would result in the "new" St. Peter's, as the Romans still call it. When the fierce but dynamic Julius II came to the pontifical throne the project received its greatest impetus. He recruited the genius Bramante to design and direct the work. When Julius died in 1513 and Bramante the next year, the building program passed into the hands of other popes and other architects. The great endeavor was plagued and impeded by bickering, controversy, indecision. Then under Paul III in 1547, the aging Michelangelo was put in charge of operations, accepting only after he was assured absolute and full authority and carte blanche for all his ideas. Michelangelo refused all monetary payment and insisted on working solely for, "the love of God, the Blessed Mother, and Peter." Determined to complete a church worthy of the Apostle, Michelangelo labored day and night under five popes for the last seventeen years of his life, until one cold February night in 1564 while sitting before the fire in his lonely apartment in the medieval tower behind Trajan's Forum he quietly slipped into eternal sleep. But he had been responsible for the greatest progress thus far on the Basilica and future architects, like Vignola, followed his ideas faithfully. The great cupola conceived and planned by the Florentine was completed under Domenico Fontana in the summer of 1588.

Meanwhile in 1585, Pope Sixtus V had asked Fontana to perform the engineering miracle of transferring the obelisk, still standing in its imperial location, though the circus had vanished, a couple of hundred yards to a point directly in front of the main entrance to St. Peter's.

Hundreds of horses, thousands of men, countless miles of rope, an elaborate network of pulleys, levers and scaffolds were needed for the task of lowering the three-hundred-ton Egyptian monument, pulling it to its new location and lifting it into position there. When the day arrived for this final step in the project, all of Rome turned out for duty as sidewalk superintendents. So precarious was the operation however — one slip, one miscalculation and the spire would shatter in a billion pieces wiping out four thousand years in one terrible moment — that Sixtus forbade anyone in the crowd to speak lest they impair the concentration of the workmen. With beasts and men tugging on the ropes with all their might, the obelisk, now crowned with an iron cross containing a fragment of the True Cross, began to rise, casting a long silhouette against the cloudy sky. When it was set at about a sixty-degree angle with the pavement, trouble struck. The ropes had stretched from the awful strain, and were in danger of snapping. It became possible neither to lift it any farther nor to lower it gently to the ground. Risking the consequences of death promised by Sixtus, a sailor in the throng yelled *"Acqua alle corde!"* ("Pour water on the ropes!"). He was escorted to the fore by police and questioned on the engineering logic of his suggestion. He explained how this was often done on ships and at length convinced Fontana and his staff. Doused in copious amounts of cold water, the ropes contracted just enough for the job to be completed. Church bells across Rome rang out the good news and the sailor was the toast of the Eternal City that night. "Whatever is your wish it shall be granted, my son," the Pontiff said to the sailor. It happened that the young man's family owned property in the south on which there were many palm trees. He asked that his family be allowed to provide the palms for services in the Basilica on Palm Sunday. To this day the hero's descendants still so serve St. Peter's.

In 1817 around the base of the monument on the pavement were traced the different directions of the winds and the twelve signs of the Zodiac by the astronomer, Gigli.

Two roaring baroque fountains sending jets fifty feet into the air provide the musical background for the daily show in St. Peter's Square, as their waters rise and fall back into great basins splashing over into miniature lakes at the bottom.

As you face the Church, the one on the right is the work of Carlo Maderno in 1613. It was perfectly matched in 1670 by Carlo Fontana, on the left side of the piazza. But the spectacular effect of the piazza is really owed to the keyhole-shaped, marble enclosure by the cavalier, imaginative Bernini. This approach to St. Peter's, requiring ten years (1657-1667) under the patronage of Pope Alexander VII, consists of two slender curved porticoes each composed of four parallel rows of columns, totaling two-hundred and eighty-four columns, fifty-two feet tall. From a focal point on each side of the square, lines were drawn along which the four columns of each set were erected. My boys like to show our guests these two points, each marked with an oval stone engraved with the words, *Centro del Colonnato* (center of the colonnade). So perfectly engineered and aligned were these columns that standing on either focus one gets the illusion that there is but a single row, as the columns in the back stand precisely behind those in front. The enormity of these porticoes cannot be fully grasped unless one realizes that in the central aisle of each, two automobiles may be driven abreast. In fact the space was laid out so that horse-drawn carriages could in terribly hot or inclement weather bring their passengers up to the steps of the Basilica sparing them the long trek across the square.

Upon reaching the gentle stairway to the church we see two giant stone figures on either side, to our right St. Peter and across from him St. Paul.

Ascending to the basilica we lose sight of the great dome as the travertine facade, now beige from the discoloration of the centuries, looms before us. Across the frieze we read the Latin dedication: *In Honorem Principis Apost. Paulus V Burghesius Romanus Pont. Max. AN. MDCXII PONT. VII* (In Honor of the Prince of the Apostles [by] Paul V of the Roman Borghesi, Pontifex Maximus, in the year 1612, seventh year of his Pontificate). Pope Paul V had the fortune of seeing the facade completed and the opportunity to so engrave it.

Now we stand at the main entrance to the basilica. Just over us is the Papal Loggia or Balcony of Benedictions from which the Supreme Pontiff on special occasions addresses the multitude and imparts his blessing to the City and to the World, and from which the name of a newly elected Pope is proclaimed.

I'm often struck at this point with the thought that St. Peter's true splendor and greatness comes not from its architectual immensity nor its artistic excellence but from the fiery zeal of Christian belief that compelled its creation.

Let us now enter this great and sacred place which was

a century and a quarter in the building. Stepping into the vestibule we watch the centuries meet, as to our left we can discern the ancient and dramatic equestrian statue of Constantine while to our right rides Charlemagne. These two benefactors of the Throne of Peter were separated in time by five-hundred years. Overhead, pigeons flutter back and forth in the upper reaches of the elegantly and lavishly ornamented vestibule, longer itself than most large churches, St. Patrick's Cathedral in New York for one. To the right of the central door is the Porta Santa, open only in a Jubilee Year. Since 1975 has been proclaimed such a year by the Holy Father a few words about this tradition are warranted at this point, I should think.

The Old Testament tells us of the Jewish custom of consecrating every fiftieth year to God by pardoning all debts. This year was called *Yobel* which, after much corruption, comes out as "Jubilee" in English. In 1300 Pope Boniface VIII declared that for all who came to Rome to pray at the great shrines there would be a plenary indulgence, or full pardon of all their sins. Boniface had intended an interval of a hundred years between Jubilees but under later popes this was reduced to fifty and finally to twenty-five. Throughout the centuries since, they have come, the Germans, the French, the Hungarians, the people of every nation on the continent, to receive this extraordinary spiritual dividend, swelling the city's population by as much as two million.

Holy Year ceremonies begin with a reading of a papal proclamation in all of the major basilicas on Ascension day of the preceding year. For our Lord passed through the Doors of Paradise on that day and the Jubilee Year represents the opening of those doors for all the faithful.

In late December the marble slab sealing the Porta Santa in each basilica is removed. On Christmas Eve, the Holy Father officially and ritualistically launches the Holy Year by striking the Holy Door of St. Peter's with a golden hammer chanting "Open the Doors of Justice for Me and I shall enter Thy House O Lord." Then he intones the solemn hymn *Te Deum* and passes through the door, followed by members of the hierarchy, to celebrate midnight Mass. After this he bestows his Apostolic Blessing to the congregation. (How I wish we could have been here this past Christmas Eve to witness it all. We had to content ourselves with watching it in our house in Jersey via satellite television.)

The ritual is repeated by cardinals, designated by His Holiness, at the other basilicas.

Throughout the year the Jubilee is marked with special solemn ceremonies. It is the hope of the Supreme Pontiff that the faithful all over the world will be motivated to come to Rome on this occasion, however great the sacrifice required, to draw inspiration from the shrines and relics and spiritual history of the Holy City and from the fervor of fellow pilgrims. Confession and Communion are required during the pilgrimage in order to derive the full measure of the indulgence.

On the following Christmas Eve, the Holy Year is officially closed by the Pope with more ritual. With a golden trowel he places mortar on the threshold of the Holy Door in the Vatican Basilica and sets a few gilded bricks in place while reciting a prayer of thanksgiving to God. A canvas is then used to cover the initial masonry work and within a few days Vatican workmen come and seal the entrance, this time until the year 2000 A.D.

Passing at last through the center door we feel the tremendous emotional impact from our first glimpse of the interior of the great church. Our attention is caught at once by the towering bronze baldachino over the main altar in the distance. Then we notice the rays of sunshine streaking through the dome and falling softly on the altar and the pavement around it. And we think to ourselves that the plans for this magnificence must have been conceived not in the minds of the Bramantes, the Michelangelos, the Berninis, but exclusively in the mind of Almighty God. For the place has the look of the forever about it, the unmistakable aura of the celestial.

When we recover sufficiently from the initial amazement we begin to observe individual features. I once complained to some friends of ours who work in the Vatican that no matter how often I visit St. Peter's and regardless of how long I stay each time, I wind up with a sense of inferiority, being unable to grasp the full meaning of the place, to do intellectual justice to its historical significance, esthetic justice to its artistic triumphs, and spiritual justice to its sanctity. They assured me that this was normal but that I ought to ignore such feelings for St. Peter's is simply beyond total human comprehension for even one who spends his lifetime at it.

Thus we go on trying. Still standing just inside the entrance we look up to see a cornice which goes throughout the church and below which are bold Latin letters with familiar passages like: "Whatsoever Thou Shalt Bind On Earth Shall Be Bound in Heaven. . . ." Don't be alarmed if walking along this ridge more than one hundred feet above us are a few men. These are the *San Pietrini* or the workmen whose task it is to keep the basilica in the best physical condition. It actually isn't too risky for it has been said that the surface is wide enough for a man to drive a horse-pulled chariot along it. That's another thing about the Basilica, what it does to your sense of proportions and dimensions. For example the *baldacchino* climbs to a height of ninety-five feet over the main altar, which is not overly impressive until we consider that ninety-five feet is the height of a ten story building. What other church that you know of could contain a ten story canopy for its central altar?

Turning to our right we see a chapel with clusters of people at the altar rail. Drawing closer we see the attraction, the world-renowned *Pietà* of Michelangelo. Who is not profoundly touched by the sight of the sorrowing mother cradling the lifeless form of her murdered son across her lap? At the age of twenty-four the Florentine genius created this masterpiece. It is the only one of his sculptures he ever signed.

One day soon after the Pietà went on display in St. Peter's the artist was mingling with the crowds gaping at it. He became distressed when time and again he heard the work attributed to this or that sculptor. Late that night he was granted permission to enter the basilica. By candlelight he chiseled into the sacred monument this message: "I Michelangelo of Florence Made This." Guides always like to ask tourists if they can find the inscription. It's really unfair for it is almost impossible for the naked eye. Perhaps binoculars would do it. There it is, on the sash across the Virgin's bosom. Because of a sledgehammer attack on the masterpiece by a madman in May, 1972, the Pietà must now be viewed through a sheet of bulletproof glass. The whole world was heartsick when it was first believed that the damage was irreparable, and not much comforted by a later prognostication that it would take from five to ten years to restore. But due to the brilliant and unexpectedly swift work of restoration artists the Pietà, its scars undetectable, was again available for public viewing within a year.

I shan't attempt to guide you completely around St. Peter's. That would require a book in itself and there are numerous such texts available that will describe in the minutest detail the twenty-seven chapels, the forty-eight altars, the four hundred statues, the eight hundred chandeliers and the endless tombs and monuments of popes and cardinals and laymen. What I hope to do is direct your attention to the things about St. Peter's (which we consider our parish church) that my family and I have come to love most.

Come then, down near the main altar on the right side to see the famous blackened bronze statue of St. Peter, the origin of which is the subject of continued debate. Some experts date it to pagan times when it was, they say, an image of Jupiter. Most others consider it to be a creation of the thirteenth century. You will notice the left hand holding the keys of Paradise, the right raised in the gesture of benediction. But look at the right foot positioned out over the pedestal! The toes have been worn smooth by centuries of kisses by millions of the devout. On the feast of St. Peter each year the statue is dressed in pontifical robes and crowned with the papal tiara.

Out in the vast nave are brass markings on the floor to help dramatize the magnitude of St. Peter's. These are the names of the world's famous cathedrals, showing where each would end if placed flush with the back wall of the apse. St. Patrick's comes just a little beyond the thirty-yard line. Then there's Paris' Notre Dame, London's St. Paul's, Milan's *Duomo* among many others.

St. Peter's, in the form of a Latin cross, is more than six hundred feet long and four hundred and fifty feet across the transept. It occupies an area exceeding six acres. Eighty thousand people may attend a ceremony here. The presence of Renaissance and Baroque genius makes itself felt throughout. A marriage of religious sentiment and artistic interest, its grandeur was intended to stimulate the spirit to thoughts of God and His promise of Life Everlasting. With its lavish ornamentation, its profusion of colors, and its staggering size, St. Peter's does just that for us. It is first, last, and always a House of the Lord and ought to be deferred to as such by every visitor. One Vatican gendarme friend of ours, Giuseppe Rincotta, occasionally draws the assignment of preventing scantily clad visitors (mostly female) from entering the basilica.

In the center rises the papal altar precisely over the tomb of Peter and under the baldacchino of twisted columns fashioned from the bronze of the Pantheon's dome by the tireless Bernini. Beneath the altar is the Confession with a marble likeness of Pope Pius VI. Twin flights of marble stairs descend to the chapel over Peter's grave. On the balustrade guarding the Confession are eighty-seven perpetually burning brass lamps, lending an indescribable solemnity to the scene. Overhead is the dome.

Supporting the dome, you will observe, are four powerful pilasters, each decorated with a beautiful loggia, below which are statues (starting at eleven o'clock and proceeding clockwise) of: a) Veronica, holding the veil upon which Christ left an imprint of His face; b) St. Helena holding the True Cross; c) St. Longinus, the soldier who pierced Christ's side with a lance and who later converted to Christianity; d) St. Andrew with the cross upon which he would be crucified.

In these pilasters are reliquaries for the actual relics represented in the statuary. On special feasts they are displayed, for public veneration, from the loggias.

At the far wall of the apse we will see another Bernini work, the *Cathedra* or Chair of Peter. A bronze throne, encasing the wooden episcopal chair actually used by the first Bishop of Rome, is held aloft by four giant (sixteen-feet-high) bronze likenesses of the Fathers of the Church. The two in front, wearing bishops' mitres, are Ambrose and Augustine representing the Western Church. In back, the bareheaded Athanasius and Chrysostom of the Eastern Rite. Above is a window with the Holy Spirit represented as a dove, more radiant than the sun.

We ought not to leave this area without stopping to ponder the lavish tombs of Paul III left of the Cathedra, and of Urban VIII to the right.

Around to the left transept are the many confessional booths where signs indicate to the people that confessions are heard in more than a dozen languages, an example of the universality of the Church.

On this same side of the church is the entrance to the sacristy and thence to the Treasury of St. Peter's, actually a small museum exhibiting some of the precious gifts sent to the pontiffs over the centuries from kings and nobility and simple folk of every land on earth. It surely merits a visit.

You may be amazed, incidentally, at the wonderful condition of all the canvas paintings that backdrop the side altars. They are in excellent condition but they are not canvas. They are mosaic reproductions of the fine paintings that were once there but are now in the Vatican Art Gallery or in churches around the city.

Beneath the statue of St. Andrew is a little sign missed or misunderstood unfortunately by the vast majority of the visitors. It reads: *Tombe dei Papi*, and points to a narrow spiral staircase that will take us down to a most interesting part of St. Peter's, the grottoes beneath, where Peter and most of his successors are buried. Following the narrow corridor around to the left we come soon to the tiny chapel of Peter's tomb on our right where, if it's morning, we will likely see a Mass being celebrated. Directly across the corridor is the peaceful chapel of Pope Pius XII where I always stop to kneel a few moments in prayer. Often there are elderly nuns, or priests, or laymen who perhaps knew the saintly man in life, saying the rosary at the kneeling bench provided.

A little farther on, the corridor opens into a wide grotto, dimly lit, where in the shadows can be seen the sarcophagi of many pontiffs. A few paces ahead on the left we see another chapel always with a cluster of the devout kneeling in prayer. This is the sepulcher of the good Pope John XXIII. Across the way is the crypt of the popular Spanish Cardinal, Merry Del Val, whom all Rome had once thought and hoped would one day be Pope.

Exiting from the grottoes we walk through an alley to a religious article and souvenir shop run by nuns. It would be worth our while to stop here if only to buy some Vatican coins and stamps and to mail some postcards from here, for this is not Italy but actually another country called the Vatican.

There is one thing we must certainly show you and that is the top of St. Peter's. So let us go back inside, take the elevator to the roof where there are more shops and where we may see close up, the twenty-foot high statues of Christ and His Apostles on the facade. From here we look up to see people waving at us from the balcony of the dome. Then we walk along the roof where there are more shops, a snack bar, and little quarters where the San Pietrini used to live but where they now merely store equipment. Up a narrow staircase and through a small door we pick our way to the interior balcony of the dome. From here we can look down into the beautiful abyss where the tour groups scurrying about down on the pavement look like a small legion of ants. Let my sons show you the whispering mosaics. Ronnie will run around to the other side and cup his ear against the tiles. Frankie or Johnny will cup his hand over his mouth which he presses to the wall and begin whispering a message. Ronald's reply travels back over the same small stones. A Renaissance intercom?

St. Peter's cupola is actually two domes, one inside the other, and the space between has an eternal stairway which puffs and groans its way to the top. As we climb we can feel the contour until, near the end of the ascent, we are listing quite markedly to the right. After the darkness and dankness of "cardiac corridor" we are greeted with a burst of light and wind as we stand stunned at the spectacle far below us. Recovering from a flash attack of vertigo, Camille and I always gingerly step out on the narrow catwalk that encircles the dome and put a vise-like grip on the waist-high, wrought iron handrail which alone keeps us from eternity. But the Brothers Korn are off and running as though they were on *Terra Firma*. Ron turns right to see if he can see the sea. ("Too repetitious!" my grade school composition teacher would have complained. Well then, Ron turns right to determine if he can discern the Mediterranean.) On clear days it's possible. John scoots round back to wave to the workers toiling in the Vatican gardens. Frank trains his field glasses on the cuties pouring from the tour buses down in the square. My signora and I and our guests content ourselves with the astonishing symmetrical beauty of Bernini's columns, the twin fountains, the obelisk, and Via della Conciliazione darting to the Tiber. Here as we stand more than five-hundred feet directly above the final resting place of the rugged fisherman who brought Christ's message to this city more than nineteen hundred years ago, and as we gaze out over the domes and spires of hundreds of magnificent temples in His honor, we sense, with deep emotion, His great triumph.

Our descent will be far less arduous so let us begin. On the way I should remind you again that it is still Sunday and that you are in luck for it is a special feast day and the Pope himself will celebrate Mass, in Latin. At last we are down from the clouds and standing shoulder-to-shoulder with our brethren in the great temple. Here he comes! *"Viva Il Papa! Viva Il Papa!"* the crowd roars as our Shepherd is borne in on the portable throne and the angelic voices of the Sistine Choir, filling every corner of the vast hall, give us a pleasant case of the chills. Trailing their Pontiff in solemn procession are the cardinals in their flaming vestments, the bishops and monsignori, the priests and seminarians. Men hold their little ones aloft, flashbulbs pop incessantly, the procession halts momentarily and His Holiness takes a baby into his arms and gives him a short ride, tears of happiness stream down every face, lumps rise in every throat, hearts palpitate ecstatically.

When the procession has reached the papal altar and the joyous uproar has subsided, Paul VI leads us in the Holy Sacrifice of the Mass:

"Introibo Ad Altare Dei"

John directing traffic in Vatican City

XXXIII

The Vatican

West Berlin is today a city entirely surrounded by a foreign country. Another European paradox is the Vatican, which is a country completely encircled by a foreign city. When a resident of Rome passes through one of the gates in the Vatican walls he is on foreign soil, on the soil of a microscopic sovereign state which at the same time is the spiritual fatherland of the world's half billion Catholics. It is ruled over by the Supreme Pontiff of Holy Mother Church.

To understand this postage stamp-sized nation of our time we must go back in time to the "last hurrah" of the Roman Empire, i.e., to its last century and a half of existence. After Constantine had rescinded the laws against Christian worship in the second decade of the fourth century, he granted a considerable piece of city property to the Church for its center of operations.

This land once belonged to the Laterani family but had been confiscated by the state under Nero and thereafter was used by Imperial families. (Marcus Aurelius was born here.) In addition to this grant of real estate the Emperor also commissioned a great church to be built in the basilical style on this property. The Basilica of St. John soon after took shape and became the logical cathedral or seat of the diocese of Rome. This mother church of the Holy City is known far and wide as *San Giovanni in Laterano*. The adjacent Lateran palace, as a result, became the residence of the Bishop of Rome who, *ipso facto*, was the Supreme Shepherd of the Universal Church. Not long after, another great basilica was erected above the final resting place of Peter, the first Bishop of Rome. The popes at this time would often go over to St. Peter's on Vatican Hill to conduct solemn ceremonies on important feasts, but would then return to the Lateran where they resided.

With the collapse of the western portion of the Roman Empire in the late fifth century, the popes, who did not join the mass exodus from the devastated city, were looked to more and more by the remaining inhabitants for secular as well as ecclesiastical leadership.

In the middle of the eighth century the Pope raised an army to defend the people of central Italy against the savage and ruthless Lombards from the North. This same pontiff, Stephen II, soon after merged his forces with those of Pepin, King of the Franks across the Alps, and together they beat back the Lombard threat. Consequently Pepin donated this territory to the Holy Father. It marked the beginning of the Papal States which were to endure through eleven centuries to 1870. They covered an area of 17,000 square miles from Umbria to Lazio and had a population approaching three million.

Throughout their existence however, the Papal States were to come under frequent attack from northern belligerents. Very early in this span of time, more precisely in the middle of the ninth century, Pope Leo IV felt the urgent need to assemble the towering walls, later named for him, around the Vatican to protect that part of the Church's territory which, being at the end of the highway from the north, the Via Aurelia, was particularly vulnerable. From the walls the Vatican gained the additional name of the

Leonine City. Also in the course of this era the popes suffered imprisonment, exile, and assassination, as Rome was beset by wave upon wave of invasions by foreigners and of attempted coups by the domestic nobility, all clearly aimed at the seizure of the Pope's temporal power.

Clement V in 1309 concluded that Rome, despite her hallowed ground and great Christian shrines, was not the best, and by no means the safest, place from which to administer the worldwide Church. Consequently he transferred the papal residence and headquarters beyond the Alps to the romantic little town in Southern France (Caesar's Gaul), Avignon.

Having lost her civil and spiritual leader, Rome became desolate and sank to her lowest ebb since the collapse of the Empire. Much of the populace evacuated. Wolves, rats, thieves, stalked the deserted streets. Palaces and churches, now abandoned, crumbled. Richly landscaped gardens were reduced by neglect to wild fields as the next six occupants of the chair of Peter completed their holy reigns in this new *Cite des Papes* on the left bank of the peaceful Rhone. Both the storybook castle and the battlemented and towered wall with which they enclosed all of Avignon still stand in remarkably sound health. Bleak indeed was the picture of Rome's future until, persuaded by Catherine of Siena to restore the seat of Christendom to the city of Peter, Gregory XI phased out operations at Avignon and set out for Rome. Instead of going back to the Lateran with all its bad memories, Gregory continued on the Aurelian Way right to Leo's walls, within which he established the new pontifical residence. From this point the true history of Vatican City begins. Upon the death of Gregory, the Vatican hosted its first conclave, i.e., a closed meeting of all the cardinals, convoked for the purpose of electing a new pope. For many centuries now the conclaves have been held in the fabled Sistine Chapel where the fresco figures of Michelangelo watch in glorious silence from their isolated vantage point on the towering ceiling.

In the 1490's the realist Alexander VI saw that the Vatican's future would be a stormy one and built a fortified passage from the papal palace to Castel Sant'Angelo which could — and did — in times of peril provide the popes with safe conveyance to the old fortress on the Tiber. Through much turbulence and strife, through the warm glow of the sun of the Renaissance and beyond, the Vatican remained as the seat of the government of the Church and of the government of the Papal States. The latter function was abruptly terminated in 1860 when these states were overrun by the troops of Victor Emmanuel, who along with Cavour and Garibaldi had in mind the unification of all Italy, even of insular Italy (Sardinia, Sicily, etc.). One decade later the troops were knocking loudly on the gates of the Pope's own city. Despite the valiant efforts of Pius IX's badly outmanned forces the Eternal City was taken and Rome became the capital of the new nation.

Hoping to fend off worldwide animosity and obloquy born out of sympathy for the Pope, the victors sought a rapprochement with the aged pontiff. But the spunky Pius, in a bitter invective, publicly denounced the "usurper" of the throne of Rome and never again, in life at least, left his little citadel, the Vatican. He became known as the "Prisoner of the Vatican." Ironically the huge square adjacent to the Vatican was named for the unification movement, *Piazza del Risorgimento*. During the funeral procession in February of 1878 which was taking his mortal remains to their final resting place in the Basilica of St. Lawrence Beyond the Walls, a gang of the King's admirers wrecked the solemnity with a futile attempt, on the Bridge of the Angels, to seize the coffin and toss it over the railing into the Tiber. They almost realized their goal as the coffin, teetering over the murky waters, was rescued at the last second by papal guards.

Pius' successors also refused to leave the enclave until

in 1929 an accord was reached between Pope Pius XI and the King. Since the Pope's Secretary of State, Cardinal Gasparri, and the King's Premier, the rising super-star of Italian politics, Benito Mussolini, signed the agreement in the venerable and historic palace next to San Giovanni it became known as the Lateran Treaty.

By virtue of the agreement the Holy Father was granted sovereignty over the Vatican territory and several extraterritorial locations including the Lateran, the property around the other major basilicas of St. Paul's Outside the Walls and St. Mary Major. Included too were the old Papal Villa out in Castel Gandolfo, and various other sites around the city such as the Gregorian College, the prestigious seminary to which the most gifted candidates for the priesthood are sent.

These then were the circumstances of the painful birth of what is the smallest nation in the world geographically but the largest spiritually and perhaps artistically, for its spiritual citizens number a half billion and they live in every country on every continent on earth. And, as Pope Pius XI used to like to point out, the Vatican contains the greatest works of Michelangelo and the other Renaissance masters; treasures of art from the Etruscan era to our own, and the most magnificent building in the world, *La Basilica di San Pietro.*

So when you enter into the great square of St. Peter's you have left one country to enter another. Frontiers of the Vatican are the ends of Bernini's porticoes and the Leonine Walls. Except for St. Peter's, square and church, which is freely accessible to the public, the Vatican must be entered through one of the gates which are constantly patrolled by the border guards from that ceremonial, fairytale Papal Army in their colorful medieval uniforms, the Swiss Guard.

Michelangelo is reported to have designed the fluffy yellow, orange, and blue outfits for the troops who reside in the barracks just to the left of Porta Sant'Anna. The Guard, numbering little more than a hundred, was once more than ceremonial. Pope Julius II first enlisted their services. In 1527 during the sack of Rome all but a dozen were killed while defending the Vatican.

A candidate must be from one of the Catholic cantons of Switzerland, between eighteen and twenty-five, of sound health, at least five feet eight inches tall, and unmarried. (He may be granted permission to marry while in the service however.)

One must either work or live in the Vatican or have official diplomatic business, and one must present his credentials, in order to get past the check points. Because of my work which brings me almost daily into the Vatican, our little family has come to know the little country quite well and to love it and its Holy Sovereign dearly. Frankie hopes to be a writer, Ronald a professional golfer. We have a problem with Johnny, though, who wants only to be a Swiss Guard when he gets big. The problem is that Johnny, while looking quite Swiss with his towhead, is not a native-born citizen of Switzerland, one of the requirements, and I'm hard put to think of how he can resolve it.

Whether one is Catholic or not he owes it to himself as an occidental to study the long history of the Vatican, since the Papacy is the only Western institution that existed in the time of Nero and still exists. It has been affecting the world profoundly — for better sometimes, for worse at others — across more than nineteen centuries and its flame, according to the promise of the Holy Spirit, will burn until the end of time.

Walk with us now, quietly and piously, yet alertly, on this sacred soil and we will call your attention to the things about the Vatican that seem to excite most visitors. And of course more than anything else they are excited by their first look at St. Peter's. But we have just come from the basilica so we will proceed to either of the two main gates the

Porta Sant'Anna behind the right colonnade or the *Arco della Campane* (Arch of the Bells) beneath the great bells at the left end of the facade of the basilica. V.I.P.'s are ushered through the *Portone di Bronzo* (the Great Bronze Door) at the end of the right colonnade. So if you are a very important person perhaps you can take us through that entrance instead.

Vatican City is dominated of course by St. Peter's but the Apostolic Palace, actually a complex of buildings, with more than a thousand rooms, around a large courtyard, also gets some notice. The palace was begun under Nicholas V. Succeeding popes expanded their dwelling again and again the way the emperors would enlarge their pad on the Palatine. The city has a population of less than a thousand but another thousand or so, clerics and laymen, come to work here every day. Actually all those who have been baptized in the Church founded by Christ are citizens. For the inhabitants, the pay is meager but almost any Roman would give his eye teeth for a chance to live here for there are no taxes and the cost of living is absurdly low, two-thirds or more lower than just outside the Vatican walls in the city of Rome. The Vatican has its own post office, railway station, radio station, passport office, fire department, medical dispensary, shopping district, jail (seldom used), and parish church (Sant'Anna). Its flag is yellow and white, decorated with the papal symbols of the tiara and crossed keys. There is *L'Osservatore Romano* the daily newspaper and semi-official voice of the state.

You might be delighted, at the far end of the city, by the sight of young black seminarians playing volleyball in their sharp cassocks with red piping and buttons. They are taking a breather from their demanding studies for the priesthood at the Ethiopian College, the only seminary inside the Vatican. Our boys have occasionally batted the ball back and forth with some of them while others looked on smilingly from their beautiful loggia.

Vatican City covers an area of about one hundred-and-eight acres. Despite its smallness, more than eighty nations around the world maintain diplomatic relations with the Vatican. For the administration of its political affairs there is a state department presided over by a Secretary of State, currently Jean Cardinal Villot of France whom many Romans consider *papabile* (papal material). Conclaves for the election of a pope are exciting times to be in Rome. In the city's taverns there are big odds boards set up with the names of all the papabili, and facilities for placing, shall we say, little wagers on favorites and long shots. And the odds fluctuate daily as rumors and claims of inside tips mount. Even non-gamblers join the speculation. At the announcement of the election of a pontiff there is gaiety in the inns and dancing in the streets of Rome, with those who collected on all bets among the gayest and dancingest. But even the losers rejoice at the news and toast their new Bishop into the wee small hours of the morning with wishes of a long life and a fruitful reign. Minutes after the conclave of the summer of 1903 elected Pius X, an aide to one of the cardinals rushed to a window overlooking St. Peter's square where a great throng waited for some news from inside. He made a gesture to a binocular-equipped friend down in the square, using two fingers to represent a pair of scissors cutting imaginary cloth. The friend interpreted the signal correctly as meaning tailor (*sarto* in Italian) and hustled about trying to place last-minute bets on Cardinal Sarto who indeed was on his way to the Loggia of Benedictions above the central doors of St. Peter's to be introduced to the world as the next Supreme Pontiff.

To help the Holy Father with the task of running the worldwide Church there is the *Curia*, sort of a cabinet, consisting of cardinals serving as directors of ten congregations (departments), or as supervisors of different ministries, or as justices on various tribunals. Among the departments there is the Congregation of the Holy Office which guards against heresy within the Church. The Pope is the constitutional head of this office, housed in the brooding grey palazzo in Piazza del Sant Uffizio just outside and left of St. Peter's Square. Then there is the Congregation of the Discipline of the Sacraments to ensure observance of all laws regarding the seven sacraments. What for centuries was known as the Congregation for the Propagation of the Faith is now called the Congregation for the Evangelization of the Peoples. Its purpose is to spread the faith around the globe — "Go and teach ye all nations." Overseeing liturgical practices is the Congregation of the Sacred Rites which also conducts hearings for beatification and canonization causes. (For an enjoyable and fast education in the canonization process my wife recommends you read "The Devil's Advocate" by Morris West.) We get a kick out of the name of the department called *Congregation of the Fabric of St. Peter's,* which is responsible for the maintenance of the immense basilica. All matters that might concern the Church in any way come under the jurisdiction of one or more of the Congregations of the Curia.

Among the tribunals of the Church government there is the Sacra Romana Rota, or court of appeals. To show the finality of when the Pope or his highest tribunal has adjudicated a matter brought before them, it is said that "Rome (meaning the highest Church authority) has spoken, the case is finished." (*Roma locuta est. Causa finita est.*) You are likely any day to see the members of the Curia coming from or heading for the Vatican in chauffeur-driven Fiats and Alfa Romeos with license plates marked S.C.V. (*Stato della Città del Vaticano*).

All the members of the Sacred College of Cardinals, the Princes of the Church, whether part of the Curia or not, are extended the same full diplomatic amenities by the Italian government that go to princes of royal blood.

They are all the chief advisers to the Supreme Pastor

in the exercise of his Holy Mission. For hundreds of years the number of cardinals (whose flaming red robes gave the name to the species of bird) was fixed at 70 until John, and again Paul, increased it to where it is now over a hundred. This was done to make the college more representative of all the peoples of the Church.

The museums of the Vatican which are open to the general public daily from nine to one for a small fee will fascinate you. These are a few of my favorite things in the museums: the majestic spiral bronze staircase leading to and from; the large urn down in the well of the staircase into which my boys and I toss coins from fifty feet up; the priceless collection of classical statuary including the *Belvedere Torso* which many believe was carved by the Greek Apollonius in 69 B.C. upon a visit to Rome and whose lines Michelangelo studied intensely; the archives containing religious and historical documents such as the transcripts of Galileo's trial and Henry VIII's request for annulment. Let us not forget the Laocoon group carved from marble by three Greek sculptors in the first century before Christ. This work is even mentioned in Latin literature. Pliny, for one, calls it his favorite work of art.

From the museums we reach the great center of international scholarship, the Vatican Library with its vast collection of ancient manuscripts of historic and cultural interest. It was begun as strictly a manuscript library. Printed books were eventually added to the collection to facilitate the study of the old materials. Also housed here are fabulous collections of papal stamps and coins. Scholars of the world can come here to examine the great documents of faith, from the Apostles and Doctors of the Church and from the Church Fathers of every age to our own.

The tour takes us next to the so-called rooms of Raphael, a series of four halls with monumental murals by the young artist from Urbino. The murals include the *Coronation of Charlemagne,* the *Disputation* (Lecture on the Holy

Sacrament), the *School of Athens*. In the latter, Raphael put the features of his contemporaries on the faces of the ancients. Archimedes looks like Bramante for example, while that contemplative fellow sitting on the steps in front is a dead ringer for Michelangelo.

A short distance from here is the luxurious and colorful Borgia Apartment laid out by the artist Pinturicchio by mandate of the decadent Borgia pope, Alexander VI. So many people on their one and only visit to the Vatican unfortunately miss the beautiful *Pinacoteca* (Picture Gallery). We shall follow the arrow signs leading to it so that we can savor its countless works of Raphael, Da Vinci, Titian, Fra Lippi et al. And while we are there we will surely look in on Room Number Two with its thirteenth century masterpiece by Giotto depicting the story of Peter and Paul. Did you know that this once served as the backdrop for the altar of old St. Peter's? Room Seven has a great *Resurrection* by Raphael's mentor, Perugino.

By now even the most artistic and esthetic of us are getting impatient for the place we have really come to see, the Sistine Chapel. Following the signs to *Cappella Sistina* through a maze of lavishly decorated corridors and exhibit halls we at last descend a flight of steps turn left and climb a couple of stairs to enter the world's most famous room. Goethe said of this solemn hall: "It is the finest artistic accomplishment in the long history of mankind." Staring incredulously at the ceiling's painted glories the German writer continued: "At this moment I am so taken with Michelangelo that after him I have no taste even for Nature herself." This undertaking, according to the well-laid plans of Michelangelo's jealous rivals, was to be the undoing of the Florentine. Bramante and others, violently upset over Julius II's admiration for the marble work of Michelangelo (who was at the time busily engaged sculpting a grand tomb for the Pontiff), persuaded the Pope to have the sculptor paint the ceiling of the papal chapel believing that the Florentine would forever discredit himself in Julius' court since he would be out of his element. Michelangelo protested heatedly at his new assignment insisting he knew nothing of fresco work. Julius was adamant.

Heartsick over being taken off what he thought would be his great life's work, the volatile Buonarotti nonetheless at once set to work on the construction of an elaborate scaffold. When this was completed he ascended to the top where he would for the next four and half years (1508-1512) labor night and day on his back, his neck contorted, his eyes burning from the paint constantly dripping on them. For long stretches of time, weeks and weeks, he wouldn't leave the chapel at all, even sleeping on a crude mattress and taking his meals high upon the scaffold. At one point, dazed by fatigue and fever, he stumbled off the platform and plunged to the pavement. When his spirits were particularly low from unrelenting harassment by his foes he would seek consolation in writing poetry. Upset by the wickedness of man he penned "Hymn to Night" in which he envied his statues: "How sweet it would be to sleep and even sweeter to be made of stone while shame and evil prevail. To see nothing, to hear nothing; that would be true joy. Ah, awaken me not; speak softly."

Yet though wracked with physical pain and tormented by the continued sniping of his enemies, he persevered. And his long agony (as Irving Stone suggests in the title of his gripping historical novel on Michelangelo) was to result in our eternal ecstasy at the sight of the great Biblical scenes across the length and breadth of the ceiling of this chapel named for Pope Sixtus IV. In rich yet subdued colors there's God creating man; the creation of the Sun and the Moon; Jonah issuing from the whale; Paradise Lost or the Fall of Man; Noah and the Flood. Side panels show the prophets Jeremiah and Ezekiel and Daniel. Others show their pagan counterparts, the Cumaean and Delphic Sybils.

When Julius II viewed the colossal masterpiece he commented with astonishment to an aide: "And he's not a painter! Can you imagine what he would have created had he been one?"

More than two decades later when he was already an old man, Michelangelo was summoned back to the chapel by Pope Clement VII to paint an immense (sixty-six by thirty-three feet) fresco behind the altar. He toiled seven years on *The Last Judgment* in which we see the righteous being raised to Heaven and the wicked cast to the horrors of Dante's Inferno.

Before we too, as did Michelangelo, get stiff necks from all the craning we will leave this wonder of wonders to complete our march through the Vatican. Let us walk in the fragrant air of the lush Papal Gardens, which are a harmonious blend of beauty, tranquillity, and solitude. In the rock garden there are flowers from around the world to demonstrate the universality of this unique country. Water plays on bronze and marble statues in the fountains that seem to turn up everywhere in this world away from the world. That elegant little stone house over there, an architectural masterpiece of harmony of proportions and tasteful beauty and of sun-baked ochre hues is called *La Casina*. It was built as a summer house for Pius IV in 1558. Pius would sometimes give his audiences here. The little villa was also the scene of Vatican seminars on poetry, philosophy, and theology. Pius' nephew, Saint Charles Borromeo, often visited him here. Notice the delicate reliefs and mosaics in the facade, and the sunny courtyard. In the course of our stroll we may hear gentle chimes playing the hymn: *Christus Vincit! Christus Regnat! Christus Imperat!* This hymn which was chanted in the arenas of Ancient Rome by the early Christians on their way to martyrdom and Paradise, is the theme song of Vatican Radio and indicates that the station has come on the air for today.

Nearby is a solitary stretch of stone wall, of recent

vintage. How Pius XII loved to walk in these surroundings each afternoon and how disappointed he would be when the weather was bad enough to deprive him of that daily respite. The wall, yellowish and vine-covered and about forty feet high, was set up so that on inclement days His Holiness could still enjoy the outdoors by walking behind it, protected from the wetness and the winds coming from the Alps.

In the period just before his death, Pope John XXIII had that tower over yonder in the Leonine wall restored, and loved to repair to it whenever he could, for a few hours of rest and solitude. From every point in the gardens the great white dome of the basilica is extraordinarily photogenic, framed by arches of shrubbery, cypresses and pines and towers and jets of water. So keep your camera handy. On our way out of the gardens we could make a stop which would, I can assure you, prove most interesting, i.e., at the Mosaic Studio. The studio came into existence upon the need to replace many of the canvas paintings in St. Peter's in the seventeenth century. Here were created the mosaics of the altars and dome of St. Peter's. You may even place an order here for a mosaic of your own. So intense is the concentration of the artists that they are not upset if you peer over their shoulders while they select with tweezers one tiny tile after another, drawing from a stock of nearly 30,000 different tints.

Time is really flying now so we will make our way out of the country, reluctantly so as always, and en route we will get the chance to pass through some of the fourteen courtyards, some awesomely vast like the Belvedere and the Pine, others charming in their smallness like the Court of the Printing House. The Vatican Gendarmes and the Swiss Guards will help us rediscover the Porta Sant'Anna and bid us farewell as we cross the border into Sunny Italy.

Au Revoir!

XXXIV

The Holy Father

Rome is waking up. Wooden seated, smoky, sluggish public buses rumble along on their first appointed rounds. Outdoor café tables are being wiped dry from the night's blanket of dew, the aroma of cappuccino beckons. Twentieth-century Fiats and Vespas scoot merrily around the first-century Colosseum.

Church bells from the Esquiline to the Aventine are ringing out their warm invitations. Nuns, seminarians, and priests, robed in a wide range of colors, their habits and cassocks flapping in the breeze, abound everywhere. The streets of the Capital are filling up with Romans already engaged in vigorous, animated conversation as they play the local sport of dodgeball with the darting vehicles.

School kids in flocks, chirping away, astound the naive tourist with their fluent Italian. All this while thousands upon thousands of wooden shutters on both sides of the venerable Tiber swing open on another page in the long history of the Eternal City.

The sun's first rays leap over the tiled rooftops and around the cupolas, stream up the Via della Conciliazione, splash across massive St. Peter's Square, while the great basilica, crowned with Michelangelo's dome, glistens.

High above the right arm of Bernini's fabulous colonnade, in the papal apartment, the curtain has already lifted
on another of Rome's daily dramas.

The Pope has been up and about for some time now.
He has already offered Mass in his private chapel, fulfilled
his breviary obligations, and breakfasted lightly. He joy-
fully anticipates another day in the service of his Lord.

Within the Leonine walls of Vatican City which are
within the Aurelian Walls of Imperial Rome, the nerve
center of the Catholic Church is revving up.

But who is this man the Pope? What is a Pope? Just
what does he do?

Webster tells us the word "pope" is derived from the
Latin "*papa*"; and in the Roman Catholic Church it is the
term used to designate the Bishop of Rome, Head of the
Church, Metropolitan of the Western Province, Primate of
Italy, and Patriarch of the West. Indeed the Pope is all of
these and more to Catholics. He is, in the eyes of the
Church, the *Pontifex Maximus* (Chief Priest or Bridge
Builder), Sovereign of Vatican City, the world's tiniest independent country (I've walked it from border to border in
a half hour), successor of Peter, the first Bishop of Rome,
holder of the keys to the Kingdom of Heaven, and most
important of all, the Vicar of Christ on earth.

The Church teaches that his mandate from the King
of Kings is the same as that given to Simon the Fisherman
from Galilee and which is in part engraved at the base of
the interior of the dome of St. Peter's Basilica in Rome in
letters six feet tall — "*Tu Es Petrus Et Super Hanc Petram
Aedificabo Meam Ecclesiam Et Tibi Dabo Claves Regni
Coelorum*" (Thou Art Peter And Upon This Rock I Shall
Build My Church And I Will Give Unto You The Keys Of
The Kingdom Of Heaven).

Pope Paul VI is the 262nd in an unbroken line of suc-
cession to the throne of Peter. The life of a Pope begins
with his election by the College of Cardinals convoked

Pope Paul VI at Castelgandolfo

upon the death of his predecessor. This solemn assembly is called a conclave, from the Latin *cum* (with) and *clave* (key) for they are indeed locked with a key in one building, until they have made a choice. While technically any Catholic male is eligible for the office, the cardinals *de facto* make their choice a fellow prince of the Church.

The voting takes place in the celebrated Sistine Chapel known throughout the world for its ceiling frescoes by the Florentine genius, Michelangelo Buonarotti.

There are two ballotings each day, until someone has received a majority of at least two-thirds plus one. After each balloting which fails to produce a new Pontiff the votes are burned with wood shavings which emit black smoke from the tiny chimney pipe atop the Sistine Chapel. This signifies to the throng overflowing the vast Piazza San Pietro that the Church is still without a Pontifex Maximus. Ordinarily an election requires several days at most. (However there was one conclave held in the old Etruscan city of Viterbo, 80 kilometers north of Rome, which took 30 months to elect Pope Gregory X.)

Back to the piazza where the murmur of the crowd crescendoes to a thunderous roar when a white puff of smoke, produced by burning only the ballots, emanates from the pipe telling the world that the conclave has finished its task. "*Il Papa è morto, Viva Il Papa!*"

The dean of the College of Cardinals soon after steps out on the balcony above the portals of St. Peter's and in flawless Latin, intones: "*Nuntio vobis gaudium magnum!*" (I announce to you a great joy!).

He waits for the deafening clamor to subside, then continues: "*Habemus Papam.*" (We have a Pope.) "*Eminentissimum Reverendissimum Dominum, Dominum Cardinalem Ioannes Baptista Montini*" . . . (the most eminent and most Reverend Lord, Lord Cardinal Giovanni Battista Montini). The Romans, since before Caesar's day always appreciative of such high drama, splendor, and ceremony, emit a roar that can be heard as far away as the Forum.

The new Pontifex who has chosen the name of Paul VI appears on the balcony and imparts his first papal benediction, "*Urbi Et Orbi*."

While his formal coronation is a week away, the Pope immediately plunges into the enormous task of shepherding the souls of more than a half-billion people around the world. He is from this moment to his death the "bearer of the awful keys" as Oscar Wilde described the burden of the Papacy. The Irish poet also once referred to the Holy Father as "the prisoned shepherd of the Church of God." Indeed in many respects the Pope has at times in history been incarcerated behind the 40-foot walls of Vatican City.

He is from this moment on acutely aware of the awesome loneliness of the job, despite the fact that he will never again be alone. The Holy Father is constantly being watched, if not by the public or his court then surely by the Vatican Secret Service charged with the safety of his person.

Paul's popular predecessor, John XXIII, found this hard to bear and enjoyed eluding the Vatican guards. He would sometimes use his chauffeur as a decoy to take the limousine around to one gate while he made his way out another with a trusted aide.

The secret service was often forced to play the frightening game of *Dov'è Il Papa*? ("Where's the Pope?") They would inevitably and exasperatedly catch up with him in the streets of the beautiful chaos that is Rome. Romans out for an evening ride would be startled to stop for a red light and see a rotund figure in white smiling and waving at them from the next car.

The Pope's work day, as mentioned before, commences with a divine service very early in the morning in his private chapel just off his bedroom. Despite his high office his apartment is frugal, his wardrobe simple, his material possessions few. His bedroom and study, with walls painted white, has three windows, one with a view of Piazza San Pietro, the others overlooking Porta Sant Angelica. Farther along Via Porta Angelica are his dressing room, bathroom, dining room, and kitchen. Three nuns do the kitchen chores and cooking for the Holy Father.

Paul follows his morning spiritual obligations with a breakfast of coffee and a hot roll. During this time he speed-reads the morning papers, keeping himself abreast of local, national, and world affairs. At about mid-morning he is ready to receive visits from his secretary of state, high-ranking cardinals of the Curia, the Pope's cabinet, and other prelates, heads of state, ambassadors and such.

As noon approaches, Paul grants group audiences. Visitors wait, in wild anticipation, in clusters of a dozen or more in the antechambers adjacent to the office of the Pope.

Usually running just slightly behind schedule, the tall Lombard, dressed in white soutane and skull cap and fingering his gold pectoral cross, sweeps into the tiny rooms, gives a brief welcome and spiritual message in each and grants an opportunity to each guest to kiss the papal ring.

Paul makes two appearances weekly to the general public. On Wednesday mornings precisely at 11 o'clock he is borne on his *sedia gestatoria* into the crowded audience hall to the cries of, *"Viva Il Papa!"* He sits upon the stage and delivers his remarks of welcome, in seven or eight languages (his French is particularly good) to pilgrims from all over the world, and then a sermon in Italian.

He comes across as holy, warm, compassionate, gentle and genuine. One is also struck by his humility. On his way to the conclave that would eventually elevate him to the Supreme Pontificate, Cardinal Montini, hearing many passersby whisper to one another, *"Il Papa,"* would roll his eyes toward heaven in incredulity.

On Sundays at noon, with the piazza jammed with

Romans and tourists, the Pope appears at his window over the square. He speaks briefly in Italian, recites the *Pater Noster* and *Ave Maria* in Latin, and imparts his Apostolic benediction to the throng below.

Paul is now ready to break for lunch. He is an extremely well-disciplined individual who eats sparingly. Pasta or soup in small quantity, some meat, a little bread and cheese, and a glass of wine, usually white, is typical fare for his mid-day meal. A monsignor or two, a visiting bishop, often old friends from seminary days, might be Paul's luncheon guests on any given day.

Soon after the meal, the Pope is ready to stretch his weary limbs and refresh his weary mind by a walk through the 16th century Vatican gardens. He enjoys the sound of rushing water from the fountains, the cooling shade of the pines, the beauty of the statuary as he strolls, customarily by himself. It is his time for contemplation, meditation, relaxation. Surely it is an important time, for the Pope's livelihood is not merely giving benedictions, granting audiences, and being carried high above the crowd in the *sedia*. He has the constant, unglamorous, overwhelming burden of making endless decisions which will have their impact on the world for decades, perhaps for centuries, to come.

The rest of the afternoon is devoted to conferences with aides who, unfortunately, more often than not bring heartache to him with new, enormous problems that demand miraculous solutions.

One small consolation is that he can, on a normal balmy Roman afternoon, hold some of these meetings out on his little rooftop garden with a splendid panorama of the seven hills.

Near 8 o'clock he takes his evening meal. Usually a few of his staff share his table. After supper the guests take their leave one by one. When all are gone the Pope withdraws to his chapel for silent prayer.

Now midnight nears. Rome is yawning. But the Holy

Father remains at his desk, catching up on important reading, correspondence, planning some new program.

It is 1 o'clock in the morning, Rome is going to bed. Still one can see, if he stands in darkened St. Peter's Square, a solitary light in the second window from the right on the top floor of the papal palace, an indication that Giovanni Battista Montini is still toiling at his desk.

But His Holiness too is human and needs some sleep. To unwind before retiring, Paul favors soft, classical music on his stereo set. A quarter hour of this is just soothing enough. Then the Supreme Pontiff of Holy Mother Church, like millions of Catholic children around the globe, gets down on his knees and recites fervently his Our Fathers, Hail Marys, and Act of Contrition.

He gets up, switches off the light. Vatican City is now in total darkness. The Pope has gone to bed.

Dormi bene, Santo Padre

Conclusion

And what on earth can compare to Rome? What city can even hold a candle to her glorious past or radiant present? Paris has quaint sidewalk cafés, to be sure; Vienna, lovely parks; Athens, solemn ruins; Milan, the opera; London, palaces. Rome? Why she has all of these in abundance, and so much, so very much, more.

Rome, the world's most beautiful, most charming, most enigmatic city, is as old as time yet eternally young. She dwells on the banks of the Tiber in the afterglow of the ages, bejeweled by the network of her ancient highways, her Colosseum and Forum, her basilicas and churches by the hundred, her endless statuary and museums, her exquisite shops and earthy flea market, her smooth white wine and bitter aperitifs, her music, her umbrella pines, her gay piazzas and seven hills. The litany of Rome is unending. And yet all of these charms pale in the mighty radiance of the great Basilica of St. Peter, where beneath the high altar rest the actual bones of the humble fisherman from Galilee, into whose hands Christ deposited the "Keys of the Kingdom."

The Pope is Rome. Seeing the Holy Father for the first or hundredth time is an indescribable thrill for every-

359

one, regardless of religious persuasion. His appearance among the throng, or merely at his window high over St. Peter's Square, evokes a unanimous, genuine joy; a joy that reaches back through time to Peter, the first bearer of the "awful keys" as Oscar Wilde has called them. This continuity of emotion at the sight of the terrestrial vicar of Christ led Chesterton to remark that, "the Church grows young while the world grows old." The city of Rome enjoys the distinction of having a foreign country, the Vatican, within its limits. Many times, my sons, their mom, and I have walked that little nation from border to border.

Rome is catching a bus which takes off before you're aboard and scrimmaging with the Fiats and Lambrettas while crossing a street. Rome is the broken aqueduct and the baroque fountain. Rome is the swank restaurant on a broad piazza ornamented with imposing monuments, and the dank trattoria down a narrow side street festooned with drying laundry; the plush hotel and the homey pensione; the garrish Via Veneto and the solemn catacombs; a lukewarm cup of espresso and a lukewarm glass of beer; a clacking carriage and a clanging trolley car.

Rome is the melodious Italian language echoing through the labyrinthian byways of Trastevere. She is a city of sandstone buildings with wooden shutters, of outdoor operas with live animals, of a thousand moonlit places with a million smiling faces.

Rome is pitting one's bargaining wits against those of the crafty street vendor; vigorous political demonstrations on the left and, happily, on the right; youngsters in their academic frocks on the way to school; women, with their purchases perched on their heads, on the way home from market.

Rome is a city of saints and libertines; of heroes, scholars, thinkers, poets, artists, sculptors, builders, cardinals, and lovers. *Rome . . . a poem in a word!*

Those who bring with them to Rome fertile imagina-

Author and family were housed in this pensione (apartment house) in the Monteverde district

tions are truly to be envied. For they are the ones who can walk through the Forum and sense the charisma of Marcus Tullius Cicero; who can sit beneath a pine on the Appian Way and watch Caesar and his legions returning in triumph; kneel in the Sistine Chapel and observe the supine Michelangelo covering the ceiling with the Book of Genesis; stand in Piazza Venezia and hear Mussolini's thunderous orations.

These are the people who can most enjoy and understand: the Colosseum, where once defenseless Christians shrank back in horror from ferocious lions, but where today innocuous alley cats shrink back in terror from untamed hordes of tourists; and the Pantheon, once a temple to all gods in the Roman pagan religion, now a Catholic Church where Mass is celebrated only on the day of All Saints; and the sprawling villas of the Borghese, Farnese, and other patrician clans, with their gardens, founts, museums, and galleries. Rome — *caput mundi* (capital of the world) the ancients called her — has a volume of history on every corner. It is here that the Apostles Peter, Paul, Simon, Jude, Bartholomew, Philip, James the Less, and Matthew are buried. It is here that the ghosts of Nero, the Antonines, Gregory the Great, Dante, Cola di Rienzo, Napoleon, Cavour, and a plethora of other historical figures are still part of the mainstream of life with reminders of each all around us.

Rome — the very sound of her name thrills me — the city that prospered because of the brilliant Augustus and in spite of the demented Caligula, is *senza dubbio* the most fascinating spot on our planet. Consider for a moment how I spent a leisurely afternoon recently. I live in the district called Monteverde, near the park where the splendid equestrian statue of Giuseppe Garibaldi looks majestically out over the capital of Italy. To unwind from my studies and my work as a guide, I motorscootered down Garibaldi Drive to the back of Bernini's fantastic colonnade that embraces Piazza San Pietro. After thrilling, as always, to the sight of the great basilica, and after a brief prayer and meditation within, I putt-putted out Via della Conciliazione, past Hadrian's mausoleum, along the serpentine Tiber, over Ponte Palatino to the Circus Maximus, the Churchill Downs of a bygone era. There I rested for a while on the slopes where once were the grandstands with a seating capacity of two hundred-and-fifty thousand. Hard put was I to resist the temptation of racing my purple Vespa around the *spina*, with an eye toward Ben Hur's record. From the race track I roared (if forty kilometers per hour or twenty-four m.p.h., can be called roaring) past the enormous Victor Emmanuel Monument, down the Via del Corso (a spur of the ancient Via Flaminia), turning right at Via Condotti (the shopping street of millionaires) to the Spanish Steps which spill prettily over the slopes of the Pincian Hill. Here in the frenzied air and amidst the young Bohemian patrons of the steps, within the welcome shade of Keats' and Shelley's adjacent flat, I, strangely enough, found just the right environment for studying for the next morning's test on the Paradise segment of Dante's *"Commedia Divina."*

Then following a relaxing glass of Frascati at a nearby outdoor café, I drove over to the Jewish Ghetto to pick up a little surprise gift (an antique coffee grinder) for my little woman and from there to the outdoor market in sunny Campo dei Fiori for a bag of fruit for my always hungry offspring. In the Campo my fellow shoppers and I were treated to an impromptu concert by a cute, barefoot waif in a tattered dress. Her *Arrivederci Roma* was particularly moving, and moved even the most parsimonious passerby to throw a few lire her way. As I mentioned earlier, the Romans really do sing uninhibitedly at work and at play just as all those Hollywood films on Rome would have you believe. Waiters, messengers, window washers, truck drivers, cops, salesgirls all intone their favorite tunes as they work or stroll through the streets. Especially is this so when the winter sun begins to blush with the anticipation of Spring, when a young man's — and young woman's — fancy lightly turns to thoughts of *amore*.

Incredible and watery Piazza Navona was my next stop where I renewed my vigor with a triple decker *gelato* which is usually enough to get me by until dinner. We Romans, you see, take our evening meal no earlier than eight o'clock. On this particular afternoon I especially looked forward to the night's feast because Camille was preparing *pasta aglio ed olio* and because our guests were to be the two pretty and brilliant Guarnaccia kids, Daniela and Paola, from across the street.

By chance, Navona that day was the forum for a political rally, and the square was ablaze with the red banners of the Communist Party and resonant with the demagoguery of young voices. This not unusual vignette arrested my attention for awhile but soon, with the early evening sun splashing on golden walks and playing on marble domes, I drove back over the Tiber and coaxed my weary bike up the incline of the Janiculum to our hilltop home, where a pre-dinner nap put a gentle icing on the whole afternoon. Where, I ask, could one spend such a typical afternoon?

"The City, the City! Residence elsewhere is mere eclipse," Cicero long ago said of Rome. And I agree with Stendhal who many centuries later said, "One may be bored in Rome in the second month, but never in the sixth. And if he remains to the twelfth, he becomes obsessed with the idea of settling here and lying in eternal rest in Roman soil, or in some Roman church."

"Ah Rome! She gets in your blood," my wife often sighs, while Henry James, America's most sophisticated traveler, expressed it this way: "It beats everything. At last for the first time I live, as I go reeling and moaning through the streets in a fever of enjoyment." The poets Shelley and Keats so loved her, that they desired to live out their lives, die and be buried in this city; and they did just that. Longfellow wrote: "There may be other cities that please us for awhile, but Rome alone completely satisfies."

Our legacy from Rome is enough to stagger the mind. For she has bequeathed to us our laws, our republic, our very language, our culture, our institutions, our institutional Church. The citizen of the Western world owes it to his intelligence to make at least one pilgrimage to Rome in his lifetime. The Christian owes it to his very soul. There is a saying among foreign students here, to wit: "See Rome and lose your faith. Understand Rome and deepen your faith." Yes! Understand Rome. Of the millions of exuberant tourists who pass through her aged gates each year, how few ever truly come to understand Rome! It has been said that only when one comes to Rome for the first time has he truly come home for the first time. For Rome is the city of the soul and therefore everyone's home town.

So do come, and let the Romans, a kindly, extroverted people who have been accustomed to tourists and pilgrims for more than two-and-a-half millennia, be your eager hosts. And when you at last come, take your shoes off and set a spell, hear? I am always somewhat bewildered by those hectic whirlwind package tours of eight countries in ten days (or some such "*If It's Tuesday This Must Be Belgium*" travesty) with a two-day stopover in Rome. To come all the way to Europe and give but two or three days to Rome borders on sacrilege.

One pope was fond of asking visitors how long they intended to stay in Rome. When the reply was, "Two days, Your Holiness," the Pontiff would say: "You of course will see all of Rome." When the answer was, "two weeks" he'd comment: "You will, no doubt, see most of Rome." Whenever the response was "two years," the Pope would put his hand on the visitor's shoulder and observe with a warm smile: "Ah you, my son, you will just begin to see Rome."

John Korn and John Cardinal Wright

The wisdom of his last observation can be supported by the visitor who returns again and again, each time realizing more and more, that he has barely scratched the surface of Rome. So here is where you ought first to come and here is where you ought to stay for as long as possible. For in Rome there is so much to be seen and learned and enjoyed that *ten* days, *ten* weeks, *ten* years — *ten* lifetimes — would not be long enough.

And while you are here, get into the spirit of the place. Don't try to Americanize her or her people, for it would be at best an exercise in futility and at worst, a source of frustration. The Romans have indeed been playing host to the world since 753 B.C. but they have never changed their ways to suit others. So when you wait an hour for stamps at the post office, or two at the bank to cash a check, when you get sardined into a public bus, when you get warm beer on a hot day and another "*subito!*" from the waiter regarding your order in a restaurant — don't be petty and small-minded and complain. Do as the Romans do. Shrug, grin, and simply go on enjoying to the fullest, every minute of every day allotted to you in this life. "Eternity," they say, "is quite a long time." *Chi va piano, va sano.*

So don't you believe Thomas Wolfe. You can go home again, by coming to our beloved Rome. Come soon and savor with us the countless charms of the Eternal City that we have tried to paint for you in this volume and those others that you will no doubt discover for yourself. Come and "reel in a fever of enjoyment." Live and breathe the spirit, the mystery, the grandeur that was, still is, and always will be . . . Rome.

"*Omnes viae Romam portant*," they were saying in Caesar's day. Modern Italian renders it: "*Tutte le strade portano a Roma.*" Surely all roads *do* lead to Rome. Do take one of them at the first chance. You shan't regret it, nor forget it, ever.

Ciao!